18 00
80k

D1588223

MSU
LIBRARIES

MICHIGAN STATE UNIVERSITY
LIBRARY

RETURNING MATERIALS:
Place in book drop to
remove this charge from
your record. FINES will
be charged if book is
returned after the date
stamped below.

WITHDRAWN

THIS BOOK RECEIVED

MAKING EXPERIENCE COUNT: MANAGING MODERN NEW YORK IN THE CAREY ERA

Edited by
Gerald Benjamin
and
T. Norman Hurd

The
Nelson A.
Rockefeller
Institute
of
Government
Albany, New York

The
Nelson A.
Rockefeller
Institute
of
Government

State University
of New York

Clifton R. Wharton, Jr.
Chair, Board of Overseers

Warren F. Ilchman
Director

James K. Morrell
Deputy Director

Alison M. Chandler
Publications Associate

Barbara A. Plocharczyk
Marketing Associate

Susan C. Lenz, Elaine Y. Young
Staff Assistants

Van de Car, De Porte & Johnson, Inc., Albany, N.Y.
Design and Production

Printing: Boyd Printing Co., Inc., Albany, N.Y.

Copyright© 1985 by The Nelson A. Rockefeller Institute of Government.
All rights reserved including the right of reproduction in whole or in part in any form.

Direct inquiries to:
Marketing & Public Relations Department
Rockefeller Institute of Government
411 State Street
Albany, New York 12203
(518) 472-1300
ISBN 0-914341-03-0

MAKING EXPERIENCE COUNT:
MANAGING MODERN NEW YORK
IN THE CAREY ERA

Edited by Gerald Benjamin and
T. Norman Hurd

TABLE OF CONTENTS

Foreword and Acknowledgements

Chapter I	Hugh L. Carey The Governor	1
Chapter II	Robert J. Morgado Secretary to the Governor	27
Chapter III	C. Mark Lawton Director of the Budget	53
Chapter IV	Barbara B. Blum Commissioner of Social Services	89
Chapter V	Robert F. Flacke Commissioner of Environmental Conservation	121
Chapter VI	Meyer S. (Sandy) Frucher Director of the Governor's Office of Employee Relations	147
Chapter VII	William C. Hennessy Commissioner of Transportation	175
Chapter VIII	James A. Prevost Commissioner of Mental Health	197
Chapter IX	Muriel Siebert Superintendent of Banks	211
Chapter X	The Carey Governorship Gerald Benjamin	235

Index

Other Rockefeller Institute Publications

Rockefeller in Retrospect: The Governor's New York Legacy
edited by Gerald Benjamin and T. Norman Hurd

1983-84 *New York State Statistical Yearbook*, 10th Edition

1984-85 *New York State Statistical Yearbook*, 11th Edition

The New York Case Studies in Public Management Series

Coping and Caring: New York in the Era of Deinstitutionalization
edited by Aaron Rosenblatt (forthcoming)

Revitalizing New York's Economy: Partners with the State
edited by Morton Schoolman and Glenn Yago (forthcoming)

Foreword

The announcement by Governor Hugh L. Carey in January of his last year in office that he would not seek a third term made it a certainty that the post-election period in late 1982 and early 1983 would be one of transition in New York state government. The governor took a number of steps, both within state government and through a specially created Council on State Priorities, to smooth the process of leadership change. And it became apparent to the Rockefeller Institute and the New York State Academy for Public Administration that a major opportunity was at hand to gain additional insight into the institutions and processes of state government in New York.

During any change in state administration, there is intense interest in the capital, in the new governor, his political skills, his management style, and his policy priorities. One area in which these are manifest is in the appointments made to top positions in the administration, including commissionerships and key staff posts in the executive chamber. As these major jobs are filled, there is discussion in the media and throughout the governmental establishment in the state about their political and programmatic implications.

But at the same time, there is little attention paid to those who, after years of service, are departing from these same positions. Yet these outgoing executives are a major resource. Their experience as managers and policy-makers at the pinnacle of state government offers a unique set of perspectives on how the process works in New York, what is right with it, and areas in which change might be needed.

In order to tap this resource while outgoing commissioners and top aides were still accessible in Albany, the academy and the institute cooperated in sponsoring a series of meetings with eight people who had held key positions in the Carey administration. Because we thought they would be more likely to feel free to comment fully and frankly, only individuals not continuing in their positions in the incoming administration were included in this group.

For each meeting, the guest participant was provided in advance with this set of general questions:

    –What do you see are the chief accomplishments of your time in office? How did you succeed in institutionalizing these accomplishments?

    –What are the chief unresolved problems left for your successor? Are they resolvable? Compare these to the problems you found when you came into office and preparations made to help you deal with them.

    –What are your chief conclusions regarding how to make the New York State system of government work? Would you particularly comment on: legislative-executive relations; organization and use of the governor's staff; relations between the governor and his office and state agencies; relations with the media and interest groups.

    –How would you change the system to make it work better?

    –If you were to begin your official responsibility again, how might you vary your course?

Though we knew that with the use of this outline, remarks might be less straightforward and free-flowing, it was our hope that these questions would give both structure to the interviews and provide points of comparison among the responses of the participants.

The edited transcripts, included here, are published after having been approved by the interviewees. Later, Governor Carey was asked if he would wish to comment upon the observations of those who had worked for and with him, and add his views to those expressed by others here. The governor agreed to be interviewed. His approved report of that interview, and other materials prepared and submitted by Governor Carey are included as well.

In addition to the editors, participants in the project included: Peter Colby, Gerald Dunn, Robert Herman, Warren Ilchman, Robert Kerker, E. Stanley Legg, Milton Musicus, Harold Rubin, Morton Schoolman, Sally Stout, Paul Veillette, and Lois Wilson.

We owe a special thanks to Warren Ilchman, director of the Rockefeller Institute, without whose support and encouragement this project could not have been completed. We are grateful, too, to James Morrell, Leah Dickerman, Roberta Bensky, Alison Chandler, Barbara Plocharczyk, and others on the institute staff whose organizational and editorial efforts made this volume possible.

T. Norman Hurd

Gerald Benjamin

Hugh L. Carey served two terms as governor of New York State, during the period of 1975-1982. Previously he had served seven terms as a U.S. Congressman from Brooklyn's 12th District. The governor now practices law in the firm of Finley, Kumble, Wagner, Heine, Underberg, Manley and Casey.

Hugh L. Carey

The Governor

The Transition

CAREY: The routes and points of access between the incoming Carey administration and the departing Wilson administration were cordial but limited. That there was little rapport was understandable since the outgoing governor was completing a 35-year skein in Albany as legislator, lieutenant governor, and governor, whereas the governor-elect had spent his entire 14-year career in public office in Washington D.C. as a congressman.

I actually had one meeting with Governor Wilson which lasted less than an hour. During that time, he identified Norman Hurd as his chief of staff who would handle all matters in the transition. This was to be my sole contact with the governor until the day of inaugural.

Immediately after election I had set up transition headquarters at the State Office at 270 Broadway in New York City. It became quickly apparent to me much more was needed than a perfunctory succession to office would afford. Not only was the access limited, as I stated above, but we would be contending with an apparatus which had held control of the state for 16 years. I wanted no void of continuity, yet clearly the times and situation required, in my judgment, drastic changes in policies, programs, personnel and philosophy.

This became even more apparent as I began the process of assuming responsibility for a takeover budget as well as the responsibilities, and indeed, liabilities of state agencies and departments. Some of the latter were in disarray—such as Health and Mental Hygiene— or dormant—to cite Commerce and the Labor Department.

To undertake this major changeover, essentially with voluntary efforts, was itself a challenge. We enlisted the aid of an overall committee of advisors drawn from a much broader base than the campaign group we had assembled. This was achieved even though the campaign team itself was a comprehensive coalition not seen in New York since the Roosevelt era. People of talent, some of whom had even been part of our primary and general election opposition, were brought together in task forces. These corresponded to key departments and functions of the state government.

The executive direction of these groups was placed under Matthew Nimetz, a brilliant young corporate lawyer who took leave

1

from his firm to provide full time direction. He was assisted by persons from the campaign staff, such as Stephen Berger, Carol Opton, and Hugh O'Neill.[1] Members of my family, my sons Michael and Donald and daughters Randy, Susan, and Nancy, attracted many other contemporaries who helped in a variety of ways.

The transition panels not only tackled issues during day and night preparation sessions, but also acted as recruitment channels to seek and screen personnel for the new state government. Through the November-December interval I made it a practice to sit in on as many sessions of the transition groups as possible to underscore issues and problems of more or less vital consequence and solicit fresh and sound ideas for solving problems. Each panel produced a series of policy recommendations, a data book on issues, and a blueprint for the guidance of the leadership in each function of the new administration.

I considered it a key function as governor-elect to relate to these panels, while at the same time gleaning whatever information I could from the government in Albany about the situation and condition of each department and agency.

During the period November-December 1974, I had more than a sixth sense that we would need to field a strong, resourceful executive team and operating administration from my first day in Albany as the state's 51st governor.

I was apportioning my time between the transition panels and a hastily assembled budget liaison group. Howard Miller and Robert Morgado began shuttling down from the State Capitol with the massive budget data, spread sheet by spread sheet. It did not take too long to determine that we faced serious difficulties. The nights at 270 Broadway grew much longer as I pored over the revenue and expenditure runs for the budget, the first that I would present in the early months of 1975.

Fortunately, my experience as a member of the Ways and Means Committee of Congress had given me a strong foundation in knowledge of fiscal and economic policies. Unfortunately, I found that: (1) I possessed limited means for altering the course of the financial plan for New York State that would have to be presented to the legislature in 60 days; and (2) not only was the budget showing a sizeable gap of nearly $700 million, but the state's basic economic situation and outlook held no hope or basis for anything but a worsening condition.

Further, collateral developments began to indicate that certain creatures of the state, public benefit corporations, were encountering difficulties as severe or worse than the state's itself. One of these came to light because I had decided to do something different from other recent governors.

The Comptroller of the State, Arthur Levitt, had a suite of offices at 270 Broadway. I had known Mr. Levitt over the past decade and shared the wide admiration and respect in which he was held throughout New York. I arranged to hold several sessions with him on the state budget and economic and fiscal outlook. He was most helpful in pointing out the practices and pitfalls that had led to the present condition. In addition, he invited me to join him at a session with his panel of private-sector advisors—a distinguished group of investment specialists and experts, including people like Gedale Horowitz of Salomon Brothers and Frank Smeel, then with Morgan Guaranty.

From these sessions I was alerted that the State Urban Development Corporation (UDC) was heading into deep distress. This was the largest, most heavily financed development facility in the United States, and it was well on its way to financial oblivion. Intense discussions were joined on the condition of UDC and other state agencies with the selected financial persons on the transition council and the budget cadre of Messrs. Miller and Morgado. By December we were joined by David Burke who would become Secretary to the Governor.

During one of our brainstorm sessions on the state situations we were posted on another untoward development. The city comptroller, Harrison Goldin issued a report in the nature of a warning that a second gap was developing in the New York City budget midway through the city's fiscal year.

Troubles were mounting and multiplying on the fiscal front. Specifically:

..the state budget was in gap by nearly $700 million;
..state agencies (UDC) and others were in jeopardy and worsening daily;
..local governments (New York City) were showing distress signals; and
..business firms were continuing to leave this state (Union Carbide, etc.) in alarming numbers.

It was becoming clear that we would need a "stress fortified" team in Albany to cope with conditions from our first day of managing the fiscal affairs of the state. I placed heavy emphasis in recruiting or getting people who could be relied upon to cope with adversity and lead in austerity. This meant business as usual in state government would not do. More and more, I began to look to the private sector. Through the transition, I tried to spot the kind of people who would be willing to come into state government and give us help.

It was in this early period that the concept of the public-private partnership was born. It was that partnership that became a hall-

3

mark of my administration in crisis after crisis, but particularly in the fiscal difficulty we faced.

Not all the woes of the state were financial, however serious they were.

In the human services agencies, e.g., Health, Mental Hygiene, Social Service, and Corrections, serious difficulties were encountered.

In Corrections, the scars of Attica were not healed. The prosecution of those responsible for the massacre was under way but lagging.

In Mental Hygiene, the dumping of patients and level of care in state mental institutions were receiving constant press and public notoriety.

In Health, a scandal in nursing homes was emerging on a wide-scale basis.

In Mental Retardation, the conditions at Willowbrook were not only the subject of major investigations in the media, but parent and public interest legal teams were suing the state in federal court, charging neglect and abuse of patients.[2]

I emphasize that this was the litany of difficulties I faced in the preview of government in the state before inaugural. I reasoned that if I became shackled with these situations from the outset, I might still be grappling for answers a year later and never get around to treating the causes of these conditions. Only by finding some way to deal with immediate conditions through extraordinary means would I gain the latitude and time I needed to prevent their recurrence through permanent preventive measures. Not only was this my concern as governor, but I felt that the incoming department heads would similarly be strapped to past mistakes and be less able to devote their time to better planning and operations.

As I saw it, there were two alternative courses of action available.

One was to use the "wailing wall and crying towel" approach. Under this scenario the new administration would devote time and energy to underscoring the gravity of the situation, using all possible resources to place the blame where it belonged. There was a definite body of opinion among well-meaning advisors that the public should be impressed that everything from the imminent collapse of the UDC to the scandals at Willowbrook were part of the same pattern of neglect and abuse of power. That theoretically would enhance the image of the new administration by pointing up the glaring deficiencies of the previous years. I rejected that approach for these reasons:

First, the nation and certainly New York had a full diet of Watergate—of corruption in high places and the short-comings of government from the federal on down. I felt the blame and shame technique, the "wailing wall and crying towel," would generate more skepticism and cynicism among the people of New York.

Second, I felt that it would be better to use our talents and energy to fix conditions instead of fixing blame. I strongly felt that, in due course, people would draw their own comparison, and we would be judged fairly on the record we would develop ourselves, rather than the negatives we could point to in the past.

From the outset, then, I determined we would not take refuge in recriminations against those who preceded us.

At the same time, for the benefit of the record, to serve the public's right to know, to have all the facts about our condition, some procedure was needed. A process was desirable, as well, to chart reliable historical analyses of the failings and shortcomings of the state.

Such process would serve to guide and counsel the new governor, his staff, and department heads, and help prevent a relapse into the same conditions and making the same errors.

I researched the powers I would have as governor, to decide what process was available to me immediately after inauguration, and decided to use the Moreland Act to conduct expert, impartial, and comprehensive oversight in two key sectors.

One, to be headed by a gifted lawyer and distinguished New Yorker, Orville Schell, would review the housing agency practices of the state with special attention to the UDC. This would give us maximum background and data to deal with the imminent collapse of that massive agency.

The other Moreland Commission would be headed by Morris Abrams, another gifted lawyer, former president of Brandeis University, with a long and distinguished record in human rights. He and his fellow commissioners would be entrusted with a thoroughgoing review and investigation of the private proprietary health care and nursing home conditions. I asked the man who would become Secretary of State in my administration, Mario Cuomo, to be liaison and work closely with this commission.

For other matters in the fields of health care and mental institutions, I enlisted the aid of Dr. Kevin Cahill to totally recast the human service side of the state government.

In December of 1974, our staff was most fortunate in securing the support and leadership of a key and central individual. David Burke, a successful executive in financial services, had been recognized over the years as one of the outstanding staff directors on Capitol Hill, where he had been chief aide to Senator Edward Kennedy of Massachusetts.

It was on the recommendations of Dr. Cahill and Mr. Burke that I decided that immediately on taking the oath, I would sign a consent

5

decree to end the litigation against the state over Willowbrook. This consent decree would acknowledge the failures of the state program, and I proposed to do more. Not only would we redress the condition at Willowbrook, but commit the state to a binding agreement with the court to extend the same warranty of drastic improvement in every other institution for the mentally retarded and developmentally disabled throughout the state.

On the eve of taking office as governor, I had so organized our transition and takeover, that our recruitment, review of issues, formation of policies and priorities, and organization of the budget and financial plan were under way.

The Moreland Commissions would serve to keep the governor's and the administration's concentration on solving problems while they would review the causes of these problems. We needed a dynamic transition because of the severity of the problems we faced.

It was reflection on the difficulties we faced in taking over that led to one of my last major decisions as governor. In 1982 I created the Council on State Priorities. This panel, again drawing on the public-private partnership concept we had pioneered in the state, was headed by AT&T President William Ellinghaus and my aide Orin McCluskey as executive director.

The council's report speaks for itself. It published, bound, and transmitted findings and recommendations on every policy and program which would confront the new governor in 1982.

We had come a long way in eight years.

There was little, if any, resemblance between the "do it yourself" transition of 1974 and the fully organized transfer of 1982.

The Governing of New York

It has been said that no governor in history faced more problems nor more trying times than we did in 1975.

I was there and I affirm that opinion with deep conviction.

With equally firm feeling, I hold that the record of our years in solving the problems we faced is a testament to the people of our administration, the team we assembled in Albany and, above all, the method we used for problem solving.

It consisted of these elements:

..Face it head on, regardless of gravity;

..Diagnose it thoroughly;

..Present it fairly to the people of New York and to all who could be called upon to help solve it;

..Offer a full solution and fight for its adoption;

..Fight equally to help reinforce the system to prevent recurrence. (Those who have suffered hardship once to solve a problem should have the reward of knowing they will not be called upon to make that sacrifice again.)

It was in that spirit that I spoke to the people of the state in the January 8, 1975, State of the State message. That speech has been called the "wine and roses" speech from one of its key passages, as follows:

The first truth, central to every problem we must confront, is that the government of New York State is in need of strong action to avert financial crisis. The last budget of the previous administration was balanced only in the most technical sense: by deferring, into the first budget of this administration, hundreds of millions of dollars of expenditures that have been made, but not paid for. Those bills are now due. At the same time, a declining national economy threatens our capacity to pay them.

In the very simplest terms, the government of the State of New York and we, as people, have been living far beyond our means. There has been scarcely an activity, a category of public spending, in which we did not lead the nation. What we did was limited only by our imagination and our desire: our buildings were the tallest and most sumptuous, our civil servants the most highly trained and paid, our public assistance programs the most expensive. Indeed, so lavish was the style of our government that we came to depend on it for life itself, forgetting that government was only the result of our industry and not its source. As the state's private economy stagnated, government became the principal growth industry in New York. Fewer New Yorkers are gainfully employed today than in 1958. But those who work now bear an enormously increased burden for the support of their fellows, and for the expenses of government. To pay for all of this, our taxes also became the highest in the nation. The extraordinary creativity and labor of our people skimmed the cream from a lush national economy; the government of the state in turn skimmed the cream from their rewards, and every interest and group and advocate came to think of the state budget and of state subsidy of local budgets, as a cornucopia, a never-ending horn of plenty that could pay for more and more each year.

Now the times of plenty, the days of wine and roses, are over. We were in the lead car of the roller coaster going up, and we are in the lead car coming down. So we must first recognize the immediate burdens we inherit. We do this not in a spirit of recrimination, nor in criticism of any man or party.

7

There is responsibility enough to go around for all. But if we would master our fate, we must first acknowledge our condition.

In acknowledging "our condition" in New York, this paradox became apparent. Although New York had the highest taxes in the nation, the most extensive and expensive of state governments, it could hardly point to any key state human service that excelled or even performed satisfactorily. That was true across the range of health, housing, corrections, mass transit, mental hygiene, commerce and, unfortunately, the justice system.

One would suppose that with this array of challenges to the system, a new governor would at least be able to field a team of his own choosing to deal with these challenges.

However, an entire year would pass, through one complete legislative session, without the State Senate confirming more than 50 percent of the governor's appointments made to the new administration .

In New York then, even during this crisis period, on appointments the slow process of confirmation prevailed.

But to the credit of those who were confirmed and given authority, they did the job in superior fashion even though we were undermanned.

People were called upon to "double in brass" and we were fortunate to have individuals who were gifted and versatile.

Peter Goldmark, who had become director of the Division of Budget, also had extensive experience in human services in Massachusetts, and was able to administer major reductions with compassion.

Judah Gribetz, counsel to the governor, was a former New York City Housing commissioner who brought special talent to the UDC, Mitchell Lama, and Co-op City problems.

John Dyson, a businessman, took over Agriculture on his way to Commerce and was a troubleshooter in a dozen ways.

Many more could be added to this list, but it is only meant to be illustrative.

At the same time we were reaching outside of government to persons like Kevin Cahill (Health Systems) and Richard Ravitch (UDC) to give us invaluable leadership on a volunteer basis.

This was the beginning of the partnership concept of government which is now a successful and accepted part of government in New York.

Having alerted the people and the legislature to our conditions in the "wine and roses" speech, it was not long before our method of dealing with problems would be tested. Downrange were all the problems of an unbalanced budget, New York City health and housing agencies in trouble, etc. But with suddenness the UDC problem came to a head. A reference to this problem and how we solved it is useful as a matrix for others that were taking shape.

Here was the largest urban improvement vehicle in the United States in the deepest trouble. It owed in excess of a billion dollars, with unfinished housing and economic development projects stalled or losing money from Roosevelt Island in New York City to the Convention Center in Niagara Falls. It had a negative cash flow of more than a million dollars a day, and no revenues on hand to service that demand. It was losing the shirt of New York State, because it was backed by moral obligation bonds carrying the state's credit in major volume.

Suddenly, the major clearing house banks withdrew their support of UDC paper. They declared them due, and demanded payment on $100 million of Bond Anticipation Notes (BAN) issued a year earlier.

Not only did I, as governor, lack access to $100 million, I did not even have a budget before the legislature to handle any request.

And not only was the credit of New York State in jeopardy, but there was more at stake. I saw in this agency, if properly conducted, a great potential for economic recovery and housing development. I did not want to lose that potential, so we put our problem-solving method to the test.

We described the condition to the legislature, the banks, the public, and the local governments. The banks refused to grant credit to the agency. The legislature said, "It's up to the governor to find a solution." We accepted the challenge. We brought in Richard Ravitch to work with Messrs. Burke, Gribetz, Goldmark, Morgado, and others, and in a matter of days we originated the rescue plan and system of restoration.[3]

We drew up the Project Finance Agency to intercept the revenues we could muster from the "live projects" of UDC as a basis for a new offering in the loan market. We asked the legislature to "bless" this issue and gave it to the new management of the agency. That new management was a team headed by Mr. Ravitch. I was called upon to relieve Edward Logue, the President of UDC. Mr. Logue was a diligent planner of projects who lacked the financial expertise or technique to manage such projects.

With the leadership of Mr. Ravitch and the eventual cooperation of the banks in handling the new paper, we could say that there was victory in the rescue of the UDC. But there had been an ordeal of endless hours of tension and uncertainty that we did not want to encounter again in New York State. To avoid recurrence we brought the agency under executive and budgetary control and invited closer legislative oversight. At the same time, we would be reinforced by the findings of the Moreland Commission.

Did the problem-solving system work? And where is the result today?

The answer is to look at Battery Park City, the South Street Seaport, the Convention Center, and Times Square renewal in New York City; the Carrier Dome in Syracuse and the Malls in Rochester, Buffalo, and Niagara Falls.

All these were worthy projects in which the new UDC took the leadership.

It was this technique of problem solving that became the hallmark of our administration in crisis after crisis. The Project Finance Agency, for instance, became the model for the Municipal Assistance Agency in the rescue of New York City only a few months after the UDC crisis.

It would take the contents of a book yet to be written to detail how our technique of problem solution applied to all the other problems we confronted. One by one, and in multiples, we had to manage:

..the state budget gap of $700 million;

..the "bail out" of insolvent state agencies;

..the illiquidity and near bankruptcy of New York City, Yonkers, and Buffalo;

..the mass transit deficit and decline;

..the Hurd and Levittown problems in education;

..double digit unemployment and the flight of industry;

..the highest taxes in the nation; and

..the failures of state service agencies to work.

All of these problems were met and solved.

We reinforced the economy of our state so that, where 700,000 jobs had left the state in the decade before we took over, there are now 800,000 new jobs and people working in New York State since our tax reduction and targeting economic development program.

To save New York City, which we did, we needed a strong center of leadership in Albany.

It must not be forgotten that in serving New York we took certain steps that so relieved the city that its future well-being is assured. First of all, in the rescue attempt, the governor at my own initiative and, in agreement with the federal government, became chairman of the Emergency Financing Control Board.

Hence in 1975, for the first time in the history of our state, the governor was responsible for the integrity of both the City of New York budget and the New York State budget and for coordination of the New York City and state financial plans.

As important as this move was, let it also be remembered that acting on our initiative, the state assumed these burdens of New York

10

City and more:

..the total budget of the City University;

..the cost of courts;

..the collection of taxes;

..responsibility for transit deficits and the nine billion dollar improvement program;

..the buildout of city facilities—Convention Center, Battery Park, Times Square; and

..the assumption of Medicaid and many health and human services costs.

About New York City, it would take another book yet to be written to do full justice to the tension and trauma of the events of New York City's fiscal crisis of 1975 through 1977. I spoke of the extraordinary and unprecedented burdens I bore as governor and I will never forget the crunch of those times. They were painful and enervating.

But they were also times of inspiration and extraordinary achievement by outstanding New Yorkers in business, labor, and government. From the onset of the crisis of New York City, a legend was born, and those who helped to shape it should not be soon forgotten. In order of appearance as they came forward to help were persons such as William Ellinghaus, Richard Shinn, Felix Rohatyn, Don Smiley, Tom Flynn, Al Casey, Herb Elish and, from the ranks of labor, Al Shanker and Victor Gottbaum, Jack Bigel and Bill Scott, Barry Feinstein and Harry Van Arsdale.[4]

For nearly a year, that team working with Mayor Abe Beame and an administration labored, with zero margin for error, to take New York City from near rigor mortis in bankruptcy to intensive care. And for the next successive three years, through MAC (Municipal Assistance Corporation) and its head Felix Rohatyn and a succession of Control Board members, such as Stan Shuman, Lee Oberst, and G.G. Michaelson, New York City was carried like a litter case by New York State until it became ambulatory.

I would be remiss here if I did not say that the budget therapy administered to the city was crafted by Peter Goldmark in tandem with David Burke, Bob Morgado, Michael Finnerty, Michael Del Guidice, and Mike Diffley. These men literally lived for several years shuttling on the turbulent thermals of the Hudson corridor between New York and Albany, to say nothing of plowing through snowstorms when they were grounded in either Albany or New York.[5]

I am deliberately omitting the details of the rescue and recovery of New York City, because of the limitations of time and space in this essay and for another reason. Frankly, that rescue story is, to me, so suspenseful and striking that it might tend to distract from another quiet but equally vital success story that was unfolding all over New

York State.

I was determined not to let the New York City and other attendant fiscal problems deter me and my administration from our fixed objectives for New York State. In short, from a state in economic decline and decadent human services, our objective was to resume our rightful place as the Empire State. I knew we could not fail and should not fail, because not only were we waging a fight for the great stake of survival, but we had a team in Albany who were bred to "even finer things than victory."

To achieve our objective of preeminence for the Empire State, we chose the techniques of "management by objective" for each key area and operating department and agency. Some examples:

In Health, Mental Hygiene, and Social Services, our aim was to increase life expectancy, decrease infant mortality, reduce dependency, and bring a higher standard of care and concern to disabled and deprived persons.

That grouping of services brought together Dr. Cahill as my architect and adviser, and leaders and planners, such as Barbara Blum, Stephen Berger, Julio Martinez, Dr. David Axelrod, Lawrence Kolb, and James Introne.[6] From scandal-ridden nursing homes and the disgrace of Willowbrook, we brought forth the highest standard of health care and disability programs in the history of New York State or any other state. And we did it while reducing the cost of health care by $2.3 billion in four years, with equivalent savings to localities and the federal government.

With savings like that, we were able to afford the opening of 800, yes 800, home-like hostels for the developmentally disabled in place of the archaic "warehouses for suffering" we found in 1975.

Just as providently, we marked many more milestones in better care such as breast cancer detection clinics; teenage pregnancy centers; drug free installations; alcohol abuse therapy centers; nutrition centers for women in childbirth (WICS) communities; and nutrition and service centers for the aged.

Most importantly, under Dr. Cahill and successive Commissioners Robert Whalen and David Axelrod, the entire house of Health was reorganized. The details of what we planned and performed is contained in the annual State of Health Messages I delivered. It is also vital to note that a new community of Health was organized, comprised of health service personnel and members of the community to represent health care clients. For the first time in New York, there was total involvement of concerned people in every phase of health care. We reconstituted every local, regional and state board under our jurisdiction.

Again, once we had achieved our objective of superior health care through better management, we wanted to make certain the system would not relapse into its previous condition. To prevent that, we founded the totally independent Commission on Quality of Care for the Mentally Disabled, empowered to inspect, review, and report on conditions in any state-supported health facility. That commission, under Clarence Sundram, has been most zealous in its mission to protect the health of residents in all facilities and is now an accepted part of the health care system.

Here again is an example of our avowed plan to cure a condition and do all possible to preclude recurrence by putting a revetment in place. In Health, the dual revetments were the Health Planning Council, the local HSAs now constituted with involved and dedicated individuals, and the Sundram Commission.

The implementation of our program required close collaboration of the heads of departments and agencies and was coordinated superbly by David Burke, as secretary to the governor, and his staff. To his credit and to the credit of the leaders of the new administration, it should be noted that our reforms were carried out under conditions of stress among state personnel. We had to adopt drastic measures to cope with the budget deficit. State employees were subjected to a wage freeze and to reduction in force and attrition of nearly 20,000 positions.

It was austerity across the board, and someone might even remember that the governor volunteered to refund ten percent of his pay until the budget was in balance. (The refund took the form of donations to the state Cancer Research Center at Roswell Park in Buffalo.)

As grave as the times were, as adverse as were the austere conditions, we nonetheless moved on our objectives in each department and agency across the board.

Let me cite a few more examples of a list which is by no means complete.

In Environmental Conservation, we began the cleanup of the Hudson and all our rivers, leading the country in implementing the Clean Waters Program with heavy fines for dumping. We secured the wetlands and new park and conservation acreage for the state. And we were so far ahead of the country in the handling of the enormous toxic waste problem that at least we had a tried and experienced team in the field to cope with the crisis at Love Canal, while the federal government dragged its feet and worse.

In Transportation, we targeted on highway safety and improvement and statewide massive support of mass transit. From the light rail system in Buffalo to the M T A downstate, we put together the innovative and sound financing to secure capital improvements valued in excess of $10 billion, while introducing and maintaining a fair fare system.

In Drug and Alcohol Abuse, we moved through prevention, treatment education, and enforcement to institute the lead programs in the country, under people like Julio Martinez and Dr. Sheila Blume.

In all of these moves, we closely coupled with local government. Secretary of State Mario Cuomo was accorded new powers for local planning as well as designated the state's first ombudsman. And he provided further leadership in the section of small business and rural affairs involvement.

To afford the changes New York needed, however, our greatest challenge and objective had to be met.

New York's economy, in decline for more than a dozen years, was worse than flat; it was moribund.

Here again, it would take a volume to recite the enormity of planning, effort, and determination that led to the rebuilding of our economy and the addition of hundreds of thousands of jobs.

Stricken as we were with deficits and excessive borrowing, we referred to ourselves in 1975-76 as a "leaking battleship that had to be turned around in a narrow strait." That turnaround was achieved with the cohesion of extraordinary efforts of the "inside team" of Messrs. Burke, Goldmark, and Morgado; the "field generals," such as John Dyson, Bill Hassett, and George Dempster; and a host of business and labor leaders.[7] "The day was gone in New York," we said, "for building monuments to the state and its government." We would finish the Mall, of course, but that would be all.

Henceforth, we would mass our energy and effort to stimulate and support the private sector initiatives. We coupled the UDC and JDA (Job Development Authority) to target aid to our most recessed areas, and under Richard Ravitch, Richard Kahan, and Robert Dormer, we zeroed in on enterprise zones in New York before these became a national buzzword.[8]

We took an agency which had been a bureaucratic extended-care facility and made the Department of Commerce an assault battalion to fight for the economic life of the future in New York State.

The rest is history. The custom-designed tax reduction program and the "I Love New York" and "Made in New York" programs, which John Dyson and I began with a few thousand dollars and the assistance of Mary Wells Lawrence, Jane Maas, and the late Martin Stern, were milestones of economic recovery.[9]

The deregulation and reform of the key industries and informational services in finance banking and insurance opened New York as the gateway and world financial capital.

The new overseas banking facility and the re-insurance exchange were beacons to business, showing that New York was ready to promote growth and profitability.

We moved to the fore of the new high tech wave under the leadership of the late George Low of RPI (Rensselaer Polytechnic Institute) with the Center for Innovation and Development, backed by Kodak, GE, Sperry, IBM, and other corporations. As New York entered the eighties, its emergence as a strong, new economic power was not an accident. It was truly our best example of management by objective. It took a tremendous team effort in Albany. I would be remiss as the leader of that team if I did not bow in the direction of the legislature.

Despite our hassles over the budget in later years, there were many occasions to share pride in common achievements in uncommon times. So much attention was paid to our budget conflicts that it is sometimes forgotten that we collaborated as well. By recruiting Assemblyman Thomas Frey to act as director of State Operations during some very difficult years, we did improve relations with the legislative leaders and members.

And due credit for the turnabout of New York should go to Speakers Fink and Steingut and my old friend Warren Anderson.[10]

In the worst of times in New York, we all had to make the best of it, and the legislature was often a partner to the governor, despite the fact that it was a legislature of divided partisanship during my eight years.

During those eight years, from the end of the days of wine and roses to the return of the Empire State to leadership in our country, ultimate credit goes to the 17 million New Yorkers. They suffered, they strived and succeeded in securing a better day.

* * * * * * * * * * *

QUESTION: Governor, you mentioned the importance of your outside circle of advisors. Was there a philosophy of government behind their use? What was the role, for example, of Kevin Cahill?

CAREY: Dr. Cahill played a very key role. In government, there is a need for clear measurements, for a way of determining what is possible, what is attainable. I gave Dr. Kevin Cahill enormous responsibility and he used it well. He was a catalyst for the entire area of health, and inspired the first "State of Health Message" in our history. He let me know what was feasible, what could be done, and what was impractical because the state lacked the resources to do it. He told me, for example, "There is something you can do about breast cancer. There is something you can do about immunization." So we set up such programs and clinics around the state, and they were successful in these and many other areas.

Dr. Cahill also helped me in the recruitment of people for the "caring" side of government. He led in totally restructuring health

15

planning, research, and operations. He changed "no show" boards into active participants in the cause of health improvement.

QUESTION: You had the reputation of being uninterested in the details of administration. Did Kevin Cahill and other outside advisors provide a link for you to the sub-areas of government?

CAREY: Certainly Dr. Cahill served very effectively to extend my contact with sub-sectors of government and, just as importantly, with the health community and the people the state is supposed to serve.

To say that I was not interested in details of administration belies the record. While I did not believe in harassing and bird-dogging key people in departments and staff, I made field trips and site visits. I held cabinet and sub-cabinet get-togethers to check and follow every function of administration. While our system was designed for management by objective, I took a deep interest in seeing that every level of government responded to needs and sectors of service. No, I didn't "nitpick" on administration, but I made sure that we had a government in New York State that worked, and the record is clear that we succeeded for eight years.

QUESTION: Compare the fiscal situation you inherited with the one Governor Cuomo inherited in his first year.

CAREY: I detailed the 1974 fiscal situation before—a real but hidden budget gap, State agencies in trouble (i.e., UDC collapse), a flat economy, jobs and business leaving, New York City's near collapse and a state badly over-extended with costly borrowing. 1974-1982—black and white, day and night—500,000 new jobs; the City of New York recovered; a stable and growing economy after a tax reduction program of $2.7 billion; most important, the governor-elect as lieutenant governor had witnessed my efforts to hold the state budget in balance for several successive years, well below the rate of inflation. As a witness, the governor-elect saw that the only budget gap he inherited was a result of the legislature overriding my budget and causing its own budget gap. In a sense, therefore, the governor-elect held the legislature at bay. Since they had caused the gap in 1982-83, they owed an obligation to close it. This the legislature refused to do in 1975 until they were forced to do it as part of the rescue plan. There could not be a more vivid contrast than 1974 with 1982.

What Governor Cuomo must reckon with is the Oneida decision of the Court of Appeals. It forces the governor to expend appropriations for local aid at the initiative of the legislature. It reduces the power of the governor to control the budget during the year of expenditure. And it presents problems. It weakens the governor's power to control spending.

QUESTION: Your comment about the Oneida decision raises the more general question of the impact of the courts upon executive power, their greater entrance into the political arena.

CAREY: There is no question that the courts have tended to legislate. Sometimes, court intervention has been welcome. For example, in the Willowbrook case, a federal court intervened and we welcomed it.

In other cases, however, such as the Flushing Bank case on the question of the governor's right to exercise emergency power, I believe the courts have gone to excess as they did in the Oneida decision to weaken fiscal authority.

QUESTION: Would you comment further about the decline of the governor's power vis-a-vis the legislature? Was this more a matter of partisan differences or of institutional conflict?

CAREY: The "majesty of the Mall" made a big difference, particularly the ornate State Legislative Office Building. It gave the legislature a sense of importance, of permanence, and they assumed more responsibility. They had all that space and they had to fill it up. The staff grew, and I had no control over that. They met year-round, not adjourning but simply recessing. This was part of a national trend, and not just confined to New York.

I remember when I first moved into the Capitol. There was a series of three offices, but I was told that the one I thought might be suitable for my needs did not have bullet-proof glass windows. When the Legislative Office Building went up, Governor Rockefeller noticed that a sniper might take a shot at him from over there, so he had bullet-proof glass installed in the bigger rooms. But the third room was the one in which he met with the legislative leaders. I guess he thought he did not have to worry about being shot from the Legislative Office Building while he was with the legislative leaders. So I guess Governor Rockefeller in his time was sensitive to legislative incursion.

QUESTION: Governor, you've attributed many of your differences with the legislature to institutional differences. How much was institutional, and how much was Hugh Carey?

CAREY: Well, it's true that I am a combative personality. I told my commissioners to fight, not needlessly, but to fight for their programs. I like a good fight.

QUESTION: But don't you think it got to be a bit excessive at times, for example, when John Dyson went down to Senate hearings in a Lone Ranger mask?

CAREY: I urged my commissioners to build their constituencies with imagination and John Dyson certainly has a gifted imagination. Barbara Blum traveled the state to build a constituency. Lillian Roberts did this well, as did many others.[11] Commissioners were encouraged to lead and they did. David Axelrod and William Hennessy are two of the most dedicated men I ever met.[12]

17

QUESTION: When you were in Washington you were in the legislature, a member of Congress. What is the difference between the "Albany game" and the "Washington game"?

CAREY: In Washington, when I was a member of the Ways and Means Committee, we worked in a true bi-partisan spirit to address and solve problems. Even with the Nixon White House, there was coordination and communication. In 1973, for example, we passed the ten percent investment credit and repealed the excise tax to restore the economy.

In 1977 Senator Bloom said that I "didn't play the Albany game."[13] Well, he was right. I didn't want to play that game.

I didn't use rollovers. I didn't use one-shots. I tried to open up government. We enacted the strictest disclosure requirements for the commissioners, our appointees. We made it clear that we would tolerate no deceit, no corruption, and there was no scandal during my terms as governor. We played the game of honest government.

QUESTION: Would you say that the nature of the causes you took up, your budget priorities, added to your trouble with the legislature?

CAREY: That's true. I made many decisions that were governmentally wise but politically costly. I worked for groups that lacked political clout. The mentally ill. The prisoners. And to get resources I sometimes had to disappoint the politically powerful.

QUESTION: What about the Goodman-Stavisky Bill, the veto override? That was historic, the first in the modern political history of the state.

CAREY: That was purely a political exercise—an election-year ploy. The education lobby is the most powerful in the state. The override had no practical effect. My veto was imperative because as governor, I was also chairman of the New York City Control Board and as such, bound by a pledge to protect the budget and financial plan of New York City.

QUESTION: You seemed to use the veto very little in your first term and then, of course, you ended with a flourish, all those item vetoes. Why were you sparing at first in your use of the veto?

CAREY: When the budget was being passed at the rate of inflation—through 1978—I didn't veto. When it came in too high, I vetoed the excess in 1980-81-82. During the crisis, great use of the veto by the governor was not necessary. After that, and after I got the $2.7 billion tax cut through in the election year, the legislature decided that they weren't going to let that happen, let me get the upper hand again.

You can see the consequence now. They have seized upon the tax cut idea this year and are running with it.

QUESTION: Were you upset about the failure of the "Robin Hood" approach to state school aid, that is, robbing from the rich school districts and giving to the poor?

CAREY: Yes, I thought that the Levittown case would come out differently, and rather hoped it would. Instead, the Court of Appeals chose to put it back in the political arena.

QUESTION: Do you think that the state bureaucracy was sufficiently responsive to your priorities?

CAREY: There are many state departments where there is no bureaucracy. People are often critical when you mention bureaucracy, but when you ask them what they think of Headstart, they say, "It's a great program. It really helps the small children." They liked the individual things government did, program-by-program, but they did not like the bureaucracy.

When you start a new program, like the breast cancer detection clinics, you don't know what portion of the constituency is for it. You know there is a need, but you don't know how many people will actually use it. A good program creates a constituency without a bureaucracy.

QUESTION: Many people thought that Bob Morgado was your link to the bureaucracy. What was your relationship with Bob Morgado?

CAREY: Bob Morgado was one of three fine men who served as secretary to the governor from 1975-1982. David Burke preceded Bob. David served for three years. Bob followed for four years and Michael Finnerty for the final year.

Bob Morgado is a man of extraordinary dedication. He was ideally suited to head up the executive chamber staff by reason of his extensive legislative, budget, and operations experience.

He had a deep grasp of the government process and he shared my short fuse for red tape and obfuscation. Bob had a quality of loyalty not only to the governor but also to the people of the state.

Rather than describing him as a link to the bureaucracy, I would say he performed the duty of liaison to the departments and agencies in order to limit the excesses of bureaucracy.

In addition, since our system was based upon management by objective, it was his job to oversee that process which kept the leaders of departments and agencies mindful of our objectives and timetables.

Bob was a superb administrator with a heart and a conscience. He had a great career in state government and New York was fortunate to have him.

QUESTION: What was the role of the program associates in your administration?

CAREY: They were essentially planners. Mike Del Giudice and

Jim Introne made major contributions here. They helped the governor organize his priorities, once he received the range of policy suggestions.

QUESTION: You mentioned the education lobby's power. What about some of the other groups in the state, Ray Schuler's group, business?[14]

CAREY: The Business Council was a welcome advent in New York. Prior to its creation, it was difficult to get an authoritative statement of the views of the business community. Without disparagement, I'd go to the Associated Industries conferences and find stationary engineers. We wanted to know where the heavyweights, the presidents, the chief executive officers were.

The governor has to build alliances, build support. The Business Council helped.

QUESTION: What about labor, that is, both in the public and private sectors?

CAREY: I appreciated their support during very tough times. The layoffs were tough on Bill McGowan and CSEA.[15] Remember that no one union leader controls New York State. Only 25 percent are organized. Many of our largest enterprises are not. IBM is not organized. Kodak is not.

QUESTION: Do you think you received fair treatment from the media?

CAREY: When I took office, during the fiscal crisis, the media decided they had not been covering the governor enough. So they increased the coverage. The stories were on television. Then the newspaper reporters brought them in and their editors said, "This is not new. Bring me something with 'color.' The people want juice." So they wrote about the personal stuff, the governor's family, the color of the governor's hair.

But they were not unfair. It is the condition of their professional lives.

QUESTION: Do you think there is any value in the GAAP (Generally Accepted Accounting Principles) legislation passed during your second term?

CAREY: It adds another layer, more paperwork. It has some value in cutting down the old abuses of "the Albany game."

QUESTION: How did alterations in federal aid, the "New Federalism," impact the state?

CAREY: We recognized during the Carter and Reagan administrations that programs were being reduced. The signs were evident. All kinds of missions were sent to Washington, but to no avail. And it was clear that the state on its own did not have the wherewithal to restore these cuts.

QUESTION: With all the decisions of significance to the state being made in Washington, how useful to New York was the National Governors' Association?

CAREY: It's a good place for governors to meet and to socialize, but not to get anything done. The rules in the committees and the organization block effective action. But the Council of Northeast Governors (CONEG), which we founded, was effective. At the first meeting in Saratoga, there was a discussion of a host of issues—industry, transportation, the environment—and we got a lot done. There was a regional community of interest, and we could more easily act together than on the national level.

QUESTION: Some people are concerned about the decline of political parties. Did you see it as one of your roles to strengthen the Democratic party in New York, and if so, how did you seek to accomplish this?

CAREY: I used to say that my predecessor as governor owned one party and leased the other.

I was not a party man. I was and am an Independent. The party did not designate me for the nomination. I had to fight for it, take it, and had to run against primary opposition.

Remember that for 16 years, this was a Republican state for statewide elections. I was very close to Robert Kennedy. No Democrat was elected statewide except Robert Kennedy in 16 years.

I did not greatly recruit from the party.

Politics today is changed. People are voting Independent. The PACs (Political Action Committees) and the groups, the teachers, the unions are increasingly important. In politics today, you've got to build your own organization. That's true in New York City, it's true for the county executives of Nassau and Suffolk.

I was the first Irish Catholic governor of New York since Al Smith, and I was very mindful of that. I modeled myself after Smith and after Harry Truman. I had Roger Tubby in Commerce, a deputy commissioner who was with Truman in his administration. We had long conversations about how Truman made decisions and I found his techniques most helpful.

QUESTION: There is always much attention given to the relationship between the mayor of New York City and the governor—Wagner and Rockefeller, Lindsay and Rockefeller. Is there conflict automatically built into this relationship?

CAREY: Differences between the mayor of New York City and the governor are historic. When I hear that a book was written [by Mayor Koch] and the governor was criticized, "What's new about that?"

As I noted earlier, I had to run the city and the state at the same time, something I wish on no future governor. We were able to do a lot for the city: on mass transit, full state funding of CUNY, assumption of court costs, income tax processing. We took over these functions while leaving the city revenue base untouched and this left the city—and the other local governments in the state—more manageable than they were before the crisis of the 1970's.

QUESTION: Why did you decide to leave office?

CAREY: I got into government because I thought the government was so much involved in my business—I was a private businessman—that I ought to get involved in its business for a while. I was in it for 22 years. I achieved what I set out to do. The state economy was turned around. New York City was restored. The caring institutions were restored. While governor, I had time for my official duties and my obligations as a parent and little else.

If I had chosen to run for a third time, I could have won. I've never lost an election when I've been at the head of the ticket. But I left a government that worked.

QUESTION: The timing of your announcement was interesting, a year before the end of your term. What was the rationale for this?

CAREY: We wanted to prepare for an orderly transition, give people time to choose a successor. We made extensive preparations. I assume you've looked at the Report of the Council on State Priorities. It's a very good, thorough report.

QUESTION: In sum, how would you assess your effectiveness?

CAREY: There are many areas that we have not discussed. Criminal Justice. The first function of the governor is to take care of the laws. The death penalty got all the attention; it distracted from our achievements in total improvement of the justice system.

And building! We didn't build a single new government building, but I was one of the biggest developers in the history of the state: Battery Park City; South Street Seaport; the New York City, Buffalo, and Niagara Convention Centers; the Carrier Dome; the establishment of the Empire State Games in Syracuse; Times Square redevelopment; and one of the most successful Winter Olympics ever.

But the major achievements were mentioned. The building of the revetments against recession, the restoration of New York's economy, the renewal of the tradition of New York as a compassionate state.

QUESTION: Would you vary your course in any way?

CAREY: I assume you mean would I have done some things differently.

The answer is yes, because second guessing yourself as governor can be a valuable exercise.

There are two things I could have done differently:

For one, I should have seen to it that there was a better organized historical record of my administration.

As an economy measure in 1975, we eliminated the position of historian of the executive chamber, the staff with the responsibility for organizing and producing the governor's papers for each year of his term.

We rationalized that over eight years this would produce a savings of one and a half to two million dollars in chamber payroll.

It was planned to have one of the educational institutions do the work for less than half that sum and provide a worthwhile exercise for the institution chosen—the City University or one similar.

Unfortunately, the succeeding administration excised the cost of this contract and now seven years of my administration are missing from the record.

I guess we should have retained the historian.[16]

For another second thought, I probably should have resisted the degree of involvement I had in the New York City mayoral election of 1977. Under pressure from newspaper editors and others in the city and a few members of my staff, I was urged to participate in securing improved leadership to move the city forward after we had rescued it during the previous three years. Mine was a no-win role, resented by the city politicians and viewed without merit upstate where city involvement is a negative. In addition I became a more proximate target in the newspaper war breaking out in New York City among some of the very editors and publishers who had urged me to participate. To put it in the vernacular in 1977, "I should have stood in Albany."

Perhaps, too, something else should have been done differently. Ten years after we began it, knowledgeable experts and business leaders tell me we should recount the "New York Experience"—an exercise in supply-side economics blended with concern and compassion that worked. They view it in contrast with the Washington record of huge deficits and in some cases crude and improvident recision of needed measures for the needy and infirm.

Before I departed for the private sector it might have been useful that I gather together members of the team, public and private, who helped me create the "New York Experience." The purpose of convening and organizing the group would be to show the federal government that we achieved in New York what they were seeking to do in Washington with better results. A comparison of New York in 1984 with other states or with the federal government attests that our way is better.

The risk of such a venture, however, would have been that I might have been viewed as trying to project myself on to the national scene. As I see the national scene in 1984, it does appear that the "New York Experience" is of even more value.

However, there is the comfort that with the record of New York's success which he helped to create, Governor Mario Cuomo is on the national scene, and I hope for the future the "New York Experience." will attract the national attention it deserves.

My last second thought is to apologize to my staff, friends, and family for some of my notorious "bloopers" which caused them needless embarrassment.

I refer, of course, to my reckless comment on "drinking PCBs," an ill-considered effort to allay fear in a moment of frustration.

And I am equally apologetic for ever entertaining the notion that my family's acre of land in Shelter Island would be more livable for me and my neighbor, the dentist, if he waited until I was no longer governor to build his house. Perhaps justice was served, because I got the punishment I deserved by paying in notoriety for what I tried to do in the name of privacy. The regret is not for me, but for the adverse effect the publicity had on those friends, family, and staff whose counsel I ignored.

Aside from those second thoughts, I would not trade my years as governor for any other experience in public life. After all, how many small boys have lived to see a governor like Alfred E. Smith, as I did at age seven, and fulfill the dream of holding the office he held. Fifty years after seeing Governor Smith attending Mass in Long Beach, L.I., I succeeded that great man. And I did my best to be worthy of his memory.

FOOTNOTES

[1]Stephen Berger, Carol Opton and Hugh O'Neill were all members of Governor Carey's Transition team; Berger later was named Commissioner of Social Services; Opton became Director of the Governor's New York City office; and O'Neill was later Deputy Secretary to the Governor.

[2]Willowbrook—located on Staten Island in New York City, is a major State facility serving the mentally retarded. A highly publicized series of revelations in the media about shocking conditions at the institution led to the signing, early in the Carey years, of a consent decree that stipulated improvement of services for the retarded in State facilities, under the supervision of the federal courts.

[3]Richard Ravitch, a prominent New York City businessman, later was named head of the Metropolitan Transportation Authority; David Burke, Secretary to the Governor (1975-1977); Judah Gribetz, Counsel to the Governor (1975-1978); Peter Goldmark, Director, New York State Division of the Budget (1975-1977); and Robert Morgado, Deputy Secretary to the Governor, Director of State Operations and Secretary to the Governor.

[4]William Ellinghaus, President, American Telephone and Telegraph; Richard Shinn, President and CEO, Metropolitan Life Insurance Company; Felix Rohatyn, General Partner, Lazard Freres and Company; Don Smiley, Chairman and CEO, R.H. Macy and Company; Tom Flynn, first Chairman of the Board, Municipal Assistance Corporation;

Al Casey, President and Chairman of the Board, American Airlines; Herb Elish, Executive Director, Municipal Assistance Corporation (MAC) (1975-1976); Al Shanker, President of the United Federation of Teachers, New York City, and the American Federation of Teachers; Victor Gottbaum, President, AFSCME, District Council 37; Jack Bigel, Consultant to Labor Unions on Pension Fund Investments and a major figure in the resolution of the New York Fiscal Crisis; Bill Scott, Assistant to the President, United Federation of Teachers (UFT); Barry Feinstein, a major New York City labor union leader, President of Teamsters Local 237; Harry Van Arsdale, President, New York City Central Labor Council (AFL-CIO).

[5]Michael Finnerty, Deputy Budget Director, later Director, Division of the Budget; Michael Diffley, a career Budget Division official. With Peter Goldmark, he did much of the fiscal analysis for the Governor during the crisis of the mid-1970's. His title was Head, Program Analysis and Revenue Section, DOB; Michael Del Giudice, Director of Policy management (1979-1981), later Secretary to the Governor.

[6]Dr. Kevin Cahill, Special Assistant to the Governor for Health Affairs (1975-1981); Barbara Blum, Commissioner of Social Services; Julio Martinez, Director, Division of Drug Abuse Services (1979-1982);Dr. David Axelrod, Commissioner, New York State Health Department; Lawrence Kolb, Commissioner of Mental Hygiene (1975-1977); James Introne, Assistant Secretary to the Governor, Deputy Budget Director, and later Commissioner, Office of Mental Retardation and Developmental Disabilities.

[7]John Dyson, New York State Commissioner of Commerce (1975-1979); William Hassett, New York State Commissioner of Commerce (1979-1981); George Dempster, New York State Commissioner of Commerce (1981-1982).

[8]Richard Kahan, President and CEO, Urban Development Corporation (UDC) (1978-1982); Robert Dormer, President, Job Development Authority.

[9]Mary Wells Lawrence, President, Wells, Rich, Greene Advertising Agency; Jane Maas, Creative team "I Love New York" Campaign, Wells, Rich, Greene Advertising Agency; Martin Stern, Creative team "I Love New York" Campaign, Wells, Rich, Greene Advertising Agency.

[10]Stanley Fink, Speaker, New York State Assembly; Stanley Steingut, Speaker, New York State Assembly (1975-1978); Warren Anderson, Majority Leader, New York State Senate.

[11]Lillian Roberts, Industrial Commissioner.

[12]William Hennessy, Commissioner, New York State Department of Transportation.

[13]Senator Jeremiah Bloom, ran against the Governor in the 1978 Democratic gubernatorial primary.

[14]Raymond Schuler, New York State Business Council, formerly Commissioner of Transportation.

[15]William McGowan, President, Civil Service Employees Association (CSEA).

[16]Funds for the publications of Governor Carey's papers were provided in Governor Cuomo's 1985-86 Executive Budget.

Robert J. Morgado was secretary to the governor from 1977 to 1983. Previously, during the Carey administration, he had successively been deputy secretary and director of state operations. During previous administrations, Mr. Morgado's experience included service with the Division of the Budget and as director of tax and fiscal studies for the Assembly Ways and Means Committee.

Robert Morgado

The Secretary to the Governor

MORGADO: It's now part of the historic record that the operation of state government from the mid-70's centered on the economic and financial turmoil that afflicted New York's largest cities, its development and financing agencies, and the state itself. While this crisis was not necessarily created by the '73 to '75 national recession, it was clearly propelled by it. To this point, except for a brief correction in 1971, the state budget had long grown in a continual, unchallenged manner. However, the truth of the matter was that the state's economy, which gave life to these budgets, was in decline from the late 60's. The public efforts initiated in the Rockefeller era remained a way of life for nearly ten years beyond the realities of what the state's economy could sustain.

The fact is that the '68 recession was the first from which the state emerged at a lower level of economic activity than before the recession. Most business cycles that we had known in our history were very much cyclical; at the end of a period of downturn, the state job level recovered to where it was before, and the process of expansion resumed. But, if you look at the position of the state in the early 70's, it never recovered to where it was in the late 60's.

So, by the time the national recession, the oil embargo, and all of the facts of national economic life hit us with full force in 1973-74, New York experienced an economic dislocation and job loss hemorrhage which rocked the very fabric of state government. Hugh Carey was confronted with the confluence of powerful forces in 1975: a heavily impacted economic recession, and severe financial and credit market problems. They're really two different problems, but obviously interrelated. Simultaneously, parallel but intensified financial problems erupted in the City of New York.

This was the backdrop when Governor Carey was inaugurated. On January 1, he gave his State of the State Address in rather somber tones. What is most striking, in retrospect, to someone who participated in the process and had a key role in helping to frame the themes of the governor's first State of the State Address, surely, was the lack of public understanding of the thrust of that address. There surely were those more intimately associated with government who had some sense of what he was talking about, but by and large, the general public did not. Nor was his articulation of political themes really broadly understood by the legislature. History erases memories very quickly, and time periods get compressed. After the fact,

27

you can intellectualize about events and separate out things that at the time were not as clearly understood. For example, the governor himself could not clearly foresee the full implications of what he said in his first State of the State Address to the New York State Legislature. Soon thereafter, the course of events became largely the determinant of the kind of government we had to put together, and the kind of strategies we would have to formulate.

Within 30 days of Governor Carey's assumption of the governorship, the Urban Development Corporation of New York State defaulted. That was the first major default of a public authority in New York State's history. It was the first in a chain of events that began to unfold throughout the year, so that by the end of that year the institutions of this state had been severely tested, and dramatically changed. By the time 1976 rolled in, New York State government was significantly different from what it was in 1974.

That singular act of default of a major public corporation was followed by the near default of the City of New York, the closing of the credit markets to all of the state's public authorities, and a dramatic change in the relationship between the federal government and the state (in terms of advancing credit to a major municipality). The state, for the first time, played a determinative role in the financial affairs of the City of New York, and by a series of other actions began to deal with local government problems from Yonkers to Buffalo, from school districts to local authorities. As a consequence of all this, not only the articulation of political wisdom, but the interrelationship of institutions in the state was substantially altered.

I have set the historical backdrop, because you can always describe political accomplishments in a series of micro-actions or policies or strategies, but I prefer to deal with government in terms of the overall forces which shape actions and the ability of executives to deal with those forces. To meet the test of those forces is indeed the best indication of success. It is in this sense that I would posit that the Carey administration succeeded. It succeeded because it met the most serious problems of our times, it met them in a way that the institutions today are healthier for it, and it met them in a way that politics changed in order to accommodate the realities of economic circumstances.

The governor's accomplishments flow from those essential actions in '75 that first created a series of economic answers to financial conditions, and then dealt constructively with the state's economy, to the degree any state government can geopolitically deal with economic development. An area of major accomplishment for the governor was his ability to deal with economic problems and the institutional changes that were wrought by those problems.

The second area that I think we take a great deal of pride in, was in coping with certain human service problems, which had been neglected for a very, very long period of time. That also had its genesis in 1975. For example, the new state concern was signaled by the signing of the Willowbrook Consent Decree in 1975.

The Carey administration put a great deal of effort and resources into dealing with the mental retardation and mental health problem in the state. By the end of the governor's terms in office, these institutions had improved remarkably. While we continue to run a significant number of large institutionally-based services, alternative and more community-based services now exist, a range of services which, at best, were primitive before 1975. The popular word "de-institutionalization" was, for the first time, given governmental substance.

Also in year one, 1975, we saw the enactment of the State Environmental Quality Review Act (SEQR). It layered environmental review process requirements onto the state regulatory system that in some ways were more severe than what one already had to go through with the federal government. But that was the way people thought about problems in 1975, and that act was a campaign promise of the governor. To some degree thereafter, our concern became one of trying to achieve the objectives of the act, but through a sane and more rational administrative process.

Or again, historically the state dealt with the banking industry as a captive industry of the state. Clearly, by the late 70's this could not be the case. Technological changes in electronics and communications meant that the banking business could not remain the same.

Of course, now it's common parlance. We are in the age of financial supermarkets, with Shearson-American Express and Merrill Lynch becoming pseudo-banks and an insurance company becoming a brokerage firm. Surely, everybody understands that today, but believe me, they did not in 1975. When we first began to talk with the legislature about having to de-regulate control of usury rates, it took us about two years to convince the leadership that we could not pretend to be masters of the money markets anymore. We almost lost half of the credit card industry to South Dakota before this recognition became substance in legislation.

Towards the end of the governor's second term, we were approaching the insurance industry on nearly the same basis. We de-regulated one area called the Insurance Exchange, creating a free zone for certain kinds of marketing of insurance policies. If, in fact, the state is the ultimate protector of the consumer, there are certain kinds of regulation that are clearly required, but when that regulation limits either choices or the kind of self-selection that a consumer may make on a purely volitional basis, we have to let the marketplace operate a little more freely.

This is to say, if a consumer purchases a $25,000 life insurance policy, that is an enormously different choice from a person insuring his thoroughbred's legs for $10 million. It's a different kind of risk insurance. To try to regulate one the same way as the other is a fallacy. Unfortunately, that's what we were doing in this state. Or again, we made little distinction between a $50,000 mortgage and a million dollar mortgage. So, we needed to make those kinds of policy separations to balance consumer protection with the marketplace. As a result, the Insurance Exchange is operating in the state today and it has created a number of jobs in New York City.

The International Free Zone for Banking was another thing we accomplished. Now other states are trying to get into the act. We regret that in almost every case it took two years to get a measure through the legislature and another year to obtain the required clearances by the federal government. By the time we had it in place, we had another dozen or so states that were then competing with us when the idea originated with this state.

I've tried to identify what I call the significant determinants of what the government was and how it performed. I obviously have emphasized what we would consider our major accomplishments in dealing with the financial structures, the economic development problems, and the large institutional complex of the state, and the political, the institutional, and regulatory changes required. Beyond that there are a series of smaller accomplishments which, while perhaps less visible, are significant in themselves.

One of the areas in which I, in particular, take a great deal of both comfort and pride is the area of corrections. When the governor's first term began, there were 15,000 state prisoners. At the end of his second term, that population had grown to 27,000. The numbers may be slightly off, but the fact is that we were able to accommodate the largest and most significant growth ever in the state's prison population. To do it in a way that, except for some minor incidents, was without a disruption or a severe prison problem was a stroke of good fortune. To an important degree, too, it was due to having a governor who was willing to be gutsy about the fact that he had to put the resources there, had to make some choices, and had to be very quick about it.

We created facilities all over the state, taking on community after community, never being loved for any of it, but getting it done. Enlarging that network from a capacity of 17,000 to a capacity of 28,000 in a period of seven years was a remarkable accomplishment. In 1975, this state ran what was basically a series of very old maximum security facilities. There were a few shorter term facilities but not many, maybe 15 units. Today, there must be 40 or 50 different correctional facility sites. The work force was increased from 5,000 correction guards in 1975 to between 11,000 and 12,000 correctional officers today. Not only was the problem of finding facility sites politically sensitive, but there were a million ways to get tangled in regulation. Yet, the administration pulled together the various institutions in order to get things done.

I operated on behalf of the governor in two very different ways. One was to provide the day-to-day management of institutions. At the same time, my other function was to provide the leadership on issues that the governor felt were important, making sure that his particular agenda was being worked on by members of his administration. So whether it was corrections or Medicaid, we continually created or re-created task forces, interposing that informal administrative mechanism to bring pressure and keep resolving more issues.

There will always be too much softness in any bureaucracy as large as the state's. And if you leave it to the regular process, programs will either get lost, frustrated, or take forever. I gained an appreciation for and understanding of both institutional actions and non-institutional actions and ended up flipping back and forth in deciding which process would be most effective for a particular issue.

We could not leave corrections to the normal process. There are too many hobbyhorses out there that continually have to be restrained. In order to build a prison, lots of things are involved: from community education to actual construction, from finding financial resources to gaining environmental approvals. Each of these has its own rigorous process of review. In cases like this, we had to cut across it all and articulate a common goal. For example, I would say to Bob Flacke at DEC, "Don't tell me what we can't do. Your job is to make sure that it's environmentally sound and not judge whether it's good environmental policy. There are other areas where you will make an environmental policy judgment, but the call here is to give me the procedural mechanism to make sure the project is sound." Bob Flacke's job was to make sure that if there were going to be hurdles, we had a way to go over them. The policy decision was already made by the governor.

Or I might say to the Office of General Services, "Your job is to tell me how we get freed from the various competitive bidding processes, which have a purpose, but, in this case, could frustrate the hell out of us." Somebody had to take the leadership on each of these issues and the sub-issues involved. I needed the commissioner of General Services to clear things through the comptroller's office so that no individual process would bog down the other. The prisoners were coming through the door at about a hundred a month, so it was obvious that the facilities were required. A schedule was drawn up. We knew what we had to have and when we had to have it. That's an example of where I would not use the institutional process, but instead would use an executive-centered, pressuring process.

QUESTION: How did the priorities and urgencies of the administration get transmitted to the agencies? Are you implying that there was some resistance or lack of clarity on the part of the top leadership in each agency?

MORGADO: Certain issues normally flow through the institutional processes, usually through the Budget Division. The fact of life is that 90 percent of all directions came from Budget. When we felt an area required a unique set of actions, then that was translated directly through the creation of an ever-evolving and changing set of ad hoc task force groups.

QUESTION: You apparently felt that in order to convey the urgency and the priority of a particular action, you needed to jolt the status quo in the agencies by creating this super-curricular mechanism. How did the urgency get conveyed down the line? Did you expect the members of that task force to do that?

MORGADO: Yes. In each case, the task force would include the head of the agency or somebody directly appointed by him. I would just convene the group and keep the score. With this kind of situation, as long as one has the energy, it was possible to change the whole nature of governmental behavior. All I had to do on behalf of the governor was to bring together Bob Flacke, John Egan, Tom Coughlin, Howard Miller or Mark Lawton, Jim Prevost and myself.[1]

Jim had a problem when it was his facilities we were trying to take away. This is a good example of a commissioner who was at war with himself. He understood what we were trying to do, but it was very difficult for him because of the constituency he represented. My job was to get this done while, from a legal standpoint, not ever asking Egan to do something wrong or Flacke to do something wrong or have Prevost, more importantly, commit suicide with the client group he also had to serve.

The most recent example of that, which the present government found less desirable, was the Pilgrim Hospital conversion. We went with a corrections facility at Pilgrim because that's the way our task force felt and that was the way Jim was best protected. There is always a series of internal trade-offs one has to do in government. The politics sank that one, but from the standpoint of institutional policy, it was the right choice. It was a facility that could be easily cordoned off from the rest of the population that Jim was serving, so that you had co-location but not really co-habitation. It's that kind of sensitivity that is needed: working with an agency on its areas of concern, but at all times understanding where you want to go.

QUESTION: Let me pull together some of the themes here, from the standpoint of a career person in Budget. Both Carey and Rockefeller had strong chiefs of staff. Carey had you; Rockefeller had Marshall and Ronan. The difference was that under Rockefeller there was, in his own words, a "creative tension." There was really a strong counsel's office in his administration, staffed by first rate lawyers like Mike Whiteman. The program staff were also strong people. (I'm talking about the hands-on groups that we had to contend with and worry about, not the leadership.) So Rockefeller had a situation where the Budget Division, as an institution, was played off against strong lawyers and strong program staff. This created tension. The Budget Division was respected during the Carey years. Although there was a strong chief of staff, the counsel's office was initially invisible and the program staff was relatively weak. It would seem that these critical defects made your job a lot harder and more demanding than the same job under Rockefeller.[2]

Why did that happen? Why were the program staffers generally a cut or two below what Rockefeller had in all but his last years? You had one or two superstars there, but it was generally not the most distinguished group in the world.

MORGADO: I agree with your analysis, but it was a matter of choice. Quite frankly, I believe that one of the weaknesses of the Rockefeller administration was that it put too much into the central, institutional processes and less in the supporting structure. When you're developing a company, you bring your managers together centrally, but once you've got the company going you export them out. Governor Rockefeller was very good at central building, but weaker, in my view, at actually running things.

We wanted to reverse that. We wanted to get the best people we could out into the agencies. As a result, it was a revolving door in our offices—bring people in for short periods and then put them out into the line agencies. We took the best people we could find in Budget and put them into the agencies. I created a different kind of central arrangement, with four or five good people around us for overall planning and strategizing, but not twenty-five functionaries. The role of the counsel ought to be clearance; they ought not to be sitting in judgment. The role of the program staff ought to be one of liaison and issue identification; they ought not to be running the agencies.

I'm sure all of this took place to the chagrin of the Budget Division. By the end of the Carey administration, the commissioner of Health was much more important to health policy development than any program staff in the governor's office. No matter how terrific the program staff were, they had issue strengths, not continual, operating, day-to-day strengths. As a result, we had the strongest commissioner of Corrections we've ever had. Obviously, there are always weaknesses. I'm speaking of the thrust of what we were trying to do.

Rather than create a tension by having the first floor exist on the first floor, I brought the first floor up to the second floor.[3] That was very different. I made the Budget Division part of the central policy process, a participant in the executive process. I forced them to understand the political judgments as well as the financial judgments in ways that they were not previously prepared to do.

Rarely did someone in the Budget Division venture to the second floor in the years between 1958 and 1974. One of the things Budget found very disturbing was that I would get on the phone and call at 8:30 if I wanted something. That used to bother Howard Miller because it upset the ingrained, central direction of that institution. Since I considered the function of the Budget Division to be a key to the operation of running government, I considered it very much a part of our second floor apparatus.

So, I saw every Budget bureau chief as part of the management team in a way that no other secretary ever viewed them. I brought the Budget Division institutionally, psychologically, and emotionally into the fabric of the second floor, and I de-emphasized the program office and made it more of a liaison office. As much as possible, we forced the heads of the major state agencies to be strong people, and to exercise executive responsibility, and not to be fearful about the Budget Division. When they had a problem, I arbitrated between them and the Budget Division.

QUESTION: Did you intend for this to happen?

MORGADO: Yes, I intended it.

QUESTION: How did you deal with those agencies where the commissioner was not one of those strong types, either by choice or by what he perceived to be non-acceptance from the governor's office?

MORGADO: I like to think that the people who complained the loudest that they didn't have the access to our office were usually the people who were the weakest. The people who were strong and very secure didn't worry about that. In fact, the process of management by exception ought to exist. The executive agencies are too large to pretend that you're going to run everything centrally. The minute you start thinking that way, you're doomed to failure. The Health Department runs itself; the Mental Health Department runs itself; Corrections runs itself.

Basically, the art of central administration is to make sure that these institutions don't collide, while at the same time trying to give them a sense of the common goals that you want them to pursue, and most importantly, trying to give them the support they require.

In almost every case where this harmony existed, there was trust and no one felt very isolated. In those cases, I would support them with the governor. They made mistakes, and we would adjust, but by and large, you support your team. I always tried to operate with that principle in mind. My concern was with the weaker agencies. Any large set of institutions is going to have uneven strength. We tried to have the best people in the most critical areas. As a result, there were seven or eight agencies that I worried about enormously. If I never saw the head of some of the other agencies, it didn't matter that much.

QUESTION: Does that imply that there were perhaps half a dozen major program areas that were your political and administrative focal points?

MORGADO: Absolutely. They were Transportation; Social Services; the three health agencies; the security agencies: Corrections, State Police, and Youth; and the economic agencies: Commerce, Banking, Insurance, and Environmental Conservation.

QUESTION: Were you willing to tolerate relatively static program operations in the other agencies?

MORGADO: Yes, and we did.

QUESTION: Through this period, how did you communicate with the governor? Did you view yourself as implementing his policies? To what extent did you use outside people? How often did you see the governor?

MORGADO: There was common sense in his style. Obviously, I largely accommodated to that style. He didn't have patience with the day-to-day administration of government. It was my job to go through the agenda with commissioners who obviously had a series of different views on the governor's program. It was rightly my job. For him to have done this would have been an inefficient use of his time.

In honesty, I always felt I had a complete communion with him. I dealt with him on all aspects of his life, from his politics to his government, from his personal ambitions to his familial expectations.

The day-to-day working relationship was always there and existed on several levels. He preferred to deal with individuals rather than with institutions. To this day, I think that perhaps I best served him by having a more intimate relationship and understanding of the institutional processes, and by trying to make those processes work on his behalf. He was always smart enough to understand both that and his personal strengths. He always considered himself the "idea person," which he was.

He said to me recently that now that he's a private citizen, he's not limited to one idea a month. And I smiled and said, "no, only one idea a week." He could spout ideas interminably. If accommodated,

I could have spent entire days staffing his ideas. My role was to listen to the ideas and cull the best. He could spout more ideas at one sitting than I could possibly ever think about in a year. The implementer-type person has to take those ideas, run with them, and make the practical ones work.

QUESTION: Governor Rockefeller would also spout ideas.

MORGADO: Yes, in the same way.

QUESTION: What did you do with the ideas you thought were crazy? Did you play the role of the abominable "no man" as well?

MORGADO: Sometimes it was a matter of listening and saying "terrific." Other times it meant coming back to him to clarify one or two points. I ignored the ideas I thought we couldn't do anything with, unless he raised them again. If he raised them again seriously or joshingly, it became a judgment call as to whether I ultimately got people working on them.

QUESTION: Is it possible for a governor to be his own chief of staff?

MORGADO: I don't think so.

Those of us who have long memories have heard the suggestion that the governor be his own chief of staff enough times in our lifetime that we can't worry about it or take it that seriously. However, the current governor seems to want to take it seriously. Mayor Koch did when he came in, and President Carter did when he came in, and so on. It goes back forever. The nature of our politics almost requires it. Of course, it defies every essential principle of management that I know.

For example, when you're scheduling a governor, he cannot think about what he ought to be doing. He has to think about what he is doing at that moment. It's not that he's incapable of doing both, but just the two roles require different kinds of people. As an anecdote, he was scheduled one day to do A, B, C, and D. He came in and complained that he wasn't going to do it. He said, "I don't like the schedule; I'm going to do this and then this." And we said, "A schedule is not a Chinese menu. This is what you should do. We have determined that you should do A, B, C, and D. I am very good at determining what you ought to do. I don't know how to deliver the speeches; I would be horrible at it. You go make the speeches and I'll make the schedule. If you don't want to do the speeches, you sit here and make the schedule, and I'll go out and give the speeches, and we'll both do a terrible job."

Any large organization requires that certain functions be done by certain people in certain ways. When a person is intimately involved in actualizing a role, it is very difficult for him to objectively judge his role at the same time.

QUESTION: Must there be only one chief of staff? Is the concept of director of State Operations and some sharing of that chief of staff responsibility unworkable?

MORGADO: It's hard to give a generic answer to it. It's a question of personalities. I could tell you very strongly that it would not have worked with Hugh Carey. And, I suspect, it would not work in most cases. To be a chief of staff to a governor is one of the most hazardous duties anybody can do. Ultimately it's very, very hard to share the responsibility. Human relations are so complex; it is inevitably problematic to put two people together and get the chemistry working so that they can develop an understanding relationship. If you try to share the responsibility among three or four or five people, you just keep multiplying the human dimension side of the equation. It's not impossible, just unlikely.

QUESTION: How did you manage the inevitable conflicts that emerged? And didn't you feel alone at some points? Despite your good relations with the commissioners, given your preeminent role in the policy-making process, there must have been some distance between you and them.

MORGADO: First, I'd like to dispel the common notion that if you have a chief of staff, somehow you have a lot of sycophants around. I'm exaggerating somewhat, but the point is that you can have a lot of very sturdy people in a decentralized process with strong central direction. These are not incompatible forces. I believe that's what we had around the governor. We did try to pick people with strength. In fact, the governor worked best with people who were strong. It wasn't a willy-nilly bunch. If I did play a preeminent role, it was a role that was occasioned by my relationship with the governor. One of the things that is often missed in all of this is that that role at no time really conditioned how the governor behaved. It was always a condition of how he behaved.

I would say to my colleagues, "If you disagree with me, the governor's office is 30 steps down the hallway. Open my door, go through one secretary, knock on his door, and he'll be happy to see you. In fact, I will ask him to see you because you have a different idea." Except for Sandy Frucher,[4] very few ever regularly took up the invitation. That created a certain amount of distance. By and large, I did have very good rapport with the group around the governor, at least the more mature ones who understood the processes, understood the governor, and worked very cohesively with him.

Yes, ultimately, it's a very lonely role. I don't know how else to do it. I thought about it a lot during my tenure and to some degree afterwards. Was there a different way? I will never know. The way I best worked with the governor, and at the same time protected him, was, to a large degree, to uphold the sanctity of our manner of relating to each other. Whether it was my pushing him or him pushing me had

37

to remain a private matter.

QUESTION: Reflecting on the personalities around him, do you predict that Mr. Cuomo will have a chief of staff by the end of this four-year term? Is there any kind of inevitability about this?

MORGADO: Personalities are vastly different. Governor Cuomo will probably try a lot longer not to have a chief of staff. Governor Rockefeller was a very strong individual and Hugh Carey was a very strong individual. It requires a certain amount of internal strength and security to deal with a strong chief of staff system, and that strength and security often comes from maturity, both personal and institutional. In my judgment, there must be some form of a chief of staff. There are two roles that must be played: one of them is inevitable; the other may be less so. The inevitable role is what I call the central administration vs. the field. In my view, matrix management rarely works between the central apparatus and the field; it doesn't matter whether one is talking about a multi-national corporation, the Catholic Church, the Boy Scouts, or New York State government. It's just too complex.

Generally, you cannot have functional relationships implementing the delegation of authority. In my view, for this to happen successfully, there is an absolute requirement of organizational maturity and a clear articulation of goals that is rarely achieved on a consistent basis by complex organizations. So, for the central administration to relate to the field through five different or six different individuals or processes is simply naive. Unless they straighten that out, New York State government will not function effectively. It cannot function that way in government any more that it can function that way in business.

I know some of the more mature corporations in America believe that they have matrix management, in which the functional relationships govern the flow of decisions. We tried it during the growth years of the divisions in our company in New York City. We're changing it today because it just doesn't work to have the sales and marketing person and the operations and engineering people who are all located centrally dealing directly with the operating or field managers. The result has been pure chaos, a conflict of our direction, and managerial paralysis. So, that's out the door; now we're changing the role of the functional groups into staff groupings. The line of authority simply has to flow from the top to the bottom.

I think Governor Cuomo is going to have to recognize that. If not, the Budget Division will run government by default, because it's the only singular, integrated unit which will exist. If the governor's office doesn't impose or interdict with a singular line of authority, and if it wants to continue to deal with six different structures, then one of two results will be obtained. Either the Budget Division will become the dominant part of government or government won't function at all. I don't think there are any other choices.

Now, how a governor operates internally with his own staff is a different matter. He can always have six people in the room if he wishes and interact with six different people at all times. Nevertheless, once decisions are made, a singular line of authority for the flow of decisions has to emerge or government will not function effectively.

QUESTION: Why was there such a delay in making some of the initial appointments in 1975? It seemed as if there were many hold-over appointees, but that they delayed filling subordinate positions.

MORGADO: There were two issues involved. One was the freshness of the government and that it had not yet developed a process for getting things done. In those days, everything was done by the governor personally. A Democratic administration had not controlled state government for 16 years, so the task of suddenly trying to create a personal appointment structure had inevitable delays. A campaign apparatus group was close to the governor; yet he remained ever-suspicious of that group. That also made him cautious.

Governor Carey also had, as is perhaps the case with any new government, a wise men process. The wise men were the political leaders, including Bob Wagner, Sr., Alex Rose, Jerry Cummins, Pat Cunningham, and David Garth, who had helped get the governor elected. In the initial weeks, they really presided over appointments with the governor. Yet they were primarily outside of government, functioning on a very part-time basis. That situation existed for much longer than I'd like to admit. It slowly changed with time, but it led to many frustrations initially. It was definitely cumbersome to work with. There was no efficiency there yet for him. He subjected the advice of this group of wise men to his own review. He would ask, "Why is he telling me this? Why is he pushing so and so?" The primary reason for the delay was that the new government had no process for making appointments that the governor had any confidence in.[5]

Secondly, right from the very beginning, he had the UDC default on his hands. He was just coming into office and did not have a clear idea of what the credit markets were all about, except that he assumed that the default was a serious problem for us. He was way-laid right from the beginning by a budget and financial nightmare and barely had the time to create the structures to help him get decisions made.

His first government was really a government of strangers in a strange land. His first secretary, David Burke, was from the Dreyfuss

Fund and prior to that out of Washington. David knew little about state government at the very beginning. And, yet, he was the secretary to the governor. Peter Goldmark, the first Budget director, was from Massachusetts and he showed up in New York State on February 1. Judah Gribetz was from the City of New York and the city government, and so had some contact with Albany. Kevin Cahill, the governor's personal advisor on health affairs, was a practicing physician from New York City. His first appointments officer was a college professor from Cortland. About six of us were his first personal aides. (For some reason, six people tend to be the collection initially in any government!) He had suddenly tossed people together who didn't really know each other. We were all strangers to each other. I was the only one who was not a stranger to New York State. For all practical purposes, everybody else was. I was also the youngest, at 32 years old, and not really in the first string in those first few months, except that the governor listened to me because I was the only one with direct knowledge about the state government.

The first thing we did was to install ourselves in the Budget Division. The first time I met the governor was around Thanksgiving of '74. We began to brief him about some of the problems he was going to face, and about the budget that he was going to have to put together between between November 20 and February 1st. He said to me, "Well, that's Wilson's budget. His Budget Division is preparing it, not mine. And I won't have anything to do with that." I said, "Your name is going to be on the cover. You become governor on January 1 by the constitution, and, by the constitution, you submit a budget on February 1, and it's going to say Hugh L. Carey on it, not Malcolm Wilson. That Budget Division's yours, whether you like it or not." It was a jarring reality.

QUESTION: How did he react to this?

MORGADO: Quietly, as was always his way. He thought about it, started sitting down and making decisions about it with us, but always he kept calling it Wilson's budget. That didn't matter, since he was also making the decisions. As long as he was making the decisions, the budget would inevitably become his. The Wilson administration was not helpful. I made the Budget Division work for us from late November on, and that was really how our administration got into the operation of the government.

QUESTION: Most public administration educational programs emphasize managerial techniques, bureaucratic rationality of a functional sort. Do you believe that the way in which such public administration/public management programs are structured would have helped to prepare you for your role in the Carey administration? And if not, how should they be altered, and how should that be related in some way to the development of an executive capacity in the New York State government?

MORGADO: I would separate the question into two areas. First a general answer. I think much of what I said, in terms of my concerns about the future, is based on the lack of understanding of some of the things that really ought to be developed in an educational setting and in people that are being trained for public life or public responsibilities. It is the humanist versus the technician argument. I will always take the path of the former rather than the latter. I came to government with training in the background and the history of the state and the state's value structure. I think that's extremely important, and I'm not just saying that because it sounds good; I believe it.

Unfortunately, too many people in government today don't have that background, and that's why they're very cavalier about institutions. Training should be not only learning the rules of the game, but understanding the philosophy behind those rules and then behaving in ways that increase the ability of government to manage itself. I am not uncomfortable or embarrassed about my own training for work in government, because I came with a good deal of understanding of the state's budgetary framework, the theories behind state government, and with a very healthy respect for it's institutions.

The one thing you can never train anybody to have is judgment; it doesn't matter whether it's in business or public life. They will develop it with time or they won't. And that outcome is rarely determined by their level of training or intelligence.

You can divide most of the world into people who are defined as bureaucratic (and that's not a negative word) and those you can define as entrepreneurial. Most organizations are also one or the other, whether they are public or private. I come from an entrepreneurial mode, and I behave that way. If there is a failing in the academy, it is in its lack of the understanding of the differences between the corporate and the entrepreneurial mentality. There's a very good recent book on the best seller list entitled *The Pursuit of Excellence*. It is about private corporations. I view private corporations as not essentially different from public corporations in terms of organizational behavior. In either case, certain things will determine excellence, and education is one of them. The private sector understands that to some degree, but not as much as they think they do. The public sector doesn't understand that at all; they really ought to be preparing administrators who are also entrepreneurs.

QUESTION: How might government change that? Some time ago, the academy was trying to get a project under way to start commissioners thinking about the responsibility they had for training in future years. The thesis there was that any administration essentially thinks in about three-year cycles. Six months are used to get organized; six months are used to campaign. Is it our fault and the fault of others at the senior executive levels that we don't think of the future enough?

MORGADO: I think the thesis is probably correct. I spoke with somebody the other night who was a member of our administration and now is with the Cuomo administration. He said he's often asked to contrast his present role with his previous role. He answered, "Well, now we have a lot of people around, and we discuss things. I always felt that when Bob was presiding over a meeting, it was like the Shogun Court." And I said, "What do you mean by that?" And he said, "You obviously always had a complex agenda and all of us were pieces in a plan. In fact, you always had your eye two steps beyond where we were and at all times knew where you wanted ultimately to go." I like to think that, whether by happenstance or direction, we were involved in a longer-term process. Personally, I always tried to figure out where we wanted to go and drove towards it, even if it meant a multi-year framework.

QUESTION: In retrospect what would you have done differently?

MORGADO: I think what most troubles me is that I failed Governor Carey by not pushing him in certain political directions which could have made the management of government a lot simpler. (Over time, we let ourselves get into situations where we were compounding our problems more than necessary.) We accomplished most of what we wanted to do, but there was a constant attempt to out-think the process, rather than to make the process work for us. It would have been relatively easy to change, had I been willing to exercise the energy to keep pushing him on the political side of his job, which he was not particularly interested in.

QUESTION: You said that New York State government was transformed in '76. Carey was a candidate in 1974. That's an extraordinarily short period of time for a transformation of government of that size. By transformation, do you mean change concerning the legislative role or do you mean concerning the premises of government, rather then the institutional structure? Was that transformation institutionalized? Could you talk, in a bit more detail, about that comment?

MORGADO: One of the most significant changes which I refer to was a revolution in the relationship between the state and City of New York. Suddenly, you had imposed upon the state's major municipality a super-structure that was managing its budget. The state was managing the city's financing, when it was going to market, its contracts, its labor union settlements. That changed the very nature of state and city relations in a very short period of time.

Except for the near default of the City of New York, I don't think there's any event that could have changed the institutional fabric as significantly.

Another drastic change was that most of the public authorities of the state were put under a Public Authorities Control Board that permanently determined the limits of their behavior. With the exception of the Power Authority and the Port Authority, suddenly the plans of all the public authorities were now subject to total executive control. Every project and every bond issue became subject to direct executive and legislative control. It's interesting to me as someone who's studied government, how drastically the public authorities of the state and their operation have changed and how little comment has accompanied the changes. In fact, most of what appears in the press assumes that we have these omnipotent authorities. In fact, the current administration still talks about public authorities in terms of getting them under control.

The executive controls everything the public authorities do today, except for the Power Authority and the Port Authority. They approve everything, right down to each nursing home that is built, each hospital that is financed, and each small housing project that is authorized. There is little difference between what those authorities do now in capital financing and what the State University does in capital financing. The executive has the same kind of control mechanism over them, if it exercises it.

QUESTION: From a management point of view, do you think that New York State government is strong enough, has enough executive capacity, to have all that authority?

MORGADO: I worry about that. The Budget Division, in my view, does not have enough executive capacity, and it's partly our fault. They have not treated that responsibility as seriously as they should have because they lack the capacity. The division pretended that it was the person who was writing the baseball line-up for the manager, rather than understanding that the manager was in fact making the decisions himself. They had the authority to do it.

If the Budget Division was exercising the authority that it should have been exercising, the Dormitory Authority would not have gotten into difficulty in 1983. Not only does it have an *ex officio* member on that authority's board of directors, but every financing arrangement that comes before the board comes not only with the bond issue but the investment agreements that make the issue possible. The decisions were made with the approval of the state executive process. We blew it.

The answer is "No." The authority which is now there is not managed by the allocation of staff responsibility commensurate with the assignment. We absolutely spent more time reviewing the clerks in the Office of General Services budget than we did on the entire financing for the Dormitory Authority.

QUESTION: It is a current feeling among newspaper editors that one of Governor Carey's failings was in terms of his dealings with the legislative leaders. How did the governor deal with the legislative leaders?

MORGADO: It worsened over time.

QUESTION: Why was that?

MORGADO: First, I'd like to separate personal issues from certain inevitable institutional trends which were determining behavior patterns to a large extent. We've seen a disintegration, over time, of executive and legislative harmony. Perhaps our government helped encourage the disharmony a bit and propelled it towards its inevitability, but the fact is that the legislature was emerging as a very different institution in the late '60's. It had changed enormously even in the last years of the Rockefeller administration.

I arrived in the state in the mid-60's and the process was beginning then. In 1965, it was the first time in 40 years that the Democratic party took a house in the legislature and it was also the first time a professional staff was created in the Ways and Means Committee. I came out of the legislative process; I spent five years there at different times of my life. I know it as well as the executive side, and I am troubled by certain institutional patterns. The legislature has the authority and the ability to frustrate policy if that is their goal.

Coming from a slightly different side of the equation, I always felt you really had to have goals that you were aiming towards. The process made it possible for you to achieve or not achieve them, but the process was not the end in itself.

Now, it seems that the process too often has become the end in itself. There is no espousal of any goals. It's all become: "How can we stop the executive? How can we do this? How can we stop that?" Nobody says, "This is what we want to do; what do you need to get it done?" There's less and less of that and more and more of neutralizing positions, and then trying to outflank each other.

I wonder whether part of this trend is due to the spirit of the times. It's not unique to New York. It clearly exists in other states, and, to some degree, at the congressional level. Until you create a greater institutional sense within people, a greater sense of their respective responsibilities, a value structure, things will not change.

The leaders are at the edge of it all. I don't deny that they are primary to making it better or worse. But we must define the core values of what we're trying to achieve and develop a greater respect for the institutional relationships. Respect for institutional roles has disintegrated, and Governor Carey was not responsible for that. It has happened over time.

I thought very philosophically and theoretically in my earlier years about a responsible legislative role, but at all times maintained a primary interest in the protection of the executive as an institution. It worries me that people don't think about that any more. Now they want to create structures to interdict the ability of the executive to operate. So the legislature passes bills that create pseudo-executive arrangements for themselves. During my years with the legislature, these approaches would never have been considered.

That doesn't mean we disputed the role of the legislature. Proper oversight is their function, and is required. There are certain elementary facts of governmental life, managerial concepts, and constitutional responsibilities, that ought to be at the core of the legislative role. When you start fragmenting the authority—but not, at the same time, changing responsibility—then you create structures that cannot work.

I can give you scores of examples. For instance, the legislature passed a bill that created a legislative commission to oversee Stewart Airport. When you read about it, you say to yourself, "Hey, they're the Department of Transportation! They have responsibility for planning allocation of resources, execution, and plan approvals. That is not the legislative function. How is the Department of Transportation, or whatever the institution that really has the ultimate responsibility within the executive, going to co-exist with a legislative body that compromises its authority without changing its responsibilities?"

These fundamental changes in the fabric of legislative/executive relationships are just magnified by the personality differences. Perhaps we handled the personal side of executive/legislative relations less than adequately; but it is naive to view this apart from the breakdown in institutional responsibilities between the executive and the legislature.

I would say, to my last breath, that while we could have changed the perception of things, we could not have substantially changed the outcomes. However, if illusion is often reality, you have to deal with illusions, and we were short on that score. As long as you leave yourself open for critical attack, it lessens your ability to operate in other ways. Style is important.

QUESTION: You focused on the institutional changes in the role of the legislature, a national phenomenon as well as a New York phenomenon. Would you see this also as in part reflecting changes in the political structure of the state? For instance, Governor Smith, Governor Dewey, and Governor Rockefeller, for a good deal of their administrations, were not just governors, they were also the dominant leaders in their party in a way that is going to be very difficult for governors to be in the future. Would that influence the way in which the governor dealt with the legislature?

MORGADO: Yes. Political authority has disintegrated; the party systems are basically non-entities today. While Governor Rockefeller could, and did, rely upon his state chairman to exercise a little discipline in the legislative process on his behalf, we had no similarly strong institution. Legislators, by and large, with the exception of those from the City of New York and the County of Nassau, do not rise up through the party ranks anymore and, therefore, they don't have a strong identity with and loyalty to their county leaders or a sense of institutional obligation. The structure is still there, but it's not a force for discipline or integration any more. I don't think any future chief executive will have that force, as far as I can tell. The process has changed. Elections are more costly today and that in itself changes how people get elected.

Parties are just not as important in an electoral sense. They clearly were not important to Hugh Carey. Political parties today are amplifiers. You must worry about their volume creating too much reverberation. If so, you turn them down. You do what you have to do so that they don't create noise in the system, but you cannot expect symphonic music from them. You are not going to get that outcome.

QUESTION: Would you have had less difficulty with the personal dimension of legislative relations if the governor were a serious candidate for president?

MORGADO: No, I don't think so.

QUESTION: Would you make a similar comment about the courts to those you made about the legislature?

MORGADO: Yes, to a substantial degree. Take the Willowbrook Master's Panel. We believed rightly or wrongly that we were trying like hell to make the consent decree work. In our government, the executive ultimately has the responsibility to balance competing values. In this particular example, the needs of retarded children and their parents must be balanced against the needs of other constituencies in the state. In their role as advocate for one set of needs, the court often interposes final judgments on the state government system, in fact imposing one value over many others. It is making it impossible for the executive to balance one set of needs against other needs, expropriating for itself a judgment call in one area, unrestrained by the need to relate that call to the needs of any other area.

COMMENT: Yet, the executive and legislative branches have really pushed a lot of decisions into the courts, e.g. property taxes and abortion.

MORGADO: On a different level, that's true. There's a fine line between decisions the court ought to be making and ones where they've taken on a managerial role. You can always get issues to court through due process to try and get some sense of what kind of legislative solutions can then crystalize.

QUESTION: Three areas of policy that you mentioned in your opening remarks—fiscal issues, deinstitutionalization, and changing of the regulatory emphasis—were essentially reactive. Were there any programs that you or the governor or the administration overtly set out to accomplish that you were unable to do? Did the climate of 1975-1976 set the framework for the whole eight years?

MORGADO: I think it did. It created the whole environment in which we had to operate. Ultimately, you can always come back and relate everything that you tried to do to that context. Some of our actions were reactive, others may have been more initiative.

QUESTION: If you knew that you were going to be in office for eight years rather than four years, what would you have done differently in the first year?

MORGADO: Probably nothing.

QUESTION: Carey's decision not to run for a third term was unusual in itself. Was it strictly a political or was it a personal decision? Did you anticipate the political malaise and the administrative malaise which followed?

MORGADO: The decision was preceded by a long introspective debate. He was very, very circumspect with whomever he talked to about it. I believe that for some time, he only talked to me about it.

I started discussing the subject with him in September of 1981. We had many, many conversations between then and the end of October. We debated the good, the bad, the pluses, the minuses, but it always came back to self-reflection. He thought, "I'm 64 and healthy, but I don't know if I will be healthy at 68. Why should I do it again? I've accomplished the things that I have been most concerned about. How can I improve upon that? Most likely I'll detract from it. On top of that, I'm going to have to go out there and raise $8 million. I hate groveling for campaign funds; it makes my stomach turn. Why do I want to do that again? What do I have to prove?"

Those were the essential reasons and they were highly personal. He said, "I don't want to run again, because I don't like doing what I have to do to win." He reflected on what he'd accomplished and whether there was much more he could do. "Would a third term add or subtract?" And he mused about his health, and what another four years as governor could do. He felt that he had five or six good years of economic production ahead, and that surrendering another four years of his life to the public sector would leave him with a net worth at the end, by the time he was 68 years old, of $100,000 or less. He'd already expended one-third of his personal net worth in his first eight years of office.

The governor has a large family. He asked himself, "I've left them with a lot of memories. Shouldn't I try to leave them with something else?" There were lots of other reasons, obviously, but basically those were the reasons.

He had also reached the point at which he really didn't want to work with certain institutions any more. In all of our discussions, I played the devil's advocate. He'd argue negative; I'd argue positive. He'd argue positive; I'd argue negative. It went on like this for two and a half months.

The first weekend or so in November, he decided he wasn't going to run. Then the question was when and how he should announce it. I argued for an early announcement, even though he knew and I knew the problems that he would assume by becoming a lame duck. But we had to look at the long term effects, and not just the short term effects. We felt the economy and the budget would be heading into a maelstrom. This convinced me that an early announcement would be better, because I was concerned about how Governor Carey would be remembered, not about a malaise in government. And I worried more about how he was perceived for the entire eight years of his tenure, rather than his last six months. Therefore, I advocated the articulation of some broad outlines of government policy and directions for the future of the state. I wanted him to occupy as high a road as possible and except himself from the political necessities that would inevitably dominate the legislative process.

I believe we succeeded in doing that. While we left behind a $500 million deficit, there is not a soul in this state that blames him, unlike most governments that have gone out of office with large deficits remaining. To me, fiscal integrity was the heart and soul of his governorship. Knowing that you're going to inevitably face history's judgment, you try to define the territory as much as possible in order to hold intact the principles which were the hallmark of your administration. It was a conscious decision to pursue this image and an early decision was required.

You could just guess how the legislature would react. It behaved exactly as we expected. We set up the budget a certain way to reinforce Governor Carey's image of financial integrity. We knew the legislature would do what they did and they did it. For example, Budget was astounded when I sat with them the night before and asked for appropriations to veto which accumulated to a total of $900 million. They said, "Well, nobody's going to believe that." I said, "No, the headline's going to read, 'Carey vetoed $900 million.'" So, we vetoed reappropriations and appropriations to reserve funds and whatever. We were creating a sense that this state was getting out of control.

Governor Carey went out of office with the state $500 million in debt, but the editorialists praised him for his stewardship of the financial affairs of state government. It wasn't a manipulated answer. We just knew what criticism we would face, and then tried to find the highest territory on which to defend ourselves, while sacrificing political options in the process. It might have been more harmonious during the last year, but when it was all over, who would have remembered that nice things were said about the governor by members of the legislature?

There was a dramatic shift in editorial opinion in the last year, which is important to the extent that it represents a public consciousness. Precisely, the editorial tenor called for "a plague on both your houses," while excepting the governor from the fiscal foolishness.

QUESTION: Was there a conscious effort to influence editorial opinion? Some legislative people in their quiet moments thought that both the governor and people like Mark Lawton took every opportunity to talk to the press. It was more an open administration during that last period. So this editorial opinion was not simply something that happened by accident, but represented a different understanding of the nature of financial problems.

MORGADO: I think so. It focused it, as I said, on the grounds we wanted it focused. The governor was very, very chagrined to face a lame duck period and potentially some malaise. But I argued that he had to separate the short-term view from the long-term view. I said, "In the long-term, you're going to be okay. You're giving up some short-term leverage, but not anything important in the long-term. The outcome is not going to be immensely different. If that is, in fact, the case, then why not occupy the highest road possible?"

QUESTION: Was Hugh Carey comfortable being governor? Did he enjoy it?

MORGADO: He was capable of great humor and was a very effective extemporaneous speaker, but he was essentially a very private person. He did not enjoy the invasions of his private life. He hated it. However, that was not very different from his behavior in the Congress.

He enjoyed the governorship; he just didn't live it. There are people in public life whose lives are totally dominated by their public careers. Carol Bellamy is one. To some degree, Ed Koch is another. Hugh Carey wasn't. He did what was necessary and sometimes, unfortunately, less than was necessary.

He enjoyed the world of ideas. However, I don't know how many creative men and women enjoy the details of anything. I don't think that he has any regrets about having been governor. Absolutely not. While he enjoyed his accomplishments in those eight years as governor, he was increasingly unable to accept the compromise in lifestyle that a public person is required to make.

QUESTION: Was he worried about his successor carrying on some of the institutional changes?

MORGADO: Yes, he was and still is.

QUESTION: You're implying that he was comfortable with the administrative mechanism in the state. Was he comfortable with your role as "deputy governor"—the day-to-day implementer and overseer of operations?

MORGADO: Yes, he was comfortable. The relationship was established over time as he began to understand what we were trying to do and I began to understand what he wanted to be done. It was not a process that occurred overnight. We went through a very nasty campaign in between. Towards the second year of his second term he was relatively comfortable with the structure.

QUESTION: Why does a private person launch upon a public career?

MORGADO: Political people must have a very, very strong ego, although you don't have to be a very public person to have a strong ego. It can be expressed in different ways. I would never want to be an elected officer. I would never want to make the compromises that would be required to do that. When you begin with a healthy sense of respect for yourself, very often events thrust you into situations which you never planned on. Hugh Carey never planned on being governor. He probably would have been happy being city council president in 1972. Had it not been for the sad experience of his wife's death in 1974, I'm not absolutely sure he would have ever run for governor.

It's often a personal tragedy that propels one to find another method of self-expression and sense of purpose. Suddenly, there was a person in office who hadn't spent 25 years of his life getting there. Increasingly, that is becoming unusual in New York. Attorney General Abrams has spent most of his adult life in public offices that could lead to becoming governor. Carol Bellamy has spent all of her professional life in the public arena—so has Jay Goldin. Not Hugh Carey. He had several careers—each very different. In my view, those who haven't spent all their lives in one arena bring a broader experiential base to the job and have a greater likelihood of being good governors.[6]

Of course, Mario Cuomo has had a relatively short public career. He has been a lawyer in private practice and a teacher. Governor Rockefeller was destined for whatever he was going to be, but it didn't have to be governor; it could have been something else. It could have been ambassador to Russia; it could have been secretary of state. He would have been happy in the Treasury in Washington, or as secretary of Defense.

FOOTNOTES

[1]Robert Flacke, New York State Commissioner of Environmental Conservation (1979-1982); John Egan, New York State Commissioner of General Services (1980-present); Thomas A. Coughlin III, Commissioner of Correctional Services (1979-present); Howard Miller, Director, New York State Division of the Budget (1978-1980); C. Mark Lawton, Deputy Director, New York State Division of the Budget (1977-1980), Director (1981-1982); James Prevost, New York State Commissioner of Mental Health (1978-1982).

[2]Alton Marshall, Secretary to Governor Rockefeller (1971-1974); William Ronan, Secretary to Governor Rockefeller (1958-1968).

[3]The phrase refers to the New York State Capitol in which the Budget Division is on the First Floor and the Governor's Office is on the "Second Floor."

[4]Meyer S. (Sandy) Frucher, Director, New York State Office of Employee Relations (1978-1982).

[5]Robert Wagner, Sr., formerly Mayor of New York City (1953-1965), directed Governor Carey's transition effort during 1974-1975; Alex Rose, long-term leader of the New York State Liberal Party, and key political advisor to Governor Carey; Jerry Cummins, Chairman of the New York State Thruway Authority, was a close political advisor to the Governor; Pat Cunningham, a major Democratic Party leader, Chairman of the State Party (1979-1980); David Garth, a campaign consultant, political advisor to Governor Carey; and Robert Abrams, New York State Attorney General (1978-present);

[6]Carol Bellamy, President of the New York City Council (1977-present); and Jay Goldin, Comptroller of New York City (1977-present).

C. Mark Lawton became director of the Division of the Budget in 1981 and served until 1982. Previously, he had been in the division as deputy director and first deputy director, and had worked for the Office of Parks and Recreation. Mr. Lawton's state service also included staff work with the Assembly Ways and Means Committee and for the 1967 Constitutional Convention.

C. Mark Lawton

Director of the Budget

LAWTON: I worked in the Division of the Budget (DOB) for five years—with only a portion of that as director. Dr. Howard Miller was the director during most of the time I was in Budget. We could sense an enormous amount of pressure for change in budgeting—new technologies, new accounting, more legislative oversight. Howard began an introspective examination of the institution and its functioning since its inception. This became an institutional history of which I think the division should be rather proud, "The Executive Budget—A Half Century Perspective." I recommend it to anyone interested in budgeting in New York State, because it's a good, lively history.

This effort gave us a perspective as to what had been accomplished. We had the comfort of knowing that the Budget Division had served the state well through many different situations for over a half century, but it became clear that the division needed updating. The changes needed to prepare for the future concerned us. It was useful to examine the past at this point, because one cannot move confidently into the future without such knowledge. The history provided the opportunity and started us thinking about what needed to be done.

I don't see it as remarkable that the legislature is seeking to expand its power and influence vis-a-vis the executive in New York State. The executive/legislative relationship will always be marked by contention and shaped by personalities and operating styles. There is a sort of creative tension inherent in the process and the relationship.

There was, however, also a change in the overall environment: a qualitative and quantitative change in the willingness of people to accept any explanation about the budget. The division had to find ways, as never in the past, to articulate a budget's themes and to educate people on its import. Beginning in Governor Rockefeller's day, this was done through a series of budget schools primarily for the benefit of the press. We deliberately expanded the process of presenting the major themes and priorities of the budget. We expanded the audience to include interest groups and the legislature, as well as the broader public. We simply recognized that there were more participants than ever before. Back in the days when we had a small representative group of leaders, it was easier to close the budget. One only had to deal with a small number of people in the budget negotiations.

Today, there's a far greater insistence on participation, and much stronger special interest group pressure throughout the process. In addition, I don't think political parties are the cohesive, conflict-resolution bodies that they have been traditionally. I do not mean that in any partisan sense; I just mean that no political party today, even within its own framework, seems to be able to reach consensus. It is part of what I refer to as "The New Reality." Other elements of "The New Reality," in addition to less cohesive political parties, were a poorer state, more demands, federal cutbacks, less tax revenue, and more accountability.

"The New Reality" meant we had to centralize controls because the business plan of the state had to be kept in reasonable balance. When one does not have adequate, on-line management information that can be aggregated to predict the results of adjustments, one must resort to strong, centralized cash control. Our chief means of expenditure control was the use of expenditure ceilings and personnel limitations. We tried to avoid setting such limits at too low a level of program activity or in too great detail. By and large, that responsibility was shifted to commissioners. Increasingly, the Division of the Budget required them to come in with plans for accomplishing the expenditure and personnel targets.

The unfortunate thing was that people neither understood nor were willing to acknowledge, for whatever reasons, that there was a new reality to deal with—that the economy of the state had changed. It was not generally accepted by the political forces and those in government that the state's basic economy had changed in the past decade. The trends and expectations set in motion in the 60's and early 70's were going to clash with this new reality. You didn't need a Budget director to say that; you needed the Budget director to be "the heavy." We had to adjust those things that needed to be and could be adjusted. In my view, the state had over-extended itself: We couldn't carry it all.

I will be very blunt with you: We can not carry the State University system as originally conceived with 100 percent state tax dollars. We probably cannot afford to do it because of the economy of the state and the competing demands on shrinking revenues. Losing close to 600,000 jobs in the late 70's was quite a dramatic shrinkage of the economy. The economic events that impacted the Northeast, and New York State particularly, changed our reality but not our expectations.

Does that mean we should not have an excellent university system? No, of course we should have an excellent educational system, public as well as private; we ought to have the best we can afford. I'm a product of the public, as well as the private, university system. We need them both.

The political and governmental leaders throughout the state did not accept "The New Reality." We tried to make people aware of the changes. I instituted a process of financial plan briefings for the commissioners. We had to bring them in and make them understand that the Division of the Budget didn't have a special and separate reserve of funds apart from the budget and the economy. The only special reserve I had was to obtain more revenue through tax increases, and we were in anything but a tax increase mood.

My approach was to include more people in the process. As I stated, financial plan briefings were undertaken, not just for the DOB staff, but for commissioners and outside groups as well. I knew, however, that I wasn't getting the message to the agencies, because the real people who were making it happen at the agency level were the finance and administrative officers. So, we extended our work to involve them in the process. We had to find a way to update the budgeting and management system and our opportunity came with GAAP (Generally Accepted Accounting Principles).

The fiscal crisis and its aftermath set the stage for the adoption of GAAP. Comptroller Arthur Levitt had been studying it for years. It was a matter of how long we could take to get there and how much control we would have over the process. The GAAP legislation that ultimately passed had artificially short deadlines and was unnecessarily convoluted and detailed. It created a lot of conversion problems. Nevertheless, we met the conversion deadline. But, far more important in the longer run is the question: Will GAAP serve government managers or accountants? Will the agencies, Budget, or the legislature have a better information system as a result of the GAAP conversion? Those concerns bothered us more than the deadlines or the uncertainty of GAAP definitions.

QUESTION: Has GAAP been oversold?

LAWTON: Absolutely oversold. Yes, it was terribly oversold.

QUESTION: There were a number of folks who didn't really understand the system, or the problems involved, or who pressured the legislature into premature action. Was that part of the problem?

LAWTON: Absolutely. Another problem with GAAP was that unfortunately it became politicized. By politicized, I don't mean Republican versus Democrat, but rather that the leaders were vying to take credit for reform. The legislature viewed it as a means to chip away at executive control over the budget process.

QUESTION: How could you possibly fight a general accounting principle?

LAWTON: You don't fight the principle, you fight the false impression that GAAP would solve problems in and of itself. It was very, very difficult. GAAP became synonymous with reform of fiscal policies, and you can't be against reform. As a last ditch attempt, we tried to gain more time for implementation. The bill, vetoed in 1980 (requiring the state to go immediately to GAAP), had to be vetoed because there was no way to implement its purposes within the time frame permitted. The governor was up the wall about vetoing it. I remember being down in New York and telling him, "You've got to veto, you've got no choice on this one; this one'll kill us. There's no way we can do it." The comptroller's office agreed. We decided to write a joint memorandum recommending veto and a joint press release outlining our reasons. We had to cover each other, because we knew a veto would be misunderstood, and it was.

QUESTION: As you said, if you give a part of state governance away to lenders, if the lenders are dependent on accounting people, and if they can't understand the system, then you're stuck. GAAP, it would seem, was an accounting thing.

LAWTON: It was a condition pressed by the market forces involved in the annual spring borrowing. When the "Big Eight" accounting firms came to do the independent audit for the comptroller, they did not understand our books. They did not know how to deal with governmental accounts. I believe that one of the major reasons we have GAAP today is because we didn't train accountants in public finance for the previous 40 years. They had little understanding of what they were looking at, yet they were required to give an opinion of reasonableness and completeness.

As you know, GAAP is still not defined insofar as governmental accounts are concerned. I've talked to university graduate faculty about this lapse. I told them that graduate schools flunked when it comes to public finance and GAAP. Most students have no awareness of GAAP principles or their impact on public finance issues. There has been no intellectual effort in the past 30 years at the graduate level to establish a conceptual framework for GAAP as it applies to public accounts and budgeting. As a result, government accounting principles are going to get defined in the process, and largely by accountants who haven't any idea what public finance issues and public policies are about.

My respect to the accountants, but it is a danger to leave it to them. The result is that we are tied to that four letter word; we must do GAAP budgeting with a piece of legislation that doesn't define what is meant by GAAP, and we don't have the benefit of any conceptual framework to develop such principles. You need 20 or 30 years of thinking about it, jockeying it around, and talking about it, in order to come up with such principles. Otherwise, there's going to be contention and confusion between public finance people and accountants. The public will not be served well, nor will it be any easier to understand what is going on.

I can remember an accounting firm coming in to do one of the first audits for the spring borrowing. They let loose a hundred bright-eyed, bushy-tailed, aggressive auditors. Do you know what they were going to do? They were going to go out and audit 20 or 30 agencies and then audit DOB's books. The idea was to reconcile the two. I guess they could do that in business; it proved impossible to do in the public sector.

The problem was that you couldn't tell them: "Don't waste your time doing it, folks, 'cause that's not the way the state operates and it won't make any sense. You can do it all between the comptroller's office and DOB." You couldn't tell them that because they would assume that you were trying to direct them or subvert the audit. So, you leave them alone and a few weeks later they come back to you and say: "Oh, you know, we can't make sense out of the agency records." Then they do what they ought to have done at the beginning.

The next year we had a new group of auditors who did the same thing. They didn't understand interfund transfers. Interfund transfers apparently don't fit any of the accounting principles. We spent hours and hours explaining to them the necessity for them. That's what we spend a lot of our time doing—educating the accountants in public finance.

QUESTION: But doesn't GAAP really contribute to your ability to explain the budget and simplify its major themes?

LAWTON: No, not really. It's been sold that way—GAAP is going to make it easier for you to understand things—baloney! Look at the experience in New York City. Everybody gets his expert and each produces a different definition of what is permissible under GAAP. A future governor is going to have to sort through all this. New York City was fortunate, because they had no comprehensive system before they converted to GAAP. The mayor now has his own group that tells him what GAAP allows him to do and not to do. Other major players have experts to advise them. All it means is that you've changed the language, definitions, and environment. There is nothing in GAAP that can make people report things accurately or enables people to understand the budget better.

QUESTION: Doesn't it force the issue of longer term planning on the part of administrative agencies and different constituencies?

LAWTON: No, not at all, certainly no more than the present system. The process is going to have to be centralized with or without GAAP, unless you eliminate the responsibility of the comptroller and the director of the Budget—unless something changes drastically. That would constitute a return to the chaos of pre-1927 (before adoption of the Executive Budget Process).

QUESTION: Well, isn't it true that there's no way you can really decentralize the accounts?

LAWTON: You can decentralize accounts if people are willing to be accountable. It would require much more training and development, however, than has been committed. It will also take time, perhaps five to ten years. In the meantime, somebody has to be responsible for certifying budgets and financial statements.

GAAP has been oversold. It won't give you truth in government, understanding of the issues, more accurate estimates of revenue and expenditures, or more resources. GAAP doesn't give you anything more than you had before. It gives you a different way of counting and more consistent definitions (if you can reach agreement on GAAP definitions). Remember there are 35 years of experience, interpretation, and precedent with the present system, and those things are not there with GAAP. So, you are going to have to define, argue, and re-define GAAP as it relates to budgeting.

For example, simply defining what constitutes the state entity is a formidable task. This definition is basic to the interpretation and meaning of future GAAP statements at the state level. Now, it is going to take some time to define the entity and achieve consensus. You're going to have Professor Anthony of Harvard helping Frank Mauro and Stanley Fink.[1] You're going to have another group of people trying to help Warren Anderson and his people, and you know the comptroller will have another group and they're going to have a fine time. Unfortunately, it is not likely that such activity will clarify anything for the public. It has been oversold as a means to clarify and purify the system. It is an unfortunate sales job; it really is selling a sow's ear as a silk purse, and it is a sow's ear at this time.

You cannot get consistent definitions of GAAP as applied to government easily. Arguments have already broken out between the two national accounting groups vying for control over GAAP (as applied to government) relative to who's going to "make the call." Government accountants have to deal with those two groups contending over whose definitions will be used. Interestingly enough, you don't get to define it by law. It will be necessary to have the professional organizations, after they're through arguing, get together and work out the definitions. Meanwhile, you have a piece of legislation saying that in two years, budgets must be prepared according to GAAP—whatever that means. The presumption is that you're going to make your best effort to do it. How? Just throw a definition up and see whether it works? The first time somebody disagrees (and he's probably got another legitimate interpretation), you negotiate and consult the experts. The consequences will be confusing for the public. Who wants to be tarred with that brush? It is a little bit like grabbing hold of a tar-baby: You're going to end up with tar on your hands or somewhere else.

QUESTION: Is Mike Finnerty going to have any problems delegating some of the controls that Budget now exercises to the departments, as a result of GAAP?[2]

LAWTON: GAAP does not require delegation of any control to the agencies by DOB. However, we've been trying to delegate such control over a number of areas for some time. Yes, he's going to have problems, but yes he must do it anyway. My experience with the departments was that they weren't really concerned. They didn't pay much attention to how such delegation would affect them.

I think what bothered the top people in the departments even more than GAAP was the appropriation of federal funds. Federal funds now had to be budgeted and accounted for as well as state funds. That bothered them a lot more, because there were different fiscal years, and the departments had to anticipate certain revenue from the federal government, which could not be easily estimated. It was difficult to combine two fiscal years into a single budget. You had to propose and submit your department budget in October, anticipating federal funds which you don't know anything about until the next April or September.

The legislature wanted to gain control over the allocation of federal funds. They therefore passed legislation that required the appropriation of federal funds. They were apparently aiming at the federal education grants in the State Education Department. The executive department had never tried to control such funds, we left that to the Regents. Therefore, we did not have much information or data on such funds except where matching funds were required. The legislature thought we were kidding, when we told them that we didn't have that kind of information. They believed we were more deeply involved than we actually were. The problem became more severe for them when the federal government changed the education funds to block grants and then reduced them by 20 percent.

QUESTION: In the eyes of the departments, all of these things are under one heading—GAAP. They think that GAAP requires federal funds to be appropriated and recorded.

LAWTON: That's right, that's exactly what the departments think. But, of course, you know it doesn't.

GAAP, to my mind, is simply an accounting methodology. But for some reason it became a totem, some sort of magic four-letter word which will save us from wrongdoers and provide us with understanding. Our legislation says we're going to do a GAAP budget. Now, I don't know what that means, and I don't think there's anybody in the world, including the accountants, who knows what it means. But you can be sure we're going to do it.

Seriously, we knew GAAP was going to mean some major changes in how we did things. The last time there was a major change in the way we counted funds and the way we allocated them and formulated them was back in the late 60's. That was when Comptroller Levitt moved, in conjunction with the Budget, into a system of accounts referred to as program budgeting. Program budgeting adversely affected an agency manager's ability to use financial information to manage resources. To my mind, GAAP was going to be a major change of a similar nature.

The program budgeting accounting conversion in the 60's did not provide a lot of useful financial information needed by agencies to manage. It was a nice system for accountants. That experience stuck in my mind, so when the GAAP conversion business looked like it was going to be implemented, I knew that we would have to prepare for it. We were determined that the management side of state government would not be short-changed as a result of a conversion in the accounting system.

As much as I understood GAAP, it seemed to be a law unto itself. I thought I understood sovereignty, but apparently GAAP overrides what you define in legislation. Essentially, what we had to do was fashion something that retained the options of the executive as best we could. Whoever the governor is and whatever party he is from, he has a statewide responsibility; he has to be able to keep the budget in some sort of comprehensive framework. We were really trying to retain management options while converting to GAAP.

One of the things we tried to do within the GAAP conversion process was to insist on time and training, and I hope that training continues. My feeling about the GAAP conversion is that it is a five to ten year process. It is not over simply because you converted a number of forms or you are in a different format. You still have to spend more money on training, upgrading skills, and developing new mind sets, if not new environments, in DOB as well as agencies.

That was the major concern I had with the comptroller's ambitious conversion program. It seemed to us that the comptroller wanted to demonstrate that GAAP conversion could be done on the cheap—that is, with $5 million in two years. Initially, the comptroller's office did not understand the larger implications and so started treating the conversion as a simple accounting system conversion. They adjusted their approach and expanded the conceptual framework after we got involved.

It was our strong feeling that you've got to have agency people involved from the start of the conversion process and, to do that, you have to start upgrading financial officers' skills. DOB had to take responsibility for upgrading their skills. The new system could not be left to develop on its own without their input.

QUESTION: How well institutionalized was this process of educating financial officers and commissioners?

LAWTON: It's too early to tell at this point. I do not believe it is well institutionalized. I put a lot of emphasis on it in the contracts between Arthur Anderson and the state.[3] I also insisted that we keep a separate GAAP conversion allocation in the budget and that a large piece of it be designated for training. My strategy was to isolate the training money into one lump sum and tie it to GAAP conversion over a long term. Rather than put it in as training money in each agency, which I think would have resulted in its being dissipated, I retained it in one central account. Meanwhile, in Budget, we prevailed on the governor to call together the cabinet to deal specifically with GAAP conversion. We called them together several times on the issue of conversion and related management information needs. I tried to warn them about what was coming down and pleaded with them to institute their own internal training and start the process of defining cost centers and key item measurements. They were going to need it to enable themselves to manage in the future. If they missed the opportunity, they were going to get jerked all over the place by outside forces.

I thought that the GAAP conversion could be used to provide the basis for management data for the future. We worked very, very hard to assure this. We developed a very good relationship with the comptroller's office. We provided major input into the conceptual design for the conversion of the 'accounting system' which made it far more than just an accounting system. We got them to change the whole conceptual framework. They worked with us cooperatively and very well.

We kept that under wraps, obviously. It was a quiet, sort of underground effort. There were weekly meetings with the comptroller's two deputies, me, and my first deputy director. We wanted to be sure that the executive did not lose the capability to plug into that system and extract data and information.

The way the system was set up, it is possible to obtain information and discrete expenditures by program categories, first by program, then by agency. It was decided that agencies would identify and define the major cost centers. My first efforts were to get the agencies to do it, because I preferred not to have the Budget examiners do it. It required time to train them before they understood what key item reporting was about and how it related to the accounting system. I really preferred that the agency managers do it.

The identification of cost centers is a very critical process that I hope receives the attention it has to have. If it is done right, we are going to be able to manage much better in the future—however we choose to manage. To me, that's terribly critical. You'll have a very bad result, if you end up with a rigid, centralized, controlled system. Today we have a centralized expenditure control system because the financial plan of the state requires it. The fact is, that budget directors must certify balance as part of the ritual of spring borrowing. The window of opportunity for an agency to address the situation is rather narrow.

I have tried to carry this message to the agencies in the past. It is in their own best interest to be involved in defining cost centers and key items. If not, Budget is going to have to do it. If Budget ends up defining the critical cost center programs, it will de facto define the boundaries of future managerial decisions. I would rather not do that. It isn't good. But an agency that doesn't actively involve itself in the process will force Budget to do it. And Budget will do it to assure expenditure control.

QUESTION: It seems that this GAAP conversion is highly mysterious.

LAWTON: No, the GAAP conversion is not mysterious, it's an opportunity. Throw away the label GAAP conversion and substitute development of a management data base. We tucked it in under the guise of GAAP, because if we had tried to develop a management data base for state government, we would not have received a dime for it. Our purpose was to make sure that, integral to GAAP conversion, a real management information system would be developed.

How wonderful it would be to be able to monitor on a real time basis the line expenditures by program and agency. The day of the computer has made it possible. Such a system will permit professionals in the Division of Budget to do important comparative and professional analysis. A major accomplishment in my short tenure was preventing the agencies and the state from irretrievably losing the capability to develop a management information data base, which could have happened if GAAP was permitted to proceed as a simple accounting conversion.

QUESTION: There is also a concern about productivity. How much have you done to encourage your staff to look into the way programs are operated to determine whether they're efficient and going in the right direction?

LAWTON: The operation has been restructured. It has probably expanded, although some people might say it shrank because where there were three units, there is now one. That unit really does management audits from the point of view of policy/program effectiveness. We reoriented the General Government Unit, expanded its scope of responsibility, and developed a concept called "commodities budgeting." (It's called that, because I didn't know what else to call it, frankly.) We folded into that unit the Management and Operations Unit, which was basically doing nitty-gritty process analysis. The result is, we have the General Government Unit looking at issues that affect all state agencies and undertaking a systematic review of these issues. You've probably seen some results in the telecommunications study—the computer policy initiatives, fleet management, and energy conservation initiatives. It was relatively easy to do a study of telephones based on personnel and cost criteria, but it is more difficult to really look at the issue of telecommunications in light of the recent decentralized changes and deciding what the state should be doing to take advantage of technological change. We're doing that in a number of areas, including vehicle management, travel, and fuel control. We brought the comptroller into this and he then decided to publicize it. Now, with microcomputers, it is possible to control fuel usage and develop accounting systems tied to specific users and cars, rather than looking at automobile usage as a result of complaints and press reports without benefit of ongoing data and measurement.

I talked over any institutional changes with the deputies and unit heads. I made sure that Mike Finnerty (my first deputy) was comfortable with them. All my time as director, I said to Mike Finnerty, "Let's make sure you can live with whatever changes we make, because you will be here, either as one of the deputies or as director." We had a lot of interaction with the staff. I involved the staff a lot in discussion about the changes and future needs of state management, asking, "What do you think? How should it be done?" That's really the way we've expanded our efforts to make everyone more aware of management needs and productivity. The problem is that all those efforts depend on information coming in to you. You have to be able to measure productivity. That's the reason why I thought it was so important to insure that, as an integral part of GAAP conversion, there be a database capability on which to build a future management information system. That information would then be integrated into an ongoing budget preparation and monitoring system.

The beginning of making a budget is pulling out what used to be the R-4 reports (the expenditure reports). You ought to be able to do that electronically (and on an ongoing basis). If you are slowly developing your key item data base, you should be able to extract information crucial to management decisions electronically, as needed. That should be the background against which you analyze a program and judge a budget request.

In selected areas we developed systems, sometimes in conjunction with the University, because they had the best information base and internal budgeting systems. The capital planning system with regard to energy conservation was devised by the University. Oscar Lanford (director of the State University Construction Fund) designed the University system and then we adjusted it so that it could be used by other agencies. It is a slow process, however. That's why I can't put enough emphasis on continuing the development of the cost center data base. It has nothing to do with GAAP as such. It is certainly not required for GAAP financial statements to be prepared, but it is central to improving the management of the state and to assuring future productivity. You can't talk about productivity and management without ongoing information and without measurement and monitoring.

By management, I mean being able to reallocate, within reasonable parameters, resources from one program area to another, to make deliberate choices and carry them through. Frankly, I do not think most commissioners manage very much, they really cannot. There are insufficient supporting systems. If a commissioner wants to do something, he goes to his fiscal office and says: "I'm going to do thus and so—find me the resources." The fiscal officer presumably has to make sure the commissioner gets what he wants. If it cannot be carved out of existing operations, it becomes a budget request. (Sometimes it is a matter of simply increasing the allowable cash ceiling for the agency.)

All commissioners usually have one or two things they want to do, and they want to get them done before they leave office. As long as these are done, they are satisfied. They rarely take a longer view. Fiscal officers in the state are not managers, they are satisfiers, and commissioners do not treat them as managers. That is terribly bothersome. The managers in state agencies are supposed to be the administrative officers, but these people tend to come out of personnel departments. Personnel people have rigged most of the civil service system to move their people into administrative offices. If you look at the background of most administrative officers, I don't think you'll find that very many of them come out of the financial or even the program areas.

In most agencies, the fiscal side is either a bookkeeping function or a budget preparation (justification writers) function. It is more stifling than it is managing. The fiscal officers are essentially doing what they have to do. They have to keep expenditures at whatever their internal plan calls for (if the agency has a plan). They are not really looking at options, and they are not managing in the way they really ought to be by bringing a commissioner options. That is what a commissioner and his top staff ought to have. However, most of the time, staff are preoccupied with reacting to DOB's activities. Usually the finance officer's job becomes one of showing what a disaster it is going to be if DOB's directive is implemented.

Your better commissioners and agency people will in fact do something. Clifton Wharton (chancellor of State University of New York) did something. He was aware. He picked up right away on what had to be done to maintain SUNY's prerogatives and independence. It happens that the State University has one of the most sophisticated accounting systems in state government. DOB can do post-expenditure tabulations, but we don't really know what's happening within SUNY Central's accounting system between reports. Especially towards the end of the year, you do not fool around with SUNY's internal accounting; you just can not. We could not—we would get buried in it. You have to remember, that Budget's total examination staff is rather small, and we don't really have the systems to do it. DOB sometimes operates like the Wizard of Oz. The very mystery feeds the power.

QUESTION: Why, then, did your office involve itself in regulating travel in the University? The impression was that your deputy was signing off on any travel voucher for the State University of New York.

LAWTON: You refer to the out-of-state travel freeze we had.

QUESTION: It might be a petty thing.

LAWTON: No, it was not a petty thing. It was idiotic. We had simply asked for a plan from each agency to control travel costs. The University, among others, did not produce and would not produce a plan. We wanted to have assurance that they had an in-house system to control travel costs. However, they apparently wanted complete autonomy with regard to travel, with little—if any—accountability. Perhaps it was a strategy on the University's part. I am sure they did not want to have a group of budget examiners looking over their shoulders, but I didn't want that either. In fact, we talked a lot about the problem internally before we took any action. (Remember the legislature had cut back on travel and the governor had announced a curtailment of out-of-state travel.) The chiefs and staff all said "What we don't want is to have to go through a pile of travel requests." So, first we gave the University major waivers by job category. We requested the plan again. We did indicate, however, that without controls by the University, we would have to take more drastic action. We did not want to review and approve their travel requests item by item. Our attempt to provide broad guidelines and waivers was unsuccessful; we ended up having to approve travel for the University, because they would not accept responsibility and be accountable.

You must impose discipline and accountability. If, in fact, you have a policy, and you're trying to implement that policy, and someone resists or is not willing to take responsibility, then it is going to end up in the papers. I must cover the governor. That is my job. My job is to take the heat when I have to. If the governor promulgates a policy, he does not want to read in the newspaper that somebody's ignoring it or running roughshod over it. There must be reasons when someone breaks from a policy line. We certainly tried to provide enough leeway. Most agencies submitted a plan, and the plan was approved.

However, that did not happen with the University, and I don't know why. When I got a note from Don Blinken (chair of the SUNY Board of Trustees), I called Clif Wharton and I told him, "I'll do whatever I can do, I'll come over and sit down with your staff and we'll do whatever works. I just need a plan."

QUESTION: Because the programs one will have are those which have been financed, a budget represents a program document. Could we talk about budgeting as a program document? To what extent did you have an input in the program?

LAWTON: We were always in a potentially unbalanced budget position to start with. We always knew that we were fighting a shortage of revenues. I used to say that ten monkeys and an adding machine can make up most of the agency budgets, because there wasn't much opportunity to analyze or think through new programs because of austerity. In one sense I could not care—I did not care—what agencies requested, because we knew that we could not afford more than a four or five percent increase in the overall budget, which just about took care of the mandated increases. It must have been incredibly frustrating to be a program person unless you were in some favored agency.

Favored agencies for Carey were, in particular, Mental Retardation, Mental Health, and in a sense, Commerce. I think there was a lot of skepticism about the "I Love New York" program, but the fact is that it worked, and then it took on a life of its own. Many people, including myself, thought it was going to be a boondoggle, but it seems to have worked.

Whenever we developed austerity measures, the governor would say, "You can't touch that program, leave them alone." Mental Retardation was one, Mental Health was the other, and to a lesser extent, Social Services and Department of Transportation's construction program. You will notice that I conspicuously left out SUNY. The feeling was that SUNY ought to come up with some sort of a plan to indicate how it was going to deal in the longer run with the new fiscal reality. The governor did not want to get into education policy. The University, however, had to come up with some way of coping with the state's reduced capability.

The increases that regularly troubled us were primary and secondary education and other local assistance programs. They had a life of their own.

With an austerity environment you could get policy direction

66

quickly. I could tell you that, under austerity, Budget was able to do 95 percent of the budget without much analysis of budget requests. By the time I got to Budget, the governor was no longer sending out his midsummer budget letter; the Division was sending out budget guidelines, budget bulletins, and austerity plans.

Howard Miller had advised me to be sure that commissioners' priorities were reflected in the budget; that is, if they didn't conflict with the governor's need and priorities. That did not mean that if commissioners had multiple priorities, they were all provided for. I would try to ascertain what the commissioner's highest priority was, and I would try to get some indication from the second floor as to whether they were compatible with the governor's program and policies. If they were, they were included in the budget.

Because we lacked the resources to initiate bold new program initiatives, we emphasized reallocation of resources from one program to another. We were trying to get the agencies to move resources around and use attrition as the major means of reducing personnel. We tried to accelerate that process as much as possible, because you can not take a human endeavor that has been around for more than a few years and not find some slack in it. I would go out of my way to accommodate agency initiatives that would reallocate and redirect resources. It was sometimes the only reward I could provide. I could not give them much more because we did not have more.

The amount of dollars a governor has for discretionary spending has been estimated by others at around $100 million. With this particular governor during this time, however, it was more like $10 to $20 million. It was really very, very slim pickings. Beyond the $10 to $20 million, it was bond proposals and restructuring existing programs. That kind of environment is easier for Budget in some ways, so long as you're willing to take the flack that is going to fly your way. The process that we used, was to get some early-on policy direction from the governor's office, and then act pretty autonomously until about halfway through the process. Shortly after Thanksgiving, we lined up the major issues and policy choices for the governor.

We tried to honor legislative intent as much as possible, because they tend to get very sticky and upset when you lower their priorities. They have a right to be concerned. The legislature is the ultimate arbitrator in setting the fiscal policy of the state. It is not really just the governor. The governor sets the agenda, controls the execution to a certain extent, manages the day-to-day affairs; he can make certain programs happen faster than others; he bargains for his program priorities with the legislature in the budget adoption/negotiation process.

As budget officials, we are the "black hats," the official "No" men, and we must be prepared to take responsibility for the ultimate decisions on allocation and execution. For example, if the State University has been appropriated a billion dollars by the legislature, but we can only spend $990 million according to the state's financial plan, $10 million has to be accommodated through expenditure limitations. We deal with SUNY Central to decide how it can be accommodated. If we get no cooperation, we have to do it unilaterally (usually on the basis of past expenditure experience). We have to, because it is necessary to maintain a balanced overall state financial plan.

Today, you have to go to the marketplace to borrow $4 billion. To borrow you have to certify the budget as balanced. You know 1975-76 really was a watershed in budget relationships, and not just between the legislature and the executive. Far more important, a piece of governance was transferred to the lenders. They became critical players in the process. That was a consequence of the fiscal crisis. Afterwards, you had to put together a financial plan that could be certified as in balance. The estimation and budget certification process was incorporated into the official statement. This is a public document available to all, and is required for the spring borrowing.

QUESTION: I wonder if Budget realizes the difficulty in determining at what point to stop cutting. When one cuts back in productivity, at what point does one know that the critical kind of services have been reached? Do you just wait to hear the screams?

LAWTON: No, Budget does not use a scream meter. We depend on our professionals and expect them to be thoroughly knowledgeable concerning an agency. That is why you need experienced people who have a long institutional memory and who will know when that critical point is being approached.

But, there is another side—the agency's willingness to deal with the problem. Agencies frequently would not take advantage of the opportunity and cooperate with us. Frequently, they preferred to avoid the hard choices. They preferred to believe that there was a better year coming up next year. Essentially, they did not want to recognize that the economy of the state had changed, and we were in for an adjustment. I thought we were in for about a decade of change, and that we would have a few years of adjustment to go. Howard Miller always used to lament: "It always seems to happen when Democrats are in." I reminded him that it has happened to Democrats and Republicans alike. So, I think it has no partisan flavor to it.

There was no doubt in my mind, after 1975—76, that for the next five or ten years the state would have to adjust to a new reality.

There's always some growth in any budget; budgets rarely go down. The problem was the existing services overhang we had. There were justifiable increases in expenditure. I couldn't really argue with commissioners who said that, programatically, many increases were justified. But we lacked the resources to meet them.

We launched a major Medicaid cost containment program, but its focus was too limited and results disappointing until we got some experience and program knowledge. The core of the cost containment program was setting rates. We set about strengthening that process. Rate increases and rate appeals were not automatically approved. And we denied many, changed methodology, and tried to force institutional and structural change in the health delivery system through rate setting. We pressed on the brake and held it down; we even had negative growth one year, but costs just drove rates right back up on us, because all the structural changes had not been accomplished. We did not alter the health care delivery system much; that would have taken another three or four years of sustained effort and some basic changes in the program's design. With regard to health care costs and the whole Medicaid/Medicare effort, in the early days nobody really knew what to do, because we lacked sufficient data and management. We constantly worked on improving and developing the data.

Education aid is still rolling along. We adjusted the school aid formula every year to provide more equity in the distribution of state aid, provided special aid to overburdened cities, and tried to address Levittown. [4]

We reduced Medicaid costs, initiated aid to mass transit, and restructured aid to transportation. We also consolidated programs of aid to localities for highways and sewage operations. We moved into mass transit in a big way. We fashioned a special mass transit package. We capped state revenue sharing, not because it was a bad program, but because we couldn't afford it. We took revenue sharing down in steps. The first year, we reduced the rate of taxes to be shared from 18 percent to 8 percent. The second year we broadened the tax base to be shared. Both approaches slowed the amount of increase, but in the midst of fiscal crisis we could not afford even that. So revenue sharing was capped at a fixed amount.

At one point the governor wanted to take it all down. He wanted to devote it entirely to education. What protected revenue sharing in the state for upstate communities was the New York City MAC bond covenants. As I stated, the governor wanted to take all the remaining revenue sharing and move it into school aid. Periodically, he would raise the possibility and we would have to remind him of the MAC bond covenants. We would go through the exercise of reexamining the bond covenants periodically. The growth in revenue sharing that would have occurred was reallocated to other areas. It was still, however, going into local aid programs.

QUESTION: Could you comment on your efforts to do something about education aid reallocation and whether you hope there will be some concrete achievement in this area?

LAWTON: I have to believe there will be eventually. We did everything but pull the trigger of the gun that was at our head. Every year we came up with an equalization formula for education aid. I think we tried every gimmick and variation that we could think of. It is nice to see that the fight is still being fought by the new governor to achieve equalization. I believe there has to be adjustment and change. I have an enormous amount of faith that it will be worked out eventually.

I do not think it is sensible to take money out of education. A lot more money needs to be spent, in different areas and for different reasons, on education. That is the spirit with which we went into most of our formula changes. We tried a lot of different variations. We really thought the legislature would buy the last one. I really thought there was a chance that the Rubin Task Force proposals would be adopted. Admittedly these were massive attempts to change how we allocated education aid. Dedicating the sales tax to education would have provided growth in education aid every year if implemented. But the interest groups did not think it was enough. They felt that they would get better growth in aid through the normal appropriation process and, therefore, rejected the proposal.

Initially, there was a lot of support for it, and it certainly would have solved the equity problem. With education aid, it was always a question of how much one could afford to do. It was never a matter of balancing a budget by not doing it. This is true even with the latest education increases. The trend is always up on education aid; it is always raised. It is like going into tax reduction. If you propose $4 million, they will propose five. It will end up a billion dollars, before you know it. One must watch out; it has a dynamic all of its own. Our problem was that the existing formulas perpetuated inequity, and the system it financed perpetuated mediocrity.

QUESTION: Perhaps we could discuss the spring borrowing?

LAWTON: Are you surprised that I did not identify it as a problem?

COMMENT: Yes, I think it is big, that it imposes borrowing costs, and that the money could be better used in other ways, if we could avoid massive borrowing in that period. It also leads to cash flow problems, and so, it might be evidence of a problem rather than a problem itself.

LAWTON: I agree with all you say. However, you'll never eliminate all temporary borrowing in government unless we find a way to squirrel money away so that you can draw upon it to flatten out the differences between your revenues and expenditures. Every business, as well as every government, must match its revenue income to expenditure outgo. That is what business and financial plans are. Interestingly, a lot of local governments and school districts do sock the money away and invest it, usually in certificates of deposit. It is not that they have no need for it; of course, they do. It is just that their revenues do not match outgo. When we had a delay in the passage of the budget and a consequent delay in aid payments, school districts did not close down. We found out that most districts had money set aside. Of course, they were worrying about state aid payments because they were losing investment income.

There is always an imbalance and there will always be. There is nothing inherently wrong with short-term borrowing. The constitution allows for it, so long as it doesn't get out of hand. It is a bad sign if the size of short-term borrowing constantly increases. The size of the borrowing in regard to total income is significant. The existing spring borrowing can be seen as an accumulated deficit— the result of what Peter Goldmark labeled the "magic window."[5] Because of the difference in fiscal years between the state and local jurisdictions, it was possible for the legislature to have the best of both worlds. The fun was in providing lots of education aid in the current fiscal year, and paying for it in the following year. Only a quarter of new aid was paid in the current year; the three-fourths balance of it was due the subsequent year. Unless you counted it as part of your expenditures in the new year to start with, it was added to your spring borrowing needs.

The other major element that added to the spring borrowing was delayed pension payments. We set a date for payment in the legislature, and pension payments are made by that date. There is a delay—an accrued liability calculated by the comptroller which has added to spring borrowing. Those are the two major elements of spring borrowing.

I do not consider the spring borrowing a problem unless it is increasing over the long run. Every year we have suggested alternative plans for reducing the size of the spring borrowing. I said several times to my legislative counterparts, that I would rather spend $200 million in program expansions dictated by the legislature (we fight so much about $10 million in a supplemental budget) than spend it on spring borrowing interest costs.

The problem is that it is relatively easy to borrow and it is yesterday's costs. The spring borrowing can be used to enforce discipline in the budget process. It was used by us in that manner. Short-term borrowing has not always taken place in the spring. Prior to '75-'76, the state borrowed short-term, not just once but whenever the director and the comptroller decided it was necessary throughout the year. You might borrow twice a year or three times a year. Naturally, each borrowing was not as large. When the crisis came along, it was decided to put all the short-term borrowing together and all of a sudden it added up to more than two billion dollars.

Two billion dollars gets your attention. It is a big number. If one borrows two billion dollars over a year in small pieces, a little bit here and a little bit there, one may not notice it. It is nothing more than what a business might do. The theory is that you borrow as you need it, for as short a time as you need it, as long as it is within the fiscal year. That way you pay less interest but you also get less investment income. The borrowing was pulled together and made to commence on April 1, the beginning of the fiscal year. The borrowing could only proceed if you had a balanced financial plan as a result of legislative action on the budget. It was an attempt to put discipline in the process and an attempt to say to the legislature: "Make whatever choices you want to, and resolve whatever it is you are trying to do. However, it must result in a balanced budget because the spring borrowing will require it."

QUESTION: It was intentional?

LAWTON: Yes, if not initially, then in the end it was intentional. Rightly or wrongly, it was one attempt to use a market mechanism as a discipline on the budget adoption process.

QUESTION: And the rating went down at the same time?

LAWTON: No, not initially and not because of delays in the passage of budgets. It was only recently that they really placed the state on credit watch. The rating agencies were concerned about the legislature coming back to pass additional spending proposals subsequent to the passage of the main budget. The lack of finality was the major reason for their concern.

COMMENT: I do not know if this is true, but I have been told that the biggest factor in the ratings has been the passing of a budget through the legislature.

LAWTON: Yes, I have heard that, but it simply is not true. There are many factors that go into a credit rating. All are subject to constant dialogue between the state, Standard and Poor's, and Moody's rating services. Among those factors are: the adequacy of revenue, the total amount of debt, and debt service as a proportion of state wealth and income, the issuer's debt coverage ratio, the soundness of the basic economy, the adequacy and availability of reserves, and whether there was closure in the budget process (sometimes referred to as finality). The first time the rating agencies considered downgrading was in the spring of 1979, and we persuaded them not to at that time because, though the budget was delayed, the result was certifiable balance. Then Standard and Poor's put out their policy statement on GAAP in May of 1980. GAAP financials were preferred; their lack was to be a negative factor in future ratings.

This past year the timing of Standard and Poor's credit watch was an inappropriate intrusion by the rating agencies into the political process, in my opinion, and I told them so. I did not think anything in the budget or the financial plan had changed from June to November. However, there was a national economic downturn from spring to fall of '82. I think the credit watch was meant to be a signal to the legislature not to unbalance the financial plan through passage of subsequent spending authorization without new revenues. Why else would the rating agencies give us a favorable rating in spring then seek to downgrade us in fall? What had we done or not done? The budget was passed in the spring, it was certified to be in balance. True, the legislature was in recess and they were expected to return. The only uncertainty was whether the legislature would unbalance it when they returned. Other than that, there was the national economic downturn.

QUESTION: Do you see the need for any basic constitutional or statutory change with respect to the responsibilities of the chief parties on fiscal matters?

LAWTON: There are further reforms that are necessary, and I suggested some of them in the report of the Council on State Priorities. I may be in a minority, but I felt that the reforms that were made in the executive budget process in 1927, through constitutional change and subsequent development of precedent and practice, were developed in a different environment with a different set of assumptions and a different reality. Specifically, in 1927 there were strong parties, less constituent and member participation, and strong legislative leaders who were able to deal as equals with the governor.

The legislature, whether part-time or full-time, is always contentious. I refer you to Governor Al Smith's or Governor Lehman's writing on the matter. They had constant problems with the legislature. The contention and the inherent conflict is not new. But the fact that they are in continuous session and have professional staff at their call is new.

Whereas previously there was focus, because of the short legislative sessions, today it takes on the feel of a floating crap game. In the past there was a very deliberate commitment to take action on the executive budget within a specific and restricted time frame. Today that is not the case. The presumption in the past was that decisions would be made, compromises would be arrived at, and the legislature would go away. I once believed it would be good to have a year-round legislature. I now can bite my tongue for having ever said it. I am less sanguine over the prospect. There is no denying, however, that the world and the process have changed. In keeping with the changes, the type of reform needed is to require the legislature to pass a balanced budget within some reasonable, but restricted, fixed time frame. After that, the legislature could pass no future expenditure bill for the year. If an executive can be held to account to submit a balanced budget, the legislature ought to be required to pass one. There must be sufficient provisions for bona fide emergencies. Since the legislature is more involved with budgeting and more contentious about revenue estimation, they should be held responsible in some way. Let us require them, by constitutional mandate, to pass a balanced budget within a fixed time period, after which, they cannot approve further expenditures.

QUESTION: Can the federal government discipline the Congress?

LAWTON: Apparently not! They have a printing press in any case. At least Congress has not reached the point where they deliberately pass an unbalanced budget and are proud of it.

QUESTION: How do you define a balanced budget?

LAWTON: I know that is difficult. But within reasonable parameters, it is possible.

COMMENT: You cannot, as a matter of fact. As you pointed out it is forward looking; it is an estimate; one cannot certify a particular number.

LAWTON: You can if you accept reasonable parameters. The whole contention over revenue is a very, very clever ploy by the legislature. It is easy to disagree if somebody is $800 million to a billion dollars from you in estimates, but there is no way to deal with it, if you're $200 million apart (on an $18 billion base). It is just not possible, with all the uncertainty and variables, to argue the exact number credibly. Yet, $200 million is a very large piece of money in the budget. The reason we are where we are right now is that the differences are too great; they are closer to $800 million than $200 million, and $800 million is not reasonable.

COMMENT: At least if the comptroller gets involved, there is going to have to be a methodology for the legislative budget. I understand there may not have been one in the past.

LAWTON: There was, though I have my doubts how reliable or certifiable it was. Last year we tried, very quietly, to offer our services to all parties. (One does not want to get the governor or anyone else into a position where he can not compromise.) Politics is compromise, and we went pretty far out on a limb by requiring budget balance for our certification prior to initiating the spring borrowing.

DOB's staff also undergoes "due diligence" sessions with the accountants and the lenders representatives. The independent auditors report to these groups whether our methodology and our range of estimates is within the "comfort level." By comfort level, they mean that $200 million, not $600 to $800 million. With the expenditure bills the legislature passed, we had no way to certify balance. To make both houses understand that there were limits, we prevailed on the comptroller to lend his best efforts to break the impasse.

We did prevail on the comptroller to have his outside accountants look at the matter. They do an independent audit and then provide the comptroller and the underwriters with an opinion as to DOB's estimates and methodology. They found that one house had a methodology which they shared and the other house had no intention of sharing any information. That blew the process apart and delayed things.

We continued to search for a way to resolve the deadlock. The final solution was to permit the governor's vetoes to stand—for the while (at least until after the spring borrowing).

I know the problems of trying to define a balanced budget are formidable. However, since we required it of the executive, why can't we require it of the legislature? You can work out the definitions. Remember, that in fiscal matters in New York State the ultimate voice is the legislature's, not the executive's.

QUESTION: But the legislature balances the budget based on its revenue estimates from the Ways and Means and the Senate Finance Committees, while the governor balances the budget based on his revenue estimates from the state comptroller's office and your office. Obviously, there are problems inherent in that.

How do you feel about techniques used in other states to constrain the state fiscal process through the constitution, for example, linkage to the percentage of income?

LAWTON: I do not favor constitutional restrictions at this stage. Every year, including the past year, we proposed an expenditure control statute. The legislature rejected them all. I think one must be realistic, and one must treat the legislature as a responsible body. Government can be responsible. I prefer a reasonable expenditure control program enacted by law, not a constitutional straightjacket. Such a program ought to be tried for a while before we fix it into the state's constitution.

COMMENT: It seems to me that that is more achievable than a constitutional provision requiring the legislature to enact a balanced budget.

LAWTON: I disagree. People can understand the need for a balanced budget; they do not easily grasp the impact of linkages. However, there is no reason to prevent both from being done in time. We have a provision in our constitution that says the legislature can pass two-year budgets. It would be interesting to see what would happen if they could only pass two-year budgets. I would favor adopting a budget for two years, with a provision for bona fide emergencies. If real problems emerge, the legislature and the governor can deal with them as required. But on the whole, a two-year budget would be more useful.

QUESTION: Would you favor a change in the fiscal year?

LAWTON: I have a little more trouble with that. I would not fool around with the fiscal year right now, in light of the fact that we have not adjusted completely to GAAP. For example, how we count outstanding vouchers for payment affects year-end balance, and changing the fiscal year would unduly complicate the matter. The present payment and encumbrance cycle is in conflict with GAAP, and the agencies do not realize it. It needs to be adjusted. They may be operating under the old principles of "hold the bill at the end of the year for rollover." In order to correct that, we submitted some amendments to the finance law in conjunction with the comptroller. We have to be aware of GAAP implications and their effect on agency behavior before we take on a change in fiscal year.

Under GAAP, when you encumber you spend. It no longer matters when you send the money out. That has to become part of the management style and the management awareness of agencies. It is ridiculous to have that encumbrance capability still open all the way through the subsequent fiscal year. It has to be foreshortened considerably. There is no doubt in my mind that there are bits and pieces like that. They have to be corrected before we think about changing fiscal years.

QUESTION: Some political scientists say that it makes no difference what constitutional limitations exist because, if necessity requires, politicians will find a way to act. Do you think that constitutional change really matters?

LAWTON: Yes I do, absolutely. I would respectfully disagree with that view, if not the underlying cynicism. I happen to believe that the key is necessity, and that concept is very important. The legislature will not transgress on constitutional limitations casually. If you have vague regulations and complicated law and a lot of gibberish, they will do it much more frequently. Al Smith fought for constitutional change because he knew the difference. I do not think it is any less important today than it was then.

COMMENT: The spirit of the restriction on loaning the state's credit to private companies would be an example. Compare the spirit of that constitutional restriction to the creation of some entities, such as the UDC (Urban Development Corporation), that in effect try to borrow the state's credit to be used for development. Now, instead, it is perceived as necessary to find a way to do something despite the constitution—its spirit. The Empire State Plaza is another example.

LAWTON: Right. The point is, that those examples are extraordinary events. One can only use that chit a few times, and it is almost self-limiting. You are not going to build 20 malls. You are going to build one. And then you are going to pay for it with more than money. You pay for it in trade-offs with the legislature. It is not an easy trip to take. A governor has to really believe that necessity requires it.

There was serious talk about taking UDC down at the beginning of Carey's administration, because it was felt that its abuses had led the way into the crisis. I argued that that would be throwing out the baby with the bath water. I remembered the struggle to establish UDC.

I worked on the Constitutional Convention. We tried to develop a community development article that essentially mirrored the UDC legislation. Of course, because of the way the new constitution was presented to the people as a single package, it failed. (Everybody forgets the issue over which the new constitution failed. It was the Blaine amendment.[6]) There was not very much difference between the ultimate UDC legislation, and what we were trying to insert into the Community Development article of the state constitution in 1965. There was a political consensus that it was desirable and necessary.

Apparently, you have to concentrate on a single issue and pick your timing to get a constitutional change to pass statewide. There has been no wholesale change in the state constitution since the eighteenth century.

That does not mean that once something like UDC is put in place, it cannot be misused. The UDC idea was an extraordinarily creative idea that was necessary and timely. I think that it was worth spilling all of that sweat and blood to get it adopted. You will not find that it led to 98 different UDCs. In my judgment, the public purpose and intent was not abused.

QUESTION: What are your contributions with respect to legislative/executive relationships, and what are your suggestions?

LAWTON: Legislative/executive relationships were, at best, always difficult. I thought that the legislature was getting more cantankerous and more difficult. I have had a little time to reflect on it and read about it. I read Al Smith's autobiography, which he wrote right after he lost the national election. I went back and read the sections on legislative/executive relationships. He talked very candidly and it sounded as if he was speaking in 1982. I recommend it for perspective.

COMMENT: A big difference is, however, that the legislature now has a staff. I don't know whether the legislature was cantankerous before they had a staff or whether the staff made them cantankerous.

LAWTON: I might be able to give you a unique perspective on it. I will begin with the premise that the legislature is a major player in the fiscal policy of the state. They really have the ultimate say. That was also true prior to 1927, and I think you have to remember that. I think the 1927 executive budget reforms were an attempt to put some rationality, responsibility, and focus into what was, up to then, a rather chaotic legislative budgeting process.

The resultant executive budget process permits governors of the state to control the agenda. By and large, depending on their political craftsmanship, they now control the issues, but they cannot determine the outcome or the timing. If you have a growing economy and growing revenues, or if you are willing to increase revenues through tax increases, then you can provide a resource for political trades and compromises. I do not see this as bad. It is, in fact, the essence of the system.

The unfortunate thing is that we do not have very much experience with a declining economy and shrinking resources combined with so much overhang. That was a unique and traumatic experience for most of the political players in New York State.

Howard Miller, the previous Budget director, was as responsible as anyone for having established a professional staff in the legislature, specifically, the fiscal staff in Ways and Means. Everyone demanded more information on the budget, and it became much more open. Legislators and constituents understood more about it and were demanding more of it.

It is amazing to see the degree to which budget news has become front-page news of late. Before, it was usually a one-day story in the middle section of the newspaper. The media rarely intruded into the business of trying to adopt a budget.

The legislature was certainly helped by staff growth. I think much of their frustration is a reaction to the Rockefeller years, when Governor Rockefeller really dominated the process. He was extraordinarily skillful and very forceful. Personalities do matter in politics. His personality was one that annealed, pulled together, and forced decisions.

COMMENT: Of course, he had more money to give away than you did.

LAWTON: Rockefeller did not just give away money. He was skillful and capable of dealing with the political process. That matters a lot in legislative/executive relationships. I worked for Perry Duryea.[7] There was a major revolt by Perry Duryea against Governor Rockefeller, when the governor went for too large a tax increase.

I think Rockefeller was able to hold back the tide for a while. However, in holding it back, pressure developed. Whoever was governor after Nelson Rockefeller was going to deal with that pent-up frustration.

COMMENT: The legislature was also dealing with bigger problems which had evolved from the Dewey days. Remember when Dewey and Senator Mahoney from Buffalo broke the billion dollar barrier? That was a serious problem. It seems to me the staffs that are being developed in the legislature are duplicating some of the things your own examiners are doing.

LAWTON: True, but the basic problem is not the staffs. I'll tell you what I believe a large part of the problem to be. The central problem in the legislature is the decline of parties. Parties no longer can impose discipline. Leaders are not able to coalesce majorities on general policies or bring together a conference vote on an issue without extraordinary personal effort. It is extraordinarily difficult for either the speaker or the president pro tem of the Senate to do that inside their own houses today. The basic function of parties today is to provide a label on which to run. They are no longer part of a cohesive conflict resolution process.

I can remember Speaker Travia, as well as Speaker Duryea, going into a conference and demanding a vote in the name of party position, not individual constituent interests. Both had made agreements with the governor based on this ability to deliver, and they did. In the last few years, neither house can do that. They could not deliver in the same manner. Senator Anderson finally admitted it publicly, and Speaker Fink has always said it. It is very unusual for a speaker of the Assembly to say: "I'm beholden to my members."[8]

In the legislature, it is not statewide needs, but district and constituent needs that prevail. Governors tend to define issues from a statewide perspective. That is inherent in being a chief executive who runs statewide. Increasingly, the leadership has had to negotiate almost issue by issue, member by member, laboriously putting together shifting majorities—depending on the issue. That MTA thing was just such an exercise.[9] They passed taxes that weren't taxes, provided aid that wasn't needed, and then ended up excluding the executive from the process, because the executive was taking the longer view. We were sure that there were going to be more problems for the MTA 18 months or two years out (and there were revenue shortfalls).

COMMENT: I found what you were saying about the relationship between passing the balanced budget and the breakdown of party discipline fascinating.

LAWTON: Now, that's my own crazy theory. It is a consequence of my experience since 1965. I can remember extraordinarily strong leadership being exercised on both the Senate side and the Assembly side. Budgets were put together between the governor and the four legislative leaders and that was that. There wasn't any nonsense dragging the thing out. The leaders told you whether they could deliver it or not, what they needed, and what they could live with. Once they committed, they delivered.

The change may also be due, in part, to two factors that are significantly different today. The Carey administration did not have as much revenue available as in the Rockefeller era. And there is also the difference in style and personality. So, we may have been missing some key ingredients.

QUESTION: What is your opinion on the role of the professional public servant?

LAWTON: The role of the professional public servant in state government is an extremely important one. There is a need for changes to be made, particularly in the middle management and senior management levels. I would preserve the essential merit system in the state. It has served the state well. New York State has an excellent cadre of professional civil servants. We should be proud of their capabilities as well as their accomplishments.

They have met challenges when they have had clear direction and leadership. For example, in DOB we had to deal simultaneously with three consecutive massive changes within a single year. Each one by itself required major effort: the appropriation of federal funds, the GAAP conversion, and the reformatting of the budget and refining of accounts to prepare for a GAAP budget. Those three tasks were undertaken simultaneously and successfully completed in less than eight months. I was so proud of everyone, that I hired the downstairs meeting rooms and threw an all-night party for them. It was impossible to express enough appreciation for what they had accomplished.

80

Unionization of the workforce, without regard to the management needs of this state, has really fouled things up. The Civil Service Law was passed before unions were permitted, and precedents have developed which are in conflict with union goals.

There is a real need to develop an environment that rewards managers who manage and permits civil servants to be responsive to direction and emerging needs. Contrary to what some people have suggested, you do not need to go to a system that has political appointees, non-statutory positions, or exempt positions.

Under the current set of conditions, most commissioners cannot control their senior managers. Change requires careful, deliberate, and delicate adjustments. You cannot violate civil servants' rights or the merit system. You should not be able to put them on the street without cause, but you ought to be able to redefine their job or redirect their efforts and put them into a situation where they can deliver. You should be able to reward people who are productive and who contribute.

There ought to be a reward system that is related to job performance, and it should be the responsibility of the supervisor to do the evaluation and deliver the reward.

Our most critical needs are to develop managerial skills, particularly above the grade 23 level. That is the seedbed for future senior state managers. I like the federal system of evaluation and testing at middle levels. I do not think you should rely primarily on written tests, when you go beyond a 23 level. After that, you ought to have a different method of evaluation and testing. One should be able to move someone up and down a grade range, depending on whether they deliver or not. You cannot avoid some subjectivity in any reward system. Also, it can be difficult to define "deliver."

COMMENT: I have seen others, not like you, Mark, who have a different definition.

LAWTON: I absolutely would not want to politicize the thing.

COMMENT: Often, civil servants are almost disloyal to the boss. Then, you have to be able to take some kind of step, if you're going to have any discipline in management. A second problem arises in getting the right person for the right job.

LAWTON: Part of the problem is the way we test for middle management and upper management and the inability to transfer people between job tasks and agencies. There ought to be far more transferability between levels and even between agencies.

I like the concept of the career executive. Even without the legislation which we submitted a number of times, we initiated some change in Budget, in cooperation with Civil Service, that was the nearest thing to a de facto career executive system. We created a special cadre of people who would be able to move across agencies and programs. We started very modestly, with maybe 25 slots, to see how we could develop the basis for a management cadre of some sort.

The answer is not "management confidential," because those people are not managers. Clearly there needs to be a management group, and they ought to be protected with a merit system. I don't think they should be removed without cause. However, they should be removable from a specific job. You should have that flexibility to reallocate and reassign them.

QUESTION: Typically, it seems the competent career service managers in the federal government are almost always despised by the secretaries and other appointed officials. Look what happened in the federal EPA.[10] Is there any way in which you can guard against that strong feeling of resentment?

LAWTON: You can educate the people who are appointees. I was a hold-over at the beginning of the Carey administration. When the new commissioner and his new people came into the agency, I organized a series of briefings for them. These briefings were on state government, not on agency issues. Perhaps a similar offer for all of the appointees of a new administration, including the commissioners, would help.

I believe that there should be a formal orientation process to explain the role of permanent civil servants, the role of permanent management, the role of control agencies, etc. Many new appointees equated civil service with permanent managers, and I think that is part of the problem; they tend to see them all as dull and unimaginative. That is far from the case, particularly in New York State. By and large, we have enormously talented people in management. Our problem is that we do not provide them the support systems they need—the training or the environment sufficient to enable them to manage effectively.

You can make a commissioner understand, but it takes effort. I have talked to a lot of new commissioners informally. Some of them came to discuss their problems. I tried to help them to use their permanent staff. They can make a difference. Leadership must be provided, however, their skills must be respected. It is important to appoint better people and motivate them. There is a need to institutionalize such a process.

COMMENT: A very serious problem in the professional service is that many of us arrived during bad economic times. During periods of good economic times, if you can remember that far back, we did not recruit the top people. As the depression and post-depression period people retire, I do not see the quality of people we recruited in the 30's and 40's and even the 50's. We have a different class of people now. We do not have the merit system and the professional class to which we have been accustomed. When are we going to recruit top-quality people again? Maybe I am being cynical about it, but I do not think that we recruited the same kinds of people in the 60's and the 70's that we recruited before.

LAWTON: I have always thought it would be fascinating to do a profile on the government executive to determine what drives him or her. There are some extraordinarily good people in government today. If there were not, the system would collapse. If they were oriented to be in private sector, they would do very well in business, but their love is government.

Budget is very fortunate, because many talented people who go into government, gravitate towards Budget. In the operating departments I do not think we have a similar circumstance, partly because society is changing. People only want to work from nine-to-five. They want limited responsibility, no overtime, and time off. This is true in business as well as in government. People approach the workplace with a different mind-set and different expectations today. If you think this is unique to government, talk to a businessman. I have and they tell me: "This next generation is nine-to-five; they don't really care about finishing the job and putting in the time; they worry about family, and they worry about their quality of life, and they worry whether they're going to be able to go to the theatre. They should be paying attention to business."

COMMENT: Part of your answer is that the way to increase the effectiveness and the impact of professional, non-political civil servants is to educate the political appointees. In other words, it is a question of giving them the latitude and the opportunity to, let us say, become less interested in the theatre.

LAWTON: As a matter of fact, I would be even more explicit. I think this is one of the major services that a place like the Nelson A. Rockefeller Institute could provide. The worst occurs when people come into government from outside who are hostile, and no one tries to counteract that urge. It doesn't matter what their party affiliation is; if they aren't helped early on, chances are they will leave early on in frustration and not have gotten much done.

It really is unfortunate. I have seen it with appointees in both political parties. Politics is not the cause. It results from the fact that there is a certain image of public workers out there. People who come in from the outside with a set of negative assumptions, unless helped early on, work themselves into a hole. It happens on the federal level, and it happens on the state level, as well.

Thank goodness, when such commissioners are appointed, they generally are not interested in running things. Nor are they actively concerned about the management and operation of government programs. Generally, that is when the permanent government takes over. We have such a good group of state employees that they carry the day.

QUESTION: Politicians come and go, but the administration stays. Unfortunately, that does not hold for the executive service in the federal government where, in attempting to do the very thing that we're discussing here, they have earned some distrust on the part of the secretaries and even the Congress. Their salaries have been frozen. Now, these good people, qualified for the executive service, are leaving government in droves the day they can retire.

LAWTON: Isn't that part of the current national administration's strategy to achieve an overall shrinkage of government? It is part of a deliberate policy to "get government off our backs."

QUESTION: How important is the press? What was the nature of your dealings with them?

LAWTON: In my opinion, the press contributes to the process in a positive way overall. However, there is too much emphasis placed on personality and gossip items rather than issues and information. Reporting on personalities is easier and more popular, but the press has a very special duty to inform the public on issues and not just entertain them. That is important. The press tends to overemphasize the personality aspect of issues—something that politicians take note of and act on. That is an unfortunate thing, but I guess it is in the nature of the media business today. Reporters write it up that way; it is understandable, even if unfortunate.

I have done a lot of thinking about reporters trying to deal with public policy issues. I have talked to publishers and editors about it, and some agree that reporting on fiscal matters can be difficult. When a person comes out of journalism school, he doesn't know much about public finance, budgets, or public issues. He or she is expected, however, to write a knowledgeable piece almost immediately. (The press corps in Albany has a big turnover.) Do they prepare journalists adequately in school? The few journalism courses I have been exposed to do not. The focus is on techniques and process, not analysis and understanding.

Well, these poor journalists cannot be expected to understand what an $18 billion budget is all about. They do not have the necessary background in government or in public finance. They frequently misunderstand the issues. So they write about personalities, because they can write about personalities without knowing anything about the issues. I spent a lot of time preparing budget schools for the Albany press corps. We gave them pre-briefings and background briefings on financial issues. I used to have a standard practice every Thursday evening at six o'clock. Members of the press could come down and talk to me about any matter in the budget or financial plan that was troubling them. I would provide them with answers, dialogue, and whatever information they needed that I could get for them. I do not know whether Michael Finnerty will continue the Thursday evening sessions, but I believe that the exchange was useful to all.

I felt an enormous responsibility to help reporters understand what was happening, because the media is the primary means of educating the public on the issues confronting them and their representatives. In addition, in the absence of good information, they would be fed misinformation—some of it pure hogwash.

Many of my sessions with reporters were off-the-record and background sessions. The purpose was not to get DOB or me into the media; it was to get the issues and information before the public. Chances are, if reporters are puzzled about something, so is the public.

COMMENT: We do not actually teach our public administrators to cultivate the reporters and teach them the substance of their work. This is a very important point. Otherwise, the reporters deal with the personality. If that personality doesn't spend time with them or shuts them off or says: "Look, I'm busy," they're going to get bad press. It has nothing to do with the quality or the rightness of the issue.

LAWTON: True. I spent a lot of effort with editors and publishers on behalf of reporters. I remember one such session in Poughkeepsie with Gannett. They had all their people together, and I butted into their business and said, "Gannett's an excellent news chain .. one of the best, and one of the most progressive, but I've always wondered why you sent a general reporter to cover an $18 billion budget that might deal with a multitude of complex issues. Every one of your papers has a business page, with staff with some financial background and experience. Some of you may even have an economist available. Why don't you ever provide those services to your general reporters covering the budget and financial issues at the state level?"

QUESTION: How did they answer?

LAWTON: I never got a satisfactory answer. Oh, we all went through a lot of chest beating and running around the issue. My purpose was not to get an answer from them, but rather to provoke them into thinking about the issue.

QUESTION: But didn't you also have a couple of good stories for these folks to write?

LAWTON: Oh yes, I almost always had a pocketful of stories, because I understood their need to make a living. The essential thing to remember about reporters is that they are good decent people trying to do a job in an environment they neither control, nor necessarily understand. I have never treated them as the devil incarnate. They have to write 800 to 1,000 words a day, and they have to have something meaningful to say. I would go out of my way to give them information with which to write a story accurately. I never expected them to pander to my preferences or to parrot my views. I expected to take my lumps when it was justified.

QUESTION: What are the prospects for the upcoming budget and for the longer term?

LAWTON: From a financial point of view, I do not think prospects for the upcoming budget are good. One can not squeeze much more from government or the taxpayers. An improved economy is what will get you out of the present bind to a certain degree. (And that prospect doesn't look too good.) I do not think any governor or any budget director enjoys the prospect of continuing austerity. Certainly, no one man can enjoy the painful task of ratcheting down the cost of government. It is not an altogether rational process; it is very uneven in program impact. Austerity allows a budget director to budget more tightly, to be the wringer, to shrink programs down to manageable limits, and to take the credit for it. But, it is not a good way to run government in the longer run. It is less fun, and you cannot address emerging needs. (And they do emerge in good times and bad.) I wish the need for austerity was over, but my guess is that there is still a way to go. The economy has not settled down. New York is better prepared than most, but not there yet.

In the longer term, I wish that budget directors could solve the major problems that confront every budget director to a certain degree—adequate resources to meet justifiable public needs—but I have a feeling that problem is going to go unresolved for awhile. Beyond that normal legacy, I left Mike Finnerty an opportunity to build an information data base which can be used by future state managers to manage. Every budget director does, in fact, produce a balanced budget for the governor to submit to the legislature. So I do not consider unbalanced budgets to be relevant, nor do I expect the system to overflow with brotherly love between the executive and the legislature. If occasionally an important public policy issue is addressed and "solved" at least for the time being—fine!

COMMENT: It certainly brought some productivity.

LAWTON: Yes, it did, but at a cost. There are no free lunches.

FOOTNOTES

[1]Professor Robert Newton Anthony, Ross Graham Walker Professor of Management Control, Harvard University School of Business; Frank Mauro, Secretary, Assembly Ways and Means Committee; formerly Secretary, Majority Program Committee; Stanley Fink, Speaker, New York State Assembly (1979-present).

[2]Michael Finnerty, Deputy Director, New York State Division of the Budget (1979-1982), Director (1983-84).

[3]Arthur Anderson and Company is a major accounting firm, retained by the State to assist in the transition to GAAP budgeting.

[4]"Levittown" refers to a lawsuit undertaken by the Levittown school district and 26 other school districts charging that New York State's school finance system was fundamentally unfair because it advantaged rich areas. After success in the lower courts, this suit failed in the Court of Appeals in 1982, eight years after it was initiated.

[5]Peter Goldmark, Director, New York State Division of the Budget (1975-1977).

[6]The Blaine amendment is Article 11, Section 3 of the New York State Constitution, which prohibits the use of public money to aid religious schools. The repeal of this amendment has been a continuous issue in New York State constitutional politics during this century.

[7]Perry Duryea, Speaker, New York State Assembly (1969-1973).

[8]Anthony Travia, New York State Assembly Speaker (1965-1968); Warren Anderson, Majority Leader, New York State Senate (1973-present).

[9]MTA, Metropolitan Transportation Authority, the principal public transportation agency in the New York City region.

[10]Federal EPA, Environmental Protection Agency.

Barbara B. Blum, commissioner of Social Services from 1977 to 1982, had previously been an associate commissioner of the Department of Mental Hygiene. Her career included extensive experience in social and mental health fields in New York City government, and five years as director of the City Office of the State Board of Social Welfare.

Barbara B. Blum

Commissioner of Social Services

BLUM: I consciously undertook, from the day that I came
to Albany, a major effort to try to change the public perception of
the welfare and services programs. In the 60's and early 70's, the
welfare case load had risen very dramatically. Looking back, one
can understand a number of factors which caused that increase, but
the public certainly never fully understood what had occurred. We
had fairly sizeable increases in the birth rate during the 60's. We had
in-migration over a period of decades that contributed to the case
load size—some people came to New York State looking for jobs and
were not able to find employment. We had some procedural slack-
ening, particularly in the New York City area. This may have contributed, although I happen to think that was a lesser factor.

At any rate, there had been a very significant increase in fiscal burden placed upon the state because of these changes in the case load
size, compounded by the fact that the public sector (both federal
and state) began to look at and publicize errors in administration.
(I'm not suggesting that they shouldn't have been publicized.) Even
during the tenure of my predecessors in the Carey administration,
any discussion of the welfare program tended to be in the context of
error rates or corrective action. This places a kind of stigma and
penalty on the client.

Consequently, from the beginning, I tried to be as accessible as
possible to advocacy groups. I charted out visits to each of the counties so that I could meet not only with local commissioners who had
sometimes viewed the state Department of Social Services (DSS) as
the enemy, but also with local legislators and county executives,
where they existed. I hadn't realized that this would be a benefit,
but I soon found that if a commissioner goes into almost any locale
outside of New York City, he becomes news. The newspaper and the
radios and the TV can be counted on to carry your message.

After a while, I got a little more sophisticated about what message
I wanted to have carried. There were really several messages. I
wanted people to know that there were people who very much
need assistance; that there were children about whom we should be
concerned in the state and outside this state, who rely on public
assistance to pay for their shelter and clothing and food; that there
were great complexities in the welfare program; and that workers
were hard-pressed to administer a program as complicated as Aid to
Families with Dependent Children (AFDC) while still having to

89

know the rules of the Food Stamp program, the Medicaid program, Supplemental Security Income (SSI), and the energy program. In a small county where specialization is not possible, workers are expected to know the differences in eligibility requirements and payment standards and a whole host of other things. I happen to think that traveling to localities was a very important set of activities. Without that set of activities, I don't believe that some of the other things that occurred could have happened.

The specific change that I feel most pleased about is the adjustment in the basic welfare grant. The adjustment was for an additional 15 percent, and it was the first adjustment since 1974. I wish that there were some way to automatically index AFDC payments in the same way we seem to be able to index payments to people who are middle income or higher income. The adjustment certainly wasn't sufficient, but at least it was an improvement over the payment standard that had existed since 1974. There was a lot of work done in many of these local meetings and with the legislature, and there was also an enormous amount of research done. We analyzed the poverty level; we analyzed with the Bureau of Labor Statistics; we tried everything we could to analyze where inflation had really hit. As a result of that very extensive analysis, it was possible to respond to the various questions from the legislators and others as we were attempting to get that change through the legislature.

Of course, there also was a very important activity during this time for which I could take no credit, and that was a coalescing of the church groups and other groups, which I think was very effective. Many, many people around the state heard about the inadequacy of the grants from individuals outside government. Sometimes the credibility inside government isn't so good, but everyone was using consistent figures which was very important. Everyone looked at what the grant was supposed to cover. Everyone advocating the change was using the same set of numbers that we had developed with our analysis.

The second major area of change was actually mandated by the legislature. This was the Child Welfare Reform Act, and it was the single most complicated piece of legislation to implement that I've ever seen, because there were a whole series of concurrent activities that had to be instituted. One was a county plan, which we managed to incorporate in this comprehensive effort. We also had to institute a uniform case record for all children in foster care and all children receiving preventive services across the state. Prior to this act, districts had used quite different approaches to recording case information.

We had to develop a review process that would identify for us instances where the plan for a child and the uniform case record

90

were not being observed. We had to develop standards that would be applied in terms of length of stay for children and types of services to be provided to children. We had to restructure a number of things in the adoption program that were complicated. We had to redesign the computerized child care review system in order to respond to both the uniform case record and the utilization review requirements. That act was implemented fully before I left, except in New York City, where they are still implementing the computer system. Even in New York City, the uniform case record is in place. While there were some time lags, for the most part, the legislative deadlines for that act were met.

In the adult service area, the greatest accomplishment was the change that occurred in the adult homes. In 1977, the adult home industry was still in deep trouble. The fact is that in Long Beach, in Rockland, and in some other places in the state, conditions in the homes were truly scandalous. The Department of Social Services did develop standards, and did work with the Department of Mental Health to improve its licensure and its inspection procedures. While you still occasionally have unacceptable incidents or situations in those adult homes, we don't have the kinds of consistently horrendous conditions that existed in 1977. Many of those homes have been closed in certain areas of the state.

I would be remiss if I didn't mention the work that the department staff did in developing protective services for adults. Those services will be enormously important in the future because of the aging of our citizenry. I do believe that New York State is ahead of most states in the nation in terms of having regulations and standards for protective services for adults. It is a very sensitive area because, unlike children, where we somehow accept that intervention can and should occur, there's a lot less certainty about when intervention is appropriate. There was some really good ground work done by the Division of Adult Services in that area.

A fourth achievement that I'm very proud of, although it's a bit more esoteric and probably will take a lot longer to have an impact than something like a change in the grant, is that we looked at the planning process in the department. The department had a legal mandate for Title XX, Income Maintenance, and Medicaid federal plans. (Actually, these are really not plans, but rather requirements, although they are called plans.) But the state law required us to produce a protective service plan for children and adults, a preventive service plan, and when the Child Welfare Reform Act came along, it was also going to require us to provide a child welfare reform act plan.

We decided that, first of all, the multiplicity of plans made little sense because there was an inter-relationship among all these services. The way you provide preventive services to children and families affects what happens in protective services and certainly affects what would happen in the Child Welfare Reform Act. A resource allocation question arises with the growing number of adults. We need to take into account the changes in that population as we're looking at state planning for younger groups.

So, we first went to the feds and said, "Will you give us a waiver for Title XX and let us plan for a three-year period, rather than planning yearly without knowing outcomes? Three years would allow us to really monitor what is happening out there." Then, we went to the state legislature with the Title XX waiver in hand and said, "We could plan for a three-year period, if you would permit us to do a comprehensive planning exercise." We got that legislation through.

Subsequently, the feds passed national legislation for a three-year planning cycle. Our changes permitted a very intensive effort to analyze, county by county, population changes, economic conditions, and service needs that are not currently covered. I hope the planning initiative will endure because it is only after a number of years that you really get payoff from a planning effort. Even at the beginning, though, the districts began to prioritize a bit better, since they were thinking over a longer range based on current and useful data from the department.

Finally, I guess I would call the management system an achievement. The legislature, in its wisdom, had dictated what we were supposed to do in the systems area, and they really had it quite backwards. They wanted a Medicaid Management Information System up before the Welfare Management System (WMS). We did what the legislature told us to do, but the fact is that WMS should have gone up first because it created the eligibility file. It was very important for the department's credibility and the administration's credibility to get those systems going.

My predecessors had already leased the equipment by the time I got to the department. I'm rather proud of the system, but I would have designed it very differently. I would have had a much less centralized system. There's just one giant computer at 40 North Pearl Street. If anything happened at 40 North Pearl, we would have some serious trouble in this state. It is, therefore, necessary now to figure out how to get the whole operation a bit decentralized. I think that anybody who has been in government knows that at times you must operate with what you've got. The state is now in that position in terms of programming, and must translate those two systems into a different mode. Frankly, the Medicaid system is always totally problematic, but there have been some good things that came out of it, such as the Medicaid Management Information System (MMIS).

QUESTION: You mentioned planning a few times, and others

92

who have been interviewed have also talked about the importance of planning. For one reason or another, it appears that this word is heard more often, which is striking for a few reasons. First of all, it's coming from the commissioner level. The idea of planning emphasizes and suggests the importance of being able to implement over a long period of time. It suggests a continuity of personnel and of coherence. What are the incentives to plan in the department?

BLUM: I observed some years ago that planning works, and that has made me have some faith in planning. My mathematical training enables me to enjoy data. I think that you learn an enormous amount by watching trend data in particular. We have done a terrible job predicting future trends and problems in this nation. For instance, I'm delighted that now, with Social Security issues and Medicare issues, we're at least beginning to think demographically. (Of course, you've got to get the economic indicators linked in there so that you don't go off the deep end with your population data.)

The first time that I realized the value of planning was way back in 1967-68, when Fred Hayes was budget director in the City of New York. He had a cracker jack staff of people that he had brought in from Washington, hot on Program Planning and Budgeting System (PPBS), which at that point I had never heard of. I was in Mental Health in the city at the time. Fred Hayes said he thought he agreed with me that resources were inappropriately flowing into Manhattan, when Brooklyn and Queens were much larger, and Brooklyn was more deprived already, Staten Island was growing, and the Bronx was in poor shape. Manhattan, one-fifth of the whole city population, was getting one-half of the mental health budget.

Hayes said, "Okay, you work with my staff and I will give you a million bucks." A million bucks then was more than it is now, but still wasn't very much. We did some very simple planning. It was really superficial. We answered questions such as where the clients come from when they enter the state hospitals and whether the majority of clients go back to the deprived neighborhoods. We looked at suicide rates, homicide rates, child abuse, and a few other factors. It was really very surface kinds of stuff, but it all correlated.

I think I was the first person who knew Far Rockaway was going to be a problem. The budget examiner said, "Oh, people vacation in Far Rockaway." He went out and drove around and argued with me about it. But we created new facilities in the East New York Mental Health Clinic and the Bedford-Stuyvesant Mental Health Center (which had been a little clinic until we put money in it). We put money into Coney Island, the South Bronx, the Harlem Inter-faith Clinic, and others. This modest funding, around a hundred thousand bucks, which went into each of these areas, permitted something to start, and each has grown. The clinics still exist. They provide aftercare for people who come out of mental health hospitals, and sometimes they prevent people from going into these hospitals.

I saw something work, and I certainly applied that experience when I went into Human Resources Administration (HRA) and childrens' services. We closed shelters and detention centers by identifying what the kids really needed, and by getting them back to their homes or into group homes or foster homes. The same set of principles apply whether you're talking about children's services or adult services. If you assess what the needs are, look at what the trends are, and at what programs exist, you can then determine what's missing and try to put your money there.

QUESTION: What, in your experience, was the main obstacle to planning? Was it lack of experience in planning?

BLUM: Everywhere I've been, the main obstacle was budget staff. Except for Fred Hayes, the budget people didn't want you to plan. It's very frightening. In New York City once Fred Hayes was gone, officials didn't want us to do it. I think there are several reasons; some are really very primitive. Budget doesn't like you to know as much, or more, than they know, which is ridiculous if you're running programs. They want to know at least as much as you know, but if you have a good planning staff, you're always going to be a little ahead, because you're always going to be thinking about different ways to go about the agency's work. Budget staff are scared to death of resource planning. They honestly don't believe, as Fred Hayes did, that preventive measures will actually reduce term expenditures. I think massive savings exist if the planning is well founded.

QUESTION: When you say Budget, are you talking about something that was pervasive at the top on down or do you mean people reacting at the lower level?

BLUM: If you're going to plan well, you have to have people on your staff who have certain skills and who are very bright and very persistent. You automatically begin to ask for a certain grade level and job description which leads you right into conflict, first with Budget, and then with Civil Service. They ask, "Why do you need that kind of job description? Why can't you use this title and use this list?" None of their suggestions produced what we needed. Meanwhile, Budget was fighting to keep their salary levels higher than ours, so they could attract people who were brighter than our people. I think Bill Hennessy was right.[1] He should have gone into Budget. I don't understand their way of operating. It is worrisome when people don't want other bright people working on mutual problems. You have a weak commissioner if the commissioner is afraid of bringing in bright people.

QUESTION: Recently, people from Budget have praised the

Medicaid Management Information System, saying that it's giving them data that will produce much more intelligent decisions and products. Is that attitude in Budget an anomaly?

BLUM: Whether or not it is an anomaly, it is a little late. MMIS went up in 1979; I think it's terrific that they find it useful in 1983. I don't mean that there weren't some people in Budget who didn't appreciate planning. All the same, last year we started a very complicated analysis of the shelter allowance, which is dreadfully inadequate. I knew that there weren't enough resources to increase it. I was trying to put the energy funds and shelter funds together in a lump sum. Mark Lawton was the only person who would listen and understand that.[2] The rest of the Budget people were adamantly opposed. You would have thought that they were down in the middle management of some other department and not responsible for thinking over the long range.

QUESTION: When you entered the state Department of Social Services and began to implement your ideas and plans, did you find the department staff reluctant? Did you feel their experience with PPBS and other unsuccessful planning attempts made them reluctant to cooperate with you?

BLUM: Yes. Actually a combination of things had occurred within the department, and as you mentioned, there had been past failure with various planning approaches over the past few years. There had been a tiny core of planning staff in existence when Phil Toia[3] was there, but he scattered them around to the divisions so that there was no planning capacity at all available to the commissioner. One of the first things I did was fight to get an office of Program Planning Analysis and Development set up. It must have taken a year and a half just to get approval from Budget for a very small group of staff, but we finally got it in place. It was never looked on with great love and affection by the divisions, although a great deal of respect began to accrue to the office after staff had done some work on planning and analysis of the basic grant. Without that group of staff, we never could have broken through in a number of areas, and so the various divisions began to respect them.

With the Reagan changes, for instance, they were the staff that tried to figure out how to strip WMS and MMIS so that we could begin to take the data and understand the impact on clients. It took a lot of work to develop any planning capacity in the department. I'm terrified that it will be the first thing to disappear.

QUESTION: Are there any unresolved problems for your successor?

BLUM: Yes. The first has to do with the Title XIX program. That came into existence when a decision was made to designate the Department of Social Services the single state agency to administer

Medicaid, even though setting of standards was in the Department of Health. For years there has been a lot of pushing and hauling about whether Medicaid should be transferred into the Department of Health. I think it reached its height in the year I came in, because it looked like an opportune time to take Medicaid away. I resisted at that time, primarily because I couldn't figure out how I would get up MMIS if Medicaid was over in Health. We were then in the middle of implementating MMIS. It was a really bizarre idea to take the program and move it, before MMIS was really up and running.

I imagine part of my reluctance was also a little bit of turf consciousness. As the new commissioner, I didn't like thinking that somebody was just going to take a good piece of the action out from the department. I have a very different opinion now. It's not just because I'm no longer commissioner; I have been voicing this opinion for about a year and a half, much to Health's dismay.

I think that now that MMIS is up, it's a perfect time for Medicaid to be transferred to the Department of Health, so that one agency can be accountable for the entire program. As things currently operate, if something goes wrong we blame Health from the Social Services point of view, and Health blames Social Services. Nobody is really accountable because it is possible to just throw up a lot of smoke and have people very confused about who does what.

The second reason I think that Medicaid should be transferred is because it consumes so much of the commissioners' time. I've come to the opinion that income maintenance is really an extraordinarily important program for the self-sufficiency of a very large group of children in this state. When you're trying to administer both Medicaid and welfare, Medicaid tends to draw attention. I can't tell you how many hours the commissioner had to spend on each of those hospitals that are in trouble. Those hours could have been spent a lot more sensibly with a single department head who had responsibility for the whole thing. The third reason Medicaid should not be in the Department of Social Services budget may sound very cynical. The cost of Medicaid outstripped welfare's costs several years ago. It is untenable for a single department to have a budget of above $12 billion in this state. It would make a great deal of sense to separate out Medicaid now, so that the income maintenance and services programs could receive appropriate attention and support.

QUESTION: Wouldn't that change the basic role of Social Services to an advocate and seeker of services as opposed to a screen to keep clients out?

BLUM: Yes, but I think this would be a much better role and becomes particularly important now that more than half of the Medicaid funds are going for nursing homes and older people. Welfare clients are getting a smaller and smaller proportion per case of

Medicaid funds, so that the advocacy role really is very important. As commissioner, you are always in a conflict situation.

QUESTION: Wouldn't that be contradictory, though, if the emphasis was on welfare, because they are in a screening out role, too? You also have contradictory roles there, don't you?

BLUM: I don't think that we are so much in a screening out role as in one to just assure that people require assistance. Some people don't require assistance or some have resources and are not eligible, but that also varies from district to district. Most commissioners try to respond to the need. The problems in New York City are really very significant.

QUESTION: Are they solvable?

BLUM: They probably are, but the system now operates very badly, and very wastefully. For instance, New York City is the only locale that is still building WMS. It will be instituted, but it has taken an extraordinarily long period of time. It's also the only locality that still hasn't got the Child Care Review System (CCRS) up for children. We've managed by hook and by crook to get MMIS up in New York City, but it was really an heroic effort on the part of a lot of fiscal and income assistance staff. New York City is a problem area that needs to be dealt with very differently, both politically and programmatically.

QUESTION: New York City is said to set a problem of scope. The city resists doing it the way that the state wants to do it.

BLUM: Part of it is scope or scale, but a lot of it is just incompetence, and I think that's what needs to be corrected. That is important at any time, but particularly when the problem and solution are quite clear.

In New York City, they're unable to think about doing things differently. There is a lot of duplication. Their income maintenance centers are poorly located in relation to their clients. All they say is, "Well, we have leases." Their service delivery system is too highly centralized; that's a system that needs to be very much decentralized. Until recently, they have had only one Medicaid office, at 34th Street. Now, these are disabled people who have to come in to get Medicaid. That's really not the way a human service agency should run.

QUESTION: What are the causes of not doing things better in New York City?

BLUM: I think it's a problem of lacking the guts to reform. You have to have a mayor who wants to do it, and you have to have a lot of people in the human resources administration who want to do it.

QUESTION: That's curious. It seems that there's been a lot of emphasis in city government on management, and that they have had some success in the management of large organizations. There are resources in the city that you might not expect to find in rural areas. The fact that there are a lot of resources and they are not properly utilized is what makes it so tragic. Have they had sustained ineptitude in their commissioners over a period of time?

BLUM: No. They have a fine commissioner now. When you go in and talk to him, he wants to do things, but then nothing happens. A very different level of commitment is necessary. The city has been through a couple of very bad decades. The door opened up in the Ginsburg administration, but Mitch was really not an administrator. He was a great person, but not an administrator. Then Jules Sugerman came in. He is probably a fine manager, given a chance, but he was busy shifting the Ginsburg policies and getting his name in the headlines every day by doing it. That does happen to administrators; to some extent, you pick up on whatever your predecessor happened to do. That administration was followed by a do-nothing period. A respected businessman was in charge, but nothing happened in the bureaucracy. The bureaucracy has just gotten worse and worse.[4]

QUESTION: Is there anything that the federal government and/or the state government could do with respect to withholding funds?

BLUM: I think so. We have withheld various kinds of monies at various times, but you really have to have a core of very powerful people moving together.

COMMENT: You have to get real leadership with support.

BLUM: Yes, and you would have to have the support of the mayor and the union people. The unions have to be dealt with if there are going to be changes of the kind I was talking about.

QUESTION: It seems that during a significant period of that development, at least in the Human Resources Administration and Social Services area, after Spiegel left, they went through their most highly publicized, highly visible era. And then, they never really grasped the extent of the managerial gap in there.

BLUM: I think that's right. But I do believe that it could be grasped, especially when WMS is up. Once that system is in, there's a real handle on the information that can be obtained from it.

QUESTION: In the transition policy review paper done for the agency, there's a fairly strong hint of a possible state takeover of the administration of Medicaid, with a regional kind of clustering outside New York. Do you think that would solve at least that component of the problem in New York City?

BLUM: I doubt it, but I just don't know enough about how it would be administered. My fear is that it would become more centralized in terms of actual delivery of services. It would be less responsive and more distant. One thing that has to be guarded against is local administration of income maintenance with state administration of Medicaid. Do we just create that many more crevices in which people can really disappear? I would have to know more about how they propose to design it.

I honestly feel that the state should spend a considerable period of time, probably two years or so, examining how one could take on direct administration of the system. It might be that the state will decide not to do that. Everyone now cites the revenue problems, the 25 percent local contribution to these programs, as a barrier. I think that there are some changes in the tax base that could be made that would permit the shift. I do believe that there is a great deal of duplication that occurs with this kind of system in place. The clients are poorly served because of some of the inconsistencies that can't be controlled very well. State administration is something that really should be looked at very closely, and I haven't seen serious work done to examine it.

In fact, there are more states doing it now than I would have expected. The states that have local administration tend to be small. Well, that's not entirely true, because California has local administration and state supervision. In my little organization, we have state demonstrations. I sit in meetings in California and observe the state and local officials doing the same kind of pushing and hauling that we always did here. I think, "Who's in charge? Who's really going to decide what the sample will be?" No matter what level you are working at, there is a considerable amount of energy that gets used in ways that really don't help clients or push the programs along very much.

QUESTION: In New York, is state-directed administration politically possible?

BLUM: Most governors would run away from it. There is protection both for the local and the state people in having the status quo stand. To support change, one would have to use the resource question. That is why we have seen some very extensive work analyzing what would be involved. It would have to be done by very objective people, because if you just had state staff doing it, there would tend to be one type of agenda, and if you have other types in the state work on it, they might produce another kind of agenda. I'm not sure who should be doing that examination, but I know that somebody should really be doing a very careful study of it.

QUESTION: You've always suggested an adjustment in the tax base. Do you have any specific ideas about that, for example tapping into the state aid payments that localities get, or is that just a generalization?

BLUM: Frankly, I don't know enough about taxation. My assumption is that if the revenues exist, there must be some way to let the counties keep their property tax, if that's what they are using for a portion of their contribution. We may be able to do some offsetting somewhere along the way.

QUESTION: If you were going to start over, what might you do differently?

BLUM: I would have taken a more hard-line stance with New York City from the beginning, which might have made my tenure a lot shorter, but maybe more satisfying.

I kept thinking that I could pursue them or we could get them to do it this way or that way. I'm fairly certain we just wasted effort, and I regret that.

QUESTION: Did the mayor keep getting in the way?

BLUM: The mayor and I had two knock-down, drag-out fights, although the governor was very supportive. The first fight took place when Blanche Bernstein was commissioner. She decided that she wanted to do a demonstration with a vendor restricted check (a check requiring two signatures) in a very large portion of the South Bronx. The housing is not so great, but evidently the mayor felt the welfare system had somehow created the housing problem. Her approach was to have the check signed by the landlord and the client.

I raised objections because I felt that if the housing was really unsafe, then it was not something into which I would want to cage people. HHS came to the rescue this time and agreed with us whole-heartedly.[5] The mayor never forgot it. He still talks about it and Blanche writes books about it.

The second fight involved the homeless. We were certainly very ineffective in dealing with the homeless at the state level, but the city was far more ineffective than we were, and heartless to boot. I thought that we needed at least one shelter in every borough because the proliferation of homeless people was becoming very evident throughout the city. The city disagreed, and for the longest time operated only one shelter for men and one for women.

When a new site was identified, the site was difficult for me to accept because it was a building I had closed when it had Willowbrook class members in it. It was a building I didn't like, but eventually the mayor opened it. The high point of all this came on a Friday afternoon at the World Trade Center when I was tired, the way you usually are at the end of the week in government. The phone rang, and it was a reporter from the *Post*. He asked, "Did you know that the mayor called you crazy today?" And, I said, "No, I didn't know that. In what context did he say that?" The reporter said that the mayor was meeting with the editorial board and he said that this crazy lady, Barbara Blum, wants to put a shelter in every community, and that this was like bringing a cancer into each neighborhood. And I said that I regretted that he had said that. I never had suggested a shelter be in every neighborhood, but I did believe that there should be at least one in each borough and perhaps more than one in some boroughs. I let it go at that. Later, when the mayor was asked about it, he was quoted as saying that he had used the term affectionately.

Recently, the mayor has begun to reach out to communities and churches. One morning I read that Harlem people had been demonstrating because they hadn't been told that he was placing a shelter across from a school. There had been no preparation for the shelter in Harlem. The mayor was now furious that people wouldn't want shelters in their communities. I sat there and thought, "This is the very same man who said it was like bringing a cancer into every neighborhood." He wonders why people demonstrate! Although I don't think that if I had gone hard at the city I would have lasted very long, I wish I had anyway.

Second, very late in my tenure, I managed to get some regional offices developed. Now, with the budget cuts, they have been pretty much dismantled. I wish I had developed those offices much earlier. We had become a very centralized department and needed to have a regional presence. Also, they would have been a terrific staging ground if ever the state decided to become a state operator. They would be a good instrument for helping to plan.

We tried to design the district offices very differently from the previous area offices. We wanted a core of three or four staff who could listen closely to the concerns of seven or eight districts around them and communicate promptly with Albany, so that if there was something that we really needed, we would be informed quickly.

QUESTION: They were not there to try to supervise in the same sense as the area office once did?

BLUM: They were very different from that, providing co-location where there were staff out there licensing or inspecting, but not supervising. Although the offices were working pretty well, they were much too young and they just didn't survive. There were seven of them. They've been killed in a funny way; one person still exists from six of the seven offices. (They didn't keep New York City at all, which is really a disaster.) There had been 30 or 35 staff members. The state kept six and called them directors, but they don't even have secretaries, so I can't think it is possible that they could accomplish very much.

The third place I would have done things differently is in employment. We got some good things going in some of the districts, but we should have done that earlier. I do think that most of the ADC

(Aid to Dependent Children) clients want to work. You really have to find a way to help them do that. Most commissioners really want to be involved in that kind of positive activity, rather than just handing out checks.

Finally, I wish we had begun work on the shelter grant much earlier. That's a very complicated area to get into with the public or with the legislature. You need a long period to develop an understanding of what changes in housing stock have occurred and what level of support is needed.

QUESTION: Was Willowbrook your career mistake, or were there benefits that came out of it?[6]

BLUM: I tend to measure benefits differently than most people. I think that a great many individuals who have gotten out of Willowbrook have benefited greatly. The consent judgment, perhaps, had unrealistic time frames. If it had time frames strung over a ten-year period, it could have been properly implemented and we would have been able to manage better. There are still 1,200 or so people at Willowbrook. I worry about those people because I think they may really never get out, and I worry a bit about the people in the community because they need a strong case management capacity that was almost lost in this budget. The minute you have people in the community without case management, you can count on a lot of abuse and damage being done to the individuals inside. Having been inside Willowbrook a lot, I think it was very important for us to get whatever group of people we could out of there. The situation was really not acceptable.

QUESTION: Within your agency, you really had competing constituencies. Did you have mechanisms for resolving conflict and competition among them?

BLUM: I have always operated with a fair amount of structure. Every Monday, all of the senior staff met for a couple of hours. We usually reviewed whatever was on the front burner, and we also tried to spend some time on long-range issues. It was a chance for people to know where I was coming from and to begin to adjust their viewpoints to that. I feel very strongly that once your objectives are clear, people have to begin to fall into line. Otherwise, you have no chance of getting the outcome you are attempting to reach. The systems people had been terribly spoiled and they wanted to run everything. That was probably the most difficult internal problem. We met frequently until everybody understood that the program people were going to dictate what was to be in the system; that they had to be specific; and that they shouldn't want the whole world in the system. It worked out eventually. That was at the very beginning and I think that was the hardest piece to handle.

The Audit and Quality Control staff were also used to very preferential treatment because no matter what you ask for them in the budget, they get more. That makes it very hard to control a division. They didn't use the computer systems as well as they should, and they didn't think about new ways to audit, but that was Budget's fault. I don't think that they operated as efficiently as they would have if funding were leaner. However, that is not a mistake of mine.

QUESTION: Phil Toia had gone to great lengths to install a management by objectives system which resulted in the Key Item System. He had brought this management technology with him out of his HEW (Department of Health, Education, and Welfare) regional experience. Did you find that kind of a formal structure useful to you? Was it still in place when you were there?

BLUM: I found it over-detailed. Some of the divisions may still use it. It's not the kind of thing that I found useful as a commissioner. If you have to get into that level of detail, except in very extraordinary circumstances, you cannot ever think about policy. It is still used in certain areas.

QUESTION: You also had different outside constituencies that you served. How did you go about reconciling the priorities among them?

BLUM: To the extent that we could, we tried to understand the changes that were occurring in the population. This state had not thought through the effects of increasing numbers of aged persons, where we now have a heavy investment. The nursing homes and health related facility programs are really essential for the old who are frail and need that level of physical care. We still don't have the kind of community services that will be required to maintain people in their own homes. It became evident that the child population was decreasing so rapidly that there needed to be a shift in resources. We tried to talk a lot about that.

We tried to do as much as we could in our department to encourage employment programs at the district level. Outside the Department of Labor, many of those are very successful. That was a fine way to really get over the problem with the competition between advocates for the working and advocates for the non-working. If there is a good employment program going, it's a real boon to the income maintenance recipient. Our competing populations are the old and the young, and the working and the non-working.

We have the welfare rights groups, and we have the legal aid groups which are really very effective.

QUESTION: Were they supportive of the department, or did they have adversarial relationships with it?

BLUM: For the most part, they ended up supporting us.

QUESTION: Did you have to make a special effort to have them do that?

BLUM: If you respond, it doesn't take very long before you have support. For instance, during one of the first trips I made to the Southern Tier, a legal aid lawyer got up and began to describe what happens if you're a migrant and you're ill or unemployed. (I hate to admit that I didn't even recognize at that point our responsibilities for migrants.) I came back here to Albany and checked out our policies; they weren't very clear and we altered them. The legal aid people know that we would listen; we may not always be able to respond quickly that way, but I think they know that too. If they know you make an effort to respond, there's less of this destructive pushing and tugging.

QUESTION: Back in 1965, the Partnership for Health Program relieved us of financial responsibility for our parents. We are now beginning to see some court action in a couple of states to reimpose at least limited liability on adult children. Is this an isolated example or part of a major shift?

BLUM: I think it will be part of a major shift. I'm basically very conservative and I believe that government substitutes very poorly for families. We do our worst service when we try to do things that family members normally try to do.

QUESTION: Do state governments do less well as family substitutes than local governments?

BLUM: I would think that the state would do it less well than local because of the distance, but I'm not certain.

QUESTION: So, do you see a shift back to family responsibility?

BLUM: I think there will have to be a shift. I don't see how we can afford to keep doing what we are doing. Look at health care costs now. Our per capita GNP is not as high as it used to be. We're not doing as well as a number of European countries.

COMMENT: As an added dimension, parents who were once willing and capable of maintaining a retarded child in the home are now reaching their 60's and 70's. There may be a state or a public responsibility that has to be assumed, and I think there's concern about that. The average age of the general population is rising.

There is a commissioner in the field who refused to contribute a penny to the support of his own child in a state institution, reflecting his view that the child was wholly public responsibility.

BLUM: I also have an adult child in an institution, and we don't contribute to his care. However, I pay more than 50 percent of my salary in taxes and that's more than it costs to keep him in an institution. It has to be one way or another. If you want to reduce my taxes, which I am more than willing to bear, I would be delighted to pay for his care. That's what this is all about at this time. The public has to enter in and pick up what people can't afford to pay, but we cannot pay for everything. You could wipe out the whole welfare program for the nation and it wouldn't pay for the increase in Medicare over the next two years. We all have to think about that. There are seven million children in this nation who are dependent on welfare and we are financing them at approximately $1,000 a child for food, shelter, and clothing for 12 months. Meanwhile, Medicare is escalating at the rate of $90 a day per client.

QUESTION: Are there any tendencies in the state government itself to dismantle programs that the state provides?

BLUM: Unfortunately, I think you'll be seeing a lot of discussion of co-payments with Medicaid. That involves a significant portion of the welfare population.

And, to add to our concerns, we may slip into an equally costly program of comprehensive health insurance through the back door, because of concern for the unemployed. Permissive legislation was signed today to allow the deduction of health insurance payments if the unemployed desire it and if there's an approved program. Now the pressure is to get an approved program. The seed is planted for a comprehensive health insurance which no one really had intended. You should also watch unemployment benefits. You now, quite frequently, see these little tiny articles in the press, adding an additional five billion dollars to the program. The escalating costs of unemployment insurance alone have a tremendous impact.

QUESTION: That five billion dollars was essentially a loan to permit insolvent systems to continue to pay. Now, for the first time, in at least three states, we have seen a cap put in place. They've reduced duration and may have even reduced benefits in the unemployment insurance system. And added to that is just the issue of who's going to pay. In Michigan, a majority of employees do not pay.

Can you define how you perceive the difference between what as commissioner of Social Services you were truly responsible for and what the public perceived you to be specifically responsible for?

BLUM: The system is a state supervised, locally administered system. The public and often the legislators themselves perceive the commissioner to be in control of whatever is happening down at the local level. In fact, the commissioner is not in control, and sometimes even the local commissioner isn't, because the local legislatures differ greatly. Sometimes, legislators would be very responsive to a very good commissioner at the local level. Other times you can have a very good commissioner at the local level who just gets the guts ripped out of his budget and can't do what he should be doing. Then, of course, you have to use your sanctions and try to force whatever can be had.

COMMENT: Beginning in 1972 and 1973 and really accelerating from 1975 when Steve Berger was commissioner, the department was playing a much more direct role in social services, as opposed to the regulatory role that it had played previously.

BLUM: The previous situation was further complicated by the fact that the department used to be headed by the Board of Social Welfare. Since I was with HRA in the city when that body existed, I can attest that confusion reigned. You never quite knew who was supposed to be doing what.

COMMENT: You were also one of the only commissioners who reported as much to Carter and Ronald Reagan as to Hugh Carey. I would argue that Schweiker and Califano were as important in your life as the governor.[7]

BLUM: The federal stuff just drove what we did. I got very frustrated the first year. I don't like the state legislative process. I like the legislators, but I think the process is a disaster. Maybe it doesn't always have to be that way. It made no sense to me at all. The big bucks were in Washington. So, we developed a liaison with our Washington office and began to work much more closely with the congressional delegation and brought in tens of millions of dollars to this state. You are playing penny ante in the Department of Social Services if you focus only on the state legislative activity. You've got to pay attention to it because it will do things to the department if you don't, but that's not really where the money is coming from. You're entirely right.

QUESTION: You said that the federal government drives the state programs, and the county controls the programs. Yet, the county perceives the state as mandating the social services programs. Would you comment on this?

BLUM: We were really serving federal mandates with the exception of the Child Welfare Reform Act (although eventually the feds picked up the same set of standards that the state had legislated for children). Since we are a kind of conduit for federal mandates we rewrote the federal requirements in the state regulation, and we were perceived as the culprit. One of the major problems in the state is that there was an inconsistent implementation of those regulations. It's unfair for clients to be treated differently from one county to another. However, there definitely is difficulty in achieving consistent implementation.

COMMENT: It is my observation that professionals in counties in rural or semi-rural conservative areas need to have someone to blame in order to deliver the services they must deliver. County administrators are always complaining about payment schedules.

BLUM: They are, but those aren't program issues; they're fiscal.

QUESTION: What are your chief conclusions regarding how to make the New York State system of government work, especially with respect to legislative/executive relationships? You certainly had an opportunity to observe them.

BLUM: During the Carey administration, I always felt uncomfortable about the adversarial tenor of the legislative session. I tend not to like confrontation at all. So, I felt uncomfortable about that and wished it were different, but I can't say to you that I honestly think it ever affected any legislation pertinent to the department. I was trying to think of some instance where relations between the executive office and the legislature impeded getting legislation that we really wanted or needed and I couldn't think of any. For instance, when the time came for the increase in the grant and we had properly justified that increase, the governor worked very closely with Warren Anderson.[8] Warren Anderson was one of our best advocates. I don't know whether I'm just forgetting some things along the way, but the confrontational tone didn't seem to have a direct impact on the department.

QUESTION: Do you see no obvious need for changes in the system?

BLUM: I told you that I didn't like the state legislative process, so, obviously I think that there is something wrong with it. It seems to me that it is overly complicated. Too many people spent too many hours on picayune things that should have been accepted more simply.

QUESTION: Is it politics that you find to be objectionable?

BLUM: No, I really like politics, but this was beyond understanding. If there were trade-offs occurring, I didn't know what they were. It's just strange. People would worry about little sentences concerning protective services; on the homeless, where we had a major problem in the city, they would argue whether Dick Berman or I would be administering a program.[9] Sometimes I couldn't figure out why they were arguing. I would say, "Well, Dick should do it," and, then, the executive office would say, "Well, you should do it." It obviously had to do with someone in the legislature feeling that they wanted a different approach, but it always seemed to me to be petty stuff. The big stuff, like the grant, just went flying through.

QUESTION: In the legislature, were you carrying the ball yourself or was somebody else carrying it?

BLUM: No, I had staff carrying the ball.

QUESTION: Was the governor carrying it?

BLUM: No.

QUESTION: How about the governor's office in general?

BLUM: Occasionally, but not very often.

QUESTION: Did you feel you did not get the support or the assistance from the counsel's office or from the governor's office that you thought you should have?

BLUM: I sometimes thought we got more assistance from the counsel's office than we needed. Some of those long sessions were beyond my understanding.

QUESTION: I can't reconcile how you felt you didn't get support, and yet you got more help than you needed.

BLUM: I'm probably not being very clear because I've never understood it myself. We got most of what we wanted, but it seemed to me to be a very inefficient way to get it. I never could understand some of those lengthy discussions about very minor issues.

QUESTION: Did you feel that most of the program changes initiated with you and the department or did they initiate outside the department?

BLUM: The grant increase was initiated inside, but there was a lot of support outside. We had been building toward that. The Child Welfare Reform Act was generated outside, but we were working very closely on that. We primarily drafted the adult home registration.

QUESTION: Were inter-agency programs largely debates between you and your fellow commissioners, or did the chamber get involved with those, too? The WIN (Work Incentive) program might be an example.

BLUM: The WIN program involved a rather unusual set of events. It was an aberration. Sometimes the commissioners worked well together.

Certainly, it was always a battle with employment. With the Office of Mental Health (OMH), I would say that half the time was a battle, but that was mostly about who was going to be responsible for the program. With the Office of Mental Retardation (OMR) I think there was very seldom a battle. Health became a non-battle when Dick Berman left. David Axelrod and I always worked well together. Lou Glasse and I argued, but she is a very good advocate. Sometimes I had to say to her, "There are other people who also need energy and attention besides older people." I think I worked well with the Division for Youth. Relations with other agencies varied along programmatic lines. The worst situation, by far, was in employment.[10]

The Work Incentive Program existed for a number of years. It was poorly designed at the federal level with both Department of Labor and Health and Human Services involvement. That dual structure was carried down to the state level so that the state commissioner of Labor and the state commissioner of Social Services were both involved. Of course, it went right on down to the local level. People wrote letters and never quite knew who was doing what to whom. Data between Labor and Social Services never conformed for a variety of reasons. We were just always being harangued by the feds and everybody else about the WIN program.

In that program, you were supposed to be able to place welfare women in employment. You registered them and sent them to Employment which was supposed to assess their capabilities. Then, they sent them back so that Social Services could provide day care service. Once you had the day care service arranged, you sent them back to Employment, and Employment did or didn't place them in employment training.

Obviously, an enormous backlog usually developed in the WIN program. So one day my deputy for income maintenance came in and was yelling about WIN again. I said, "Okay, Sydelle, what would you do to change this nutty program?"[11] She answered, "Well, you have to put responsibility in one agency or the other. I think we should have it, because Labor never places welfare mothers." And I said, "Okay, you draft what you think would be necessary." So she drafted some language and it looked fine; it was a demonstration, now called the WIN demo.

An older man named Lloyd Rader, a commissioner in Oklahoma, once told me that years ago a commissioner here in New York State had been instrumental in getting a very good Medicaid reimbursement rate for Oklahoma at a time when Oklahoma couldn't afford to come into the Medicaid program without a preferential rate. He also told me, when I became commissioner, that if he could ever do anything to help New York, by all means call. So I called him and said, "Lloyd, how do you feel about WIN?" And he said, "It's dreadful." And I said, "I think we can do something about it." And I read him Sydelle's draft. He said, "Well, you send it right over." He got Senator Boren to move it and Moynihan got on as a co-sponsor. It just whipped right through committee and right into the Budget Reconciliation Act, and we had the WIN demo, which 22 states have now gotten into. Everybody in the department was thrilled, Sydelle most of all, because she had done it. The WIN demo required that the feds be notified three months before you were planning to take over administration of the program. I put forward the plan to do that, but it was one of those awful times in government when timing is all off. Phil Ross had left and Lillian Roberts was coming in just as I was trying to take WIN out of Labor. I'm convinced that if Phil had still been there, there would not have been a problem, but Lillian viewed it as a real power grab. She threatened to resign. So we are one of the minority of states that still has dual administration.[12]

QUESTION: Is that the same reaction you had when you came in with Medicaid?

BLUM: Yes. Timing is really very important.

QUESTION: What conclusions have you reached with respect to the relationships between the department head and other agencies that you haven't mentioned?

BLUM: The Civil Service was a mixed bag. Sometimes we seemed to get really good responses and other times, inexplicably, we didn't break through, even on very minor things. Division of Budget (DOB) would give us the big things and fight over the small things. There's a certain theme here that worries me, one that I hadn't thought of before this evening. With the comptroller's office, although we had a few audits, I think that, for the most part, the recommendations were implemented and were on target. I can't recall anything with them that was alarming or that I disagreed with enormously. The Office of General Services (OGS) was kind of fifty-fifty. In terms of our department, we received very good responses. With the World Trade Center, we received less response. We had our worst problem with our Fair Hearings Operations, which is a very large operation in New York City. It took about four years to get some minor renovation in an air conditioning duct. I never could quite figure that out. I'm not certain why the uneasiness occurred with OGS.

QUESTION: Bill Hennessy implied that the cabinet may not have been collectively unicentered. There was a group of maybe half a dozen commissioners with somewhat common interests, of which you and he were part, that together could reconcile issues before they became major problems. What's your impression of that?

BLUM: I think that Bill Hennessey was very active; of that group, David Axelrod was certainly an active member; John Egan was also an active member of that group and then I guess Robert Flacke and Orin Lehman were included. A number of things were handled before they ballooned out.[13]

QUESTION: How did you convey those kinds of decisions to your staff once you had reached agreement at the commissioners' level? How did you insure it was an agency commitment? Or was that never a problem?

BLUM: It usually was not a problem. I didn't have as much to do with the entire group as I did with David Axelrod and with OGS. The others did a great deal together on environmental and certain other issues. However, there were times when Jim Prevost[14] and I would come to an agreement, and then the middle management would never quite accept that agreement. That was never true with agreements I would come to with David Axelrod. I don't know why. Perhaps it was because I worked with a different division of my department when I worked with Health than when I worked with OMH. With Health, I would be working with my Medicaid division. So maybe they were simply more responsive to what I was saying, or maybe David's people were. I would be working with my Division of Adult Services when I worked with OMH. I'm not quite sure whom Jim was working with on these issues. But there certainly was a response on those health issues. Whenever Egan said to me that something was going to be done, he did it.

QUESTION: What conclusions have you with respect to the relationship between your department and the executive chamber? Are the basic responsibilities and the sharing of commitments and obligations in that relationship sound? Should the department have greater independence, a greater degree of responsibility, or should they have less?

BLUM: I had almost total autonomy. Except for this WIN thing, I have no complaints at all. I was allowed to run the shop and I got support when I needed it, as with the MMIS move up here to Albany. The governor could really have thrown me in very easily, but I had total support from his staff. When some hospitals were failing, there was a tendency, not so much on the part of the executive office, but rather the Department of Health, to use our department as a scapegoat. But I think that I overcame that.

QUESTION: Did you have total support because you and the governor or you and Bob Morgado saw eye to eye, or do you think it was because there was not a great deal of concern about what you were doing, and hence you were given latitude?[15]

BLUM: If I had gotten into more trouble there might have been more supervision exercised.

COMMENT: It sounds as if the governor had no program in the welfare area.

BLUM: That is not true. Look at what happened in this state compared to other states during the same period.

QUESTION: Where was the initiative in this state?

BLUM: Well, I think the initiative logically came out of the department, but it was supported by the executive office. It should have come out of the department, but it would never have gone anywhere if it wasn't supported. I don't know whether it will ever be recognized, but from the time Hugh Carey was in Congress until he left the governorship, he was almost overly generous in the human service area. The program associates and Bob Morgado were also very supportive.

QUESTION: When you had any problem with reconciliation, did you take it to them?

BLUM: The program associates did a lot of coordination work to smooth the way on certain things or to advise us about what was happening in other agencies that we weren't aware of. I went to Bob Morgado only when I really needed support.

QUESTION: Did you have trouble getting to him?

BLUM: No, but I very seldom tried.

QUESTION: Do you feel you had control over appointments to your agency?

BLUM: Yes, I had total control.

QUESTION: How about termination?

BLUM: Again, I had total control. In fact, I was very slow about bringing people in and changing positions. I came in during the year before the election and was urged to do a housecleaning. I don't believe in housecleanings. I think you should test people out. After the election, I let a few people go, and brought in a few people of my own, but for the most part, there was a great deal of stability.

QUESTION: Were you satisfied with the quality of people who came into the agency through the normal processes of state recruitment?

BLUM: For the most part, yes, I find that I had an amazingly competent young staff, and there were some older persons there who gave really good continuity. Since there had been quite a bit of expansion under Stephen Berger, there was a mix in the Department of Social Services that you didn't find in many departments.[16] I thought that the people who wanted to come into the department were, for the most part, very committed and bright.

The same problem existed in other agencies and also in New York City; the writing skills are not what one would want. People get highly credentialed without seeming to know how to write a paragraph. I never understood how anyone could get a doctorate and not be able to write well.

QUESTION: Do you have any further comments with respect to the competitive exam system in the state? Are there needs for important changes?

BLUM: There could be significant improvements if the material tested was made to relate more closely to actual job responsibilities.

I read through the current exam. There wasn't a single question about the characteristics of the population that the department serves. It was so distant and mechanistic. It was not what I would want to test a person on. I'm not sure a commissioner has the time to get involved with that kind of thing. Maybe I didn't get involved as much as I should have. The system could be improved. I believe very strongly in the Civil Service system, but the testing criteria have to be relevant.

QUESTION: Does the system have built-in incentives that are sufficient to encourage and stimulate the employees, particularly those who have real potential, or is there some tendency for them to become discouraged and leave for something else?

BLUM: I think that the salary structure and the benefits are now sufficiently high, if they stay at the levels they have reached, for people who are willing to live in Albany (which I find a charming community). In the department, we have a good many people who are very bright and who certainly could make it in New York City, if they wanted to live there. Unless they received slightly higher salaries, however, I think they'd be at a living disadvantage there. There may be some agencies where people are too entrenched.

I did not like the lack of flexibility when I was working in the old Department of Mental Hygiene. In that instance, I would make two observations. Despite the fact we were under the Willowbrook consent judgment, it was extremely difficult to get OGS to locate our space and to get telephones and stationery. Then, since we were taking people out of Willowbrook, I needed a very different kind of staff than had been in that department before. I felt that I needed some social workers and staff for them, and I needed some case managers who didn't have to be social workers, but needed to have a different and specific background. It was very difficult to get the staff I wanted. I never knew whether it was Civil Service or the department, or both, that caused the problems. All of us were out there fighting like crazy to try to get what was really essential, and we had a court breathing down our neck.

We were dealing both with people in the central administration who really didn't realize the urgency of our needs, and with people outside who couldn't appreciate the different skills that were required.

QUESTION: You said earlier that one strength of the Social Services Department is that there are a lot of exempt positions. Could you elaborate a little?

113

BLUM: It gave me a fair amount of flexibility in moving people around. There were an amazing number of exempt positions. It's rather tragic that the assumption has now been made that those positions were political appointments. As a consequence, the people in those positions were fired. Many of them were certainly not political appointments. They were hired simply because of the enormous technological revolution the department was going through. Suddenly, you needed to recruit at high levels and literally transform the department overnight.

I think we started too late to try to institutionalize those positions. I know I started only about a year ago. I kept saying to myself, "This position could be competitive; that could be non-competitive." You can keep only two exempt positions in your division. Of course, everybody looked on these exempt positions as terrific things to have, because if somebody left, you could go out and get someone who really met your needs. We had the largest proportion of exempts in any department. We may even have had more exempts in the department than any other department in the state, but I'm not sure of that. It just gave me a feeling of being in control.

QUESTION: Was your relationship with the media and with special interest groups satisfactory, or were there ways in which they might have been improved? Were they a problem for you? Were they constructive or useful?

BLUM: Usually those kinds of contacts are very useful because you can learn so much from them. It is very important both to hear what people's perceptions are of what the department is doing, and to be able to interpret and respond where there are misunderstandings.

I was talking to a group of new commissioners from other states a couple of weeks ago and I said that, looking back, I probably would have set aside more time at the beginning to speak to the media and the special interest groups. Reporters always need a story immediately and they miss a great deal except for a few like Bob Pear at *The New York Times*. Most of the reporters just want that instant explanation and they don't dig very hard. You can use that, but you can sometimes get hurt by it also.

QUESTION: To what extent do you think your public relations office was effective in giving your side of the story to the media?

BLUM: I think it was modestly effective. We had difficulty keeping good people.

My first director of public relations was terrific, but he got recruited to the governor's office. Then I brought in an excellent person who was there for a year, and he got recruited as well. After that, I had difficulty recruiting someone who really related well to the press.

QUESTION: We've heard several other former commissioners talk about their responsibilities. Did you feel you had the real responsibility and other commissioners had only administrative challenges?

BLUM: Well, sometimes I did. Yes.

QUESTION: There's a qualitative difference in the kinds of things you had to grapple with and the kinds of things others have talked about here.

You had an extraordinary responsibility. You had a legislative mandate that was incredibly complex, you had a set of information problems, and you had a public opinion problem. Did you feel that you had the hardest job in the Carey cabinet?

BLUM: Some of the time. But I saw other commissioners getting hung. For instance, I think OMH is probably the roughest job in the state. I think there's a whole lot of history to that. I was inside OMH. I think that there is not a more Byzantine bureaucracy, and I've been in a lot of bureaucracies also.

COMMENT: There have been some Byzantine commissioners, too.

BLUM: That may contribute to the status of the bureaucracy. I would find that the most interesting agency to reshape.

There were several lucky breaks for me at DSS. First of all, a great deal of work had been done, as early as the Rockefeller administration, in beginning to look at errors and in realizing it was important to clean-up the errors. I don't think you have to get too public about an error unless you want to show who is responsible. Often it is the people who are ripping off the system (and who tend not to be clients, for the most part).

I already had a strong audit capacity when I entered office. I gather that when Steve Berger became commissioner he really stomped around on the second floor and got permission to have some flexibility at the executive level, which is very important when you have that range of programs. You've got to be able to count on some people in each of these areas. The department probably had more positions than any other department in the state, although we are not by any means the largest department in terms of staff. We're about 4,500 people.

QUESTION: I assume that your quantitative approach has had a good deal to do with your success. In so many instances, one assumes that a person has to be a professional social worker to be able to succeed in this field. Your undergraduate training in math contradicts this assumption.

BLUM: I trained in math, and then started to raise a family. My second child, whom I mentioned previously, was very handicapped, and so I did a lot of volunteer work. Therefore, it was a natural evolution to move into the mental health field in the city. There I had a very fine person above me. I was deputy, and the director was an old military man who was also a psychiatrist. He started to teach me about personnel. I learned civil service at the city level before I learned anything outside. I also learned the budget, which was fun for me.

A good deal of my career evolution was based on chance, but I don't think that I would have had many of these opportunities without my math training. The good thing about mathematics education, when it is well taught, is that you learn to arrive at the same solution in many different ways. In government, that is a very important concept because if one thing doesn't work, something else eventually will.

QUESTION: Your achievements were largely management achievements concerning management information and planning, but your problems were ones that required addressing major political concerns. Has Cesaer Perales, your successor, been in touch with you about some of these problems?

BLUM: No. I've seen him at a ceremony and we've talked. Before I left, I started work on some materials that were later incorporated into a book. I assume that he's had access to those materials, but contacting predecessors doesn't seem to be something that occurs.

QUESTION: Were you in touch with your predecessors?

BLUM: When I was recruited, I went to talk to Phil Toia about taking the job. My greatest concern was about the commuting that I had to do. Phil assured me that he commuted all the time, which I found out later was not true. Anyway, we talked mostly about commuting.

QUESTION: How long do you figure it took you to get accustomed to being commissioner?

BLUM: Well, it certainly took until I was confirmed. The period before was very traumatic. I started in December, and I wasn't confirmed until April. I found it to be a very demeaning process. I became accustomed to the role only a month or two after I was confirmed.

When I came in, Phil Toia had already left to go to the Budget. (He subsequently left the Budget very quickly.) Carmen Schang, who had been counsel, was made acting commissioner. Then, I was asked to become acting commissioner. There is a little quirk in the legislation that needs to be amended. (I'm not sure whether it has been amended or not; I've recommended a number of times that it be changed.) It gives the commissioner the power to appoint an acting commissioner. If you already have an acting commissioner, there's a question of whether the acting commissioner may appoint another acting commissioner.

It all started on the wrong foot, because nobody mentioned this problem to me until I was there. Then, I guess Bob Morgado won, and I became acting commissioner. They kept talking about scheduling a confirmation hearing, but it kept being delayed and delayed. Finally, a hearing was scheduled for March. That day, I went up to Senator Smith's office, because the hearing was to be held in his conference room, and he told me that they had an emergency and wouldn't be having the hearing that day.[17] There's nothing worse than preparing for a hearing and then being told in that way that it was canceled, which I thought was unconscionable. A phone call to an office is perfectly possible under those circumstances. So, I told him that if I wasn't confirmed in the next week, I wasn't interested in the job. They had it scheduled and I was confirmed.

QUESTION: Why do you figure you were chosen for the job? Did sex have an effect?

BLUM: Oh, I'm sure it did. I think they were having a little trouble in getting somebody to take the job. A lot of people thought I would last about six months.

QUESTION: What do you think is the optimal length of service for a commissioner?

BLUM: I've always thought three years. I was there longer than I intended to be because of the Reagan changes. I was starting to look for other things at that point.

QUESTION: You mentioned two things that you would have done earlier; however, there is a finite amount of time and energy. Why do you say three years?

BLUM: I think different people have different cycles. I take at least 12 months to know what I'm doing.

QUESTION: Would you say that the public sector has, by definition, a shorter time frame or is it related in some way to the electoral cycle?

BLUM: No, I hadn't thought of the electoral cycle, although maybe subconsciously I had. I usually can plot out what I'm going to do in a second year and get it started in a third year. Even in minor government positions, you make hundreds of decisions. Some of those decisions are based on information that is sound, some of them are based on information that is moderately acceptable, and some are not much more than educated guesses. I have always found that by the third year some of my wrong decisions were coming back. I was always afraid that I wouldn't be able to be honest enough to say, "That was a mistake that I made."

It's very hard to say that one of your decisions was wrong. I think it's easier for somebody else to take the corrective action.

QUESTION: Yet three of the four regrets you mentioned were things that you wished you had done sooner.

BLUM: I think I did those things because I was hanging on. I didn't have long enough to get them done. I probably couldn't have gotten them done with everything else I was doing at the beginning. I always wanted to develop regional offices, and I did it during the last year and a half. At least I started the ball moving with regional offices and the shelter stuff. We also did a little bit with employment, which I think will continue to grow. I don't think I could have lasted another two years.

FOOTNOTES

[1] William Hennessy, New York State Commissioner of Transportation (1977-1982).

[2] C. Mark Lawton, Director, Division of the Budget (1981-1982).

[3] Philip Toia, New York State Commissioner of Social Services (1976-1978).

[4] Mitchell Ginsberg, Commissioner of Human Resource Administration, New York City (1968-1970); Jules Sugerman, Commissioner of Human Resource Administration, New York City (1970-1974).

[5] Federal Department of Health and Human Services.

[6] Willowbrook, located on Staten Island in New York City, is a major State facility serving the mentally retarded. A highly publicized series of revelations in the media about shocking conditions at the institution led to the signing, early in the Carey years, of a consent decree that stipulated improvement of services for the retarded in State facilities, under the supervision of the federal courts.

[7] Richard Schweiker, Secretary of Health and Human Services, for President Reagan; Joseph Califano, Secretary of Health and Human Services, for President Carter.

[8] Warren Anderson, Majority Leader, New York State Senate (1973-present).

[9]Richard Berman, Director, State Office of Health System Management (1979-1981).

[10]David Axelrod, New York State Commissioner of Health (1979-present); Lou Glasse, Director, New York State Office for the Aging (1976- 1982).

[11]Sydelle Shapiro, Deputy Commissioner for Income Maintenance, New York State Department of Social Services (1977-1982).

[12]David L. Boren, United States Senator from Oklahoma (1979-present); Daniel Patrick Moynihan, United States Senator from New York State (1977-present); Philip Ross, New York State Industrial Commissioner (1976-1981); and Lillian Roberts, New York State Industrial Commissioner (1981-present). [The Industrial Commissioner is the head of the New York State Department of Labor.]

[13]John Egan, New York State Commissioner of General Services (1980-present); Robert Flacke, New York State Commissioner of Environmental Conservation (1979-1982); Orin Lehman, New York State Commissioner of Parks and Recreation (1975-present).

[14]James Prevost, New York State Commissioner of Mental Health (1978-1982).

[15]Robert J. Morgado, Secretary to Governor Carey (1977-1982).

[16]Stephen Berger, New York State Commissioner of Social Services (1975-1976).

[17]William T. Smith, New York State Senator (1962-present).

119

Robert F. Flacke served as commissioner of Environmental Conservation between 1979 and 1982. Previously, he had been an elected local official and chairman of the Adirondack Park Agency.

Robert F. Flacke

Commissioner of Environmental Conservation

FLACKE: I am a native of the city of Albany, and moved to the Adirondacks after serving three years in the navy as a gunnery officer. It was my profound desire to go out to the midwest. I never made it, for a wide variety of reasons.

Since 1958, I have held several positions in education, business, and government, all at the same time. I am an English teacher, a guidance and a psychiatric counselor (if one wants to take a look at the old credentials in the Education Department). I enjoyed my work in these roles at Queensbury School for a number of years. I worked in school administration and also with program development for what today is called learning disabled children. At that time, the field had a number of different names. I developed a program in the early 60's for dyslexic children. As a result, I have a great deal of experience with certain behavior characteristics and interaction with both individuals and groups.

I became involved in a business enterprise called the Fort William Henry Corporation. In the 60's this company was very small. I've been the chief executive officer for almost 20 years, and have worked with that company until it reached its present state of development. It now owns two motor inns, several gift shops, restaurants, taverns, and an historic attraction.   I began to participate in government elections as a minority candidate (the area being quite heavily Republican), and as an advocate for improvement of local government programs. I served on the town planning board, formulated a zoning and master plan for my community, and ran for supervisor. After being elected, I served approximately ten years. I then reluctantly accepted a role in the Adirondack Park Agency. Governor Malcolm Wilson was looking for someone with local government experience. The agency was under Republican leadership.

When Governor Carey was elected, he was seeking a Democrat to be the chairman. At the same time, the Adirondack region was in a state of expansion because of the agency's program. I agreed, after discussions with Bob Morgado, to be chairman of the Adirondack Park Agency for a year.[1] At the end of the year, I felt the program was more acceptable to local governments and that management reforms were in place. It was a very grueling experience. The Adirondack Park Agency and its programs were in a great deal of difficulty. Bob Morgado talked me into staying another year. I remained another year and a half, and again asked to be relieved. At

121

that point, Governor Carey asked me if I would be the commissioner of the Department of Environmental Conservation.

I brought a variety of management and experience skills to the department. I had completed graduate work in both education and management. I also served as a consultant, working with Harris Kerr in the hospitality industry, primarily doing economic feasibility studies.[2] I was competent in a variety of management skills, and I thought that this was a great opportunity to bring improved management to the agency.

Many private sector people feel that they can easily apply private sector skills to the public sector. But after working in government for 20 years, I recognize that it is not exactly true. The goals are quite diverse. The bottom line for the private sector is always profit and loss. It is very objective. The bottom line for the public sector is ethereal at times, perhaps a perception rather than a reality. The goal, of course, is services to people. How people perceive those services varies widely.

The first thing I tried to do in the Department of Environmental Conservation was to intelligently assess where environmental management was nationally, relate it back to a regional basis, and from there determine the needs of the state. My analysis was that environmental management was a very new national concept. It was ten years old, formed under President Nixon, and a unique concept in our society. Our country had determined that it was going to take a portion of the economic resource base and spend it to maintain the quality of the environment. As you study the department, you'll find out that this affects a wide variety of things.

Nixon decided to assess the merits of the regulatory growth of the Roosevelt era, a time when there was tremendous growth of regulatory agencies. As a result of that study, Nixon and Congress came to the conclusion that many of the regulatory agencies failed in their mature years. An attempt was made, in the establishment of the Environmental Protection Agency, to rectify the regulatory problems of the past. Most regulatory agencies had been fairly independent, rather than part of the executive branch. They were given a broad directive to assess what was needed and then perform. It was later noted that the regulatory agency usually ended up being a tool of those who were regulating.

Therefore, Congress, in its wisdom, said that they would make the Environmental Protection Agency (EPA) a branch of the executive department, and would put the environmental standards and time tables in the law. This was a radical departure.

If you follow the maturity sine curve for any large social issue in this country, the process of developing legislation calls for an examination of problems by our society. The ensuing debate is long and volatile. A determination of whether the issue is regional or national is necessary. There's an involvement of the intelligentsia, the media, and the people. Poems and editorials are written. Songs are sung. Then Congress determines what they're going to do about it. And, if the tempo is high enough, usually as a result of conflicts, we end up with a law, a law which is a compromise of the positions of the left and right.

At the implementation stage of these laws, the decision makers generally turn the agencies over to the people who were the advocates. Usually, those people make very poor managers. Their desire is to administratively seek the goals that were not achieved as a result of legislative compromise. This was the story of the Adirondack Park Agency and of the Department of Environmental Conservation. We saw, in the beginning of the environmental movement nationally, and in New York State, a continued effort to advance environmental management beyond where the legislation took it—in fact—by ignoring the law.

When I came to the Department of Environmental Conservation (DEC), we were in the up-swing of a backlash against the abuses of the first managers. The environmental movement did not have the numbers, the money, or the constituency to have a counter backlash. The constituencies, the Sierra Club, and the Natural Resource Defense Council (NRDC), for example, were blamed for the first management abuses. There was a backlash against regulation, believing it hurt the economy. I think it reached its zenith during the middle of the Carter years. There were tremendous breaches of the law in EPA during those years.

In talking with the governor, I advocated that in New York State we should take a middle road. We would obey the law, and rigorously enforce it. Within that law, we would try to take the agency from its adolescent management stage into maturity and, hopefully, leave the agency in a condition where it would be able to protect the environment of New York State in spite of political change. That was my goal. It was a management-oriented goal. Such a goal is generally not evident with the chief executive officer of a state agency.

QUESTION: Did the various environmental groups actually perceive your role as one of being consciously and conscientiously managerial?

FLACKE: No, they were very, very bitter with me, because they thought that I should continue to be an advocate beyond the law and not a manager. They said to me, "You're too structural, you're too much of a manager."

QUESTION: To what lengths did they go to express this?

FLACKE: Well, towards the end, when the administration changed, they saw their opportunity to recapture the agency. They became quite vocal at that point. The environmental movement in New York State is an oligarchy of about 20 people who are left over from the heyday of the movement. They perceive an environmental agency as an advocacy agency. They would like to use the agency, and use the administration, and use the laws to achieve goals which aren't necessarily legislative goals, but their own preconceived goals. When these people attain a high level position in a state agency, there are problems because they don't represent the public—they represent themselves and a very narrow viewpoint.

As an example, the Environmental Protection Agency caused Carter difficulty because he gave the management of the agency to the oligarchy of environmental advocacy leaders. The loyalty of the management was not to Carter, but rather to this ethereal group of environmentalists and their narrow view of society.

QUESTION: Tell us by what qualifications and reactions to constituents you were able to move the department away from the Sierra Club?

FLACKE: I tried to stay in the middle. I tried to be very fair and equal with both industry and the environmentalists. There's a degree of violence in the constituency of this agency that's missing in other state agencies. Most state agencies can muster a unified goal. Our constituents take far left or far right attitudes. The swing from the extreme left to the extreme right probably destroyed the federal Environmental Protection Agency. Carter had essentially given the agency to the Sierra Club. The Reagan administration did a complete reversal. As a result, there was no management and no cohesion. It is ending with such an extreme degree of conflict that the environmental agency at the federal level is probably destroyed.

QUESTION: How did you deal with the fish and wildlife group and the forestry group? They're both pretty strong.

FLACKE: It was easy because I considered myself one of them. I'm a north-country person. I fish and I hunt. I live in a natural resource world. As the Chief Executive Officer of Environmental Conservation, I wasn't overly friendly with my friends, because the more friendly I was with them, the more the environmentalists would hate me. Many of my good old friends in the conservation days said, "Gee, why don't you pay more attention to us?" I did, however, bring them back. They had, under the growth of the environmental quality part of the agency, been given the back seat. That was too bad because natural resource management in this state is very important to the state's future.

I used my tenure in the agency as a great opportunity to make the system work. I enjoyed every minute of it. But that's not the perception of the commissioner's role by other people. When you tell people that you're really spending your time managing an agency, they

124

think, "What does that mean?"

QUESTION: Do commissioners regard themselves as managers?

FLACKE: I don't think they regard themselves as managers, per se.

QUESTION: Would you say they regard themselves as advocates for a particular policy?

FLACKE: They regard themselves as a combination of things, including that. They do not concentrate time and effort on management and structure. I spent about 30 percent of my time on internal management. What is the structure of the organization? How could it best serve to meet the goals? Is the actual structure viable? Is it growing? Are the managers good? Can they be better? Are they meeting the goals? Are they off to the left? Are they off to the right? And so forth.

It is a very diverse agency. Many of the programs that it manages don't even relate to each other. For example, there's very little relationship between a forest ranger and a hazardous waste technician. They have separate skills and separate constituencies and so forth. The agency as a whole has many constituencies, many of which don't or won't communicate.

There were also residual loyalties to the old divisions that were combined to form the Department of Environmental Conservation. You'd say to Mr. Smith, "Mr. Smith, where are you from?" "I'm from the Health Department." Or "Where are you from, Mr. Jones?" "I'm from the old Conservation Department." Most would not perceive that they were members of the Department of Environmental Conservation.

The new set of problems that were upon us required immediate integration. Let me give you an example. If a smokestack had soot coming out of it, it was very easy to identify, because it was quite apparent—you either saw the smoke or you smelled it. As a result, money went into the air program, and they managed to stop the soot. The soot then went into a landfill, and the landfill then became a problem. The federal government allocated money to solve them both—the landfill problem and the air problem. But the programs had different appropriations, different public laws, different groups of activists and constituencies. The waste people, however, didn't communicate with the air people. The air people didn't talk to the water people.

New environmental problems involve all three disciplines, but the ability to resolve problems became quite acute as a result of the divisions not wanting to work with one another. Each was very independent. Each had its own money. Each had its own resources and was protective even to the point of hiding them. I had to say, "Come tell me how much money you have, before we really have a problem." It was like creating a symphony orchestra. We had to get all of the musicians to play one song.

QUESTION: How did you approach this departmental dilemma? Was it resolvable?

FLACKE: It required two things: work and time.

First of all, I recognized that there was a problem of no integration of programs. I created an integrating element by integrating senior management, a measure I considered vital.

The department had about 20 people reporting to the commissioner. There had been a succession of three or four commissioners. As a result, the bureaucracy had gone back into its shell. Each section of the department guarded its own rights, its own budget, its own constituency, and its own federal leads, and wouldn't talk to other divisions. Lo and behold, if anyone in the Water Division wanted to borrow one of the automobiles belonging to the Air Program, all hell would break loose. I created an integrating level. I divided the department into realistic categories, and combined and integrated functional levels.

It had been done once before. The library will show you all of Stan Legg's work in the formation of the agency.[3] I emerged with a great deal of respect for Mr. Legg and considered that he did what was economically and legislatively achievable—at the time.

I asked Vic Glider one day, "Vic, why is the Water Division of the agency under Lands and Forests?"[4] He said, "Well now, Stan Legg couldn't get away with separation then." When you reorganize structurally, you must deal with what is achievable—the ultimate programmatic approach is important. Don't fight for a structure that is not achievable.

We were finally able to put all the water people under "Water," and all the land people under "Land," and all the air people under "Air." Then, we worked with natural resource people to improve managers. The natural resource people had to be treated and regulated just like anybody else, because they are the users of the natural resources. They just happen to be responsible for public natural resources. They're using public water, using public land for recreation, and using public air. We began to make these distinctions at the senior management level. We created a senior management group of about seven people who would be the integrators. Their primary functions were to bring the divisions together, to eliminate bureaucratic in-fighting, and to enable us to combine our dollar resources.

QUESTION: Did you choose all of your subordinates?

FLACKE: Yes. I only brought three people into the agency. They were Dick Persico, who worked with me at the Adirondack Park Agency and was a lawyer; Peter Lanahan, who is an excellent public administrator; and Roy Torgelson from Budget to control the money.

The rest of the top positions were from the agency. We picked Eldridge Rich to run Environmental Quality. We wanted a person there who would be able to work as a co-equal with the others, rather than as a super boss. That's why we picked Eldridge. He was excellent as a coordinator. Air, Water, and Land had very strong people. Gene Seebold was in Water, Bud Hover in Air, and we had just put Norm Nosechuck in Hazardous Waste.

We had to take some of the water money and the air money, and use it for hazardous waste. And we had to do this legitimately, with all groups participating in the process.

QUESTION: Did you have any opposition to this?

FLACKE: Quite a bit, but, nevertheless, we did it. It was possible because we had the cooperation of our professionals.

I saw myself as an agent of change. I enjoy the science of change. There's not too much written on change as a science, but nevertheless what is available is good. Change on a management basis could be quick and radical. I decided, however, that we would do it slowly and incrementally. The people who are in this bureaucracy are wonderful people. If they sense you're ready to spend the time to manage and lead and work with them, they will respond. And they really did respond.

I emphasized retraining people. I forced them to study management material. For me, management was a high priority issue. The leaders actually got sick of listening to me about management. I circulated hundreds of periodicals and gave them opportunities to talk about management improvements and directions.

People reach the epitome of career through technical expertise. The traditional problem with an agency like DEC is that management expertise is lacking. Being an excellent wildlife biologist does not mean that you're a very good manager. We needed good managers. We needed good lawyers to manage a legal department. We didn't need more lawyers who could fight legal cases.

For example, there was a problem with hearing officers. Hearing officers were more advocates than objective judges—the department lawyers retained that mode of thinking. Most lawyers are trained in a conflict orientation. However, the ability to resolve problems without conflict is quite necessary today.

In the beginning of a movement, the only way to solve a problem was to go on strike, overturn milk cans, or cause a riot. It was imperative to gain a conflict, an explosion, and get to court. But in the real world, whether it's public or private, going to court does not resolve the problem; it just transfers it to somebody else and extends it. Love Canal will be in the courts for 10 or 15 years.[5] Conflict is all right to start a movement, but it destroys problem resolution. Laws are to be obeyed or changed, not used as advocacy goals.

QUESTION: The Minnewaska Project in New Paltz has been in the works for several years now.[6] It appears that this project is being killed by indecision—the length of the process, the litigation, the number of pending court cases. Do you see, as a result of your experience, any way to create a decisive, decision-making process that incorporates environmental goals, yet lets things happen by confining it to a certain amount of time? Is there any way to get out of killing something just by stretching it out?

FLACKE: Some of the structures and systems we put in were intended to do that. In pre-Bob Flacke days, the way to solve Minnewaska was to become an adversary. I asked people in the department, "How did you guys decide to oppose a project?" I learned that if the air people really didn't like it, the water people and the solid waste people would go along with the air people.

First, we changed the legal structure. We copied the pre-trial conference from the legal system and then innovated. It's now been copied by many other states, but we were the first to do it. A lot of things are solved in pre-trial conferences. We called them "scoping meetings." At formal scoping meetings, you bring all the adversaries around the table and isolate the issues, then narrow them down. Once you narrow the issues down, you cannot use the hearing process as a way of dragging settlement out. Much is discovered through this quasi-formal scoping process. You try to bring in the Sierra Club. You bring in NRDC. You bring in industry. You bring in all the interested parties and sit them down at the table and you begin to narrow the issues. It is easy to get a lawyer to sue, but not easy to get a lawyer to negotiate.

In a public hearing, the parties begin 180 degrees apart and fighting each other. Then, in court, you begin to open ways to negotiate. The process can be shortened with these scoping meetings. If this reaches maturity in the next four or five years, I expect you will knock out many of the public hearings. They won't even get that far. This process offers better hearings, better quality, better examination of the issues, more objective facts.

QUESTION: There must be a certain limit on size. It doesn't happen with every issue.

FLACKE: Oh, no, we're just talking about the larger ones.

QUESTION: Would you talk about your predecessor and successor? Did they move in a management direction also?

FLACKE: Jim Biggane was the quintessence of management. He is a brilliant administrator. He did much to bring some semblance of order to what Henry Diamond did. Apparently, Diamond had little direct interest in management. Ogden Reid opposed the bureaucracy. I think the bureaucracy eventually just "threw-up" all over him, and he left. Peter Berle was an outstanding individual and a very fine lawyer, but was not management-oriented and did not hire good managers. His top managers were leftovers from the environmental oligarchy—very poor.[7]

QUESTION: Do you think your programs will be carried through the transition?

FLACKE: About 50 percent of them were institutionalized. I think that the bureaucracy itself, the bureau chiefs, the section heads, and the division heads liked the work I did in management.

I don't think that Mario Cuomo has the environmental management sense that I do, and I don't think Hank Williams does either.[8] Their approach is traditional. The agency is now a political arm of the governor's office. The leaders are loyalists rather than competent managers.

QUESTION: Do you think that they're fearful that your priorities will define what they're doing?

FLACKE: No, I just backed the wrong candidate for governor. It is a political reality.

QUESTION: I notice in the paper that your successor is going to fire most of the assistant commissioners that you put in place.

FLACKE: Yes, he's getting rid of that senior management group that we put in place, the integrators and the coordinators. He's going back to what I call entrepreneurial management. I don't know if he'll do too well.

When I first started my business, I did the payroll, I put the flags up, I hired the people, and I bought the merchandise. That is entrepreneurial management. If you're not there, the business folds up. If you want to grow, you have to understand management, understand leadership, understand delegation, and understand communication. Hank has gone back to entrepreneurial management; he wants everyone to report to him. You can do it if you want to. Henry Ford did it for a while. But I don't know whether you can do it in today's world, with the bureaucracy the way it is. The bureaucracy will be the one that will survive. The bureaucracy is a very positive thing, but it is part of the game, too. You have to understand what the bureaucracy is and what it represents.

QUESTION: What is your estimate of the New York State professional civil service?

FLACKE: It is probably the best in the world. Of course, I'm limited to my experience in the agency.

QUESTION: In what way can the management levels of the career service be improved? Are there practical ways of recognizing performance and rewarding it appropriately? Is it a problem to ask these individuals to continue without the flexibility and reward for performance that is often justified?

FLACKE: Most of the leading professionals in the department have had their careers wrapped up in that agency for a number of years. I enjoyed working with them, and I felt that they got a great deal of satisfaction out of being able to participate in the management of the department. They got a great deal of reward from that. At least I sensed that they did. I suppose you'd have to ask them. With my predecessors, they had been used to going off into the corner and waiting to see what would happen.

Peter Berle began to try to put it together again. If he had more time, I think he would have been able to do that. I recognize the way politicians used the civil service to run the agency. They established the goals and then said, "I want you to carry them out." I got a great return for allowing them to participate in determining the goals for the agency.

Take our publication, *Challenge of the 80's*. That started out as a slick political document. As the 1980's approached, there was pressure to do something to usher in the new decade. We did not really push a great deal in the beginning. The senior staff in central office wrote *Challenge of the 80's*, and then we began to circulate it among the division and section heads and the people out in the regions.

It exploded. They said, "What about us? What about our careers and our goals?" So, I said to myself, "Let's throw the whole thing away. If there really is that much interest in it, let's write a macro thing on participative management and see what the agency staff people would like to see in the 80's." And that is what you see now. It's their perception of the agency's goals for the 1980's put together in that package. It is not necessarily Governor Carey's or my own.

The existing document, *Challenge of the 80's*, is not a slick document. It was highly criticized by the environmental oligarchy because it doesn't seek out new goals. It's a practical, programmatic analysis of our great difficulty with funding, with Civil Service job classifications, and with dioxins and hazardous and toxic wastes. It concludes that these problems are not going to be easily resolved, because no one is going to throw money at them. It is, in fact, a sober document.

QUESTION: Did you feel that you lost many competent people because you didn't have salary flexibility?

FLACKE: No.

QUESTION: What about anticipating environmental problems? It seems that part of the responsibility of the agency is to try to defuse and depoliticize conflicts and prevent the negative outcomes that occur when they are, in fact, highly politicized. Might this be furthered by trying to systematically identify what might be conflicts of the near future?

FLACKE: A lot of that is in the *Challenge of the 80's*. From the way I structured my time and the way I structured the senior management of the agency, I figured it would take about eight to twelve months to go from crisis management—reacting to problems—to where we would anticipate problems. I thought it would take eight to twelve months, but we did it in about six months. The integrators were to resolve the conflict between the various competing divisions within the agency that had their own constituencies and their own sources of money. Those were the people who were to plan out into the future. I think they did an excellent job. They identified the problems presently out there, and then began to put time and money into setting up structures for problems that were going to come down the pike.

The biggest immediate problem facing the State of New York as a whole is domestic waste. The second problem is that, as a result of the growth and maturity of the environmental movement, the state and the private sector are unable to site anything. If you are either in the public or the private sector today, you have to remember that pre-environmental movement laws did more than protect the environment. Those laws opened up the process, and that did not exist before. When I lived over on Second Avenue in Albany, I thought every neighborhood had a dump. The Second Avenue dump was in back of the Delaware Theatre.

QUESTION: Does the gradual, but what appears to be steady, changeover in the New York infrastructure from heavy industry in the past to more service-oriented industry and high technology place less pressure on the environment, or does that bring with it a new sense of pressure?

FLACKE: I used to work a lot in demographics in the private sector. Demographic skills are necessary to survive in the hospitality industry. The leadership of state agencies rarely used the statistics that came out on population movements. People today are locating primarily for quality of life. I talked with the governor at some length about it, and he agreed with me. Nevertheless, if you subscribe to the two-tier economic theory, New York State is essentially lessening its manufacturing base. The manufacturing of consumer products that are not related to a geographic location are all going overseas.

People are seeking quality of life. New York has great supplies of water. If you examine the movement of people in New York State, there have been great shifts. The Hudson Valley has had a 25 percent population increase in the last 25 years. People leave New York City, but where are they moving? Places like Poughkeepsie and Plattsburgh are growing. Each place that's growing has a high natural resource base with a high quality of life.

If we enhance those opportunities and make them better (set up programs for Lake Ontario, for example), we can attract more people. You must keep giving people the opportunity to use those resources. Our water resource is unbelievable, but we practically give it away. Some municipalities make money on it, but some sell it to people at such a low cost that they can't keep up the infrastructure. The limits of growth in the south and the west and the midwest have been reached. They have severe environmental problems. They ran out of water in southern Florida and in New Orleans. In the eastern states, water is the issue. New York has all that. Everybody says, "our infrastructure is declining and in bad shape." That's true, but it's still in pretty good relative shape.

QUESTION: Should environmental concerns be a part of the definition of infrastructure?

FLACKE: Yes, but what is infrastructure? There seems to be an emphasis on roads. That's probably a mistake. The reason for that is that road contractors have been highly organized on a political basis.

QUESTION: How did concern over the tax base during your tenure conflict with what you saw as the staff's overall environmental job?

FLACKE: I never saw it as a conflict. If you don't find some type of a middle ground, you will go into a self-destruct mode very quickly. You cannot blindly accept all economic goals.

Environmental management is really just another section of economics. When you examine internalization of cost, you're saying to the world that the product or service that's being provided now includes its effect upon the quality of life; therefore, you must pay for it. The state will now provide the services and the money for the standards, but you who are using the environment's natural resources must internalize and pay the costs necessary to maintain the resource.

DEC had its budget decline at a rate of about 8 percent to 12 percent a year. As a rule of thumb, we were allowed to grow by one half of the inflation rate. We identified the main problems, and we had to find funding. So, we developed internalization of cost formulas.

Then we began to develop programs which will probably come into reality in this legislative session. The program on television recently, "Give a Gift of Wildlife," aids us in gaining proper funding for the agency. I think my major accomplishment was to take the agency from adolescence (and that is not a negative word at all, it's just an analysis of any type of growth), and give it a pretty good start by working and training managers and developing a structure that will have some validity in the near future.

What is the environment? What are we really doing? What is the broad economic theory behind environment management? It is to regulate everybody who uses the natural resources according to a standard, so that they do not cause an economic leak to another group, or to another generation, or to people down the river.

The formation of the new laws took place over a period of ten years. The time was spent developing case laws, defining standards that had been nebulous and weak, and then training people to understand the standards. This lengthy process enabled us to determine what Congress and the people of the State of New York really wanted.

For example, we operated in nine regions simultaneously. In Buffalo, we might have had a wildlife biologist reviewing a project and putting 80 hours into it on wetlands, because his professor taught him that wetlands were good. A similar project in Twin Forks on Long Island might have been examined by somebody else, who had been taught by someone who didn't stress the importance of wetlands and therefore spent less time on wetlands. So we needed equity and consistency. The problem with the agency was that many of the people that were hired in the early days were advocates. As a result of being advocates, they did not want to be bothered with standards or consistency.

An agency employee examining a wetlands project who doesn't want it to go through can stop it, even though the law says this project can be done in this wetland. Many reviewers had a built-in interest not to give a permit.

The law says there must be a public hearing. In the early days, the legislature began to see hearings abused and therefore instituted the 90-day law to correct the problem. A permit had to be issued 90 days after the hearing. But the way the reviewer examining the wetlands beat the process was to never approve a completed application. He lost the application, or said, "It's not correct; go fill it out again; it doesn't have enough information." Even the environmental textbooks say the best way to beat any project is to drag it out until it dies its own natural death. The left side of the environmental movement perceives that conduct as acceptable and desirable. The right side feels that it is bad and will sue on it.

As a manager, I believe this conduct is not acceptable in a professional agency. The manager must have standards; he must go through peer review. The standard should be developed through management by participation. Then, if an individual does not agree with the structure, he should leave. It came out that the Left believed we were not operating the agency according to the way it should be—that is, by allowing everybody to advocate according to his own conscience. The Right saw that we were putting some order into the system, but they did not particularly like what we were doing, because we were also tough on them. They did, however, feel a sense of justice and honesty.

QUESTION: You mentioned that acid rain was one of the important problems facing us in the future. Is it resolvable?

FLACKE: Sure. Acid rain is strictly an economic problem, tied to the cost of energy in the Midwest.

The Clean Air Act, which came into effect 15-odd years ago, was a compromise. And the first series of changes in the Clean Air Act was another set of compromises, all of which worked to the disadvantage of the Northeast. When those compromises were negotiated, we didn't have OPEC. As a result, the East could continue to use cheap, low sulphur oil and the West could continue to burn coal.

Then the imbalance surfaced and it turned into one big mess. You end up with the midwestern states not cooperating with the Clean Air Act. They fought it bitterly. They did not develop what is called State Implementation Plans (SIPs). They didn't do anything the way we do it in the East.

The one thing they did do was to implement a tall stack policy. They had over a hundred tall stacks built, because the letter of the law said if you cleaned up your own air, that was all you had to do. The easiest way to clean up your own air was to build a tall stack and give your dirty air to somebody else. Eight years into this system, you've got high power rates here (for a combination of reasons) and low power rates there. If you go to a midwestern congressman, they say, "Yes, we know, but if I go back home and say that I want to raise my power rates to protect New Yorkers, they'll laugh at me and throw me out of office." So until we can get 51 percent of the votes in Congress, we're not going to get anywhere.

Governor Carey developed our two-fold strategy on this basis. We allowed the attorney general to sue in the courts (although he's not going to get very far, because the Clean Air Act allows them that and he knew it), and we went on the bandwagon, creating coalitions. We formed a 31-state coalition and signed agreements with the provinces of Quebec and Ontario.

QUESTION: A few years ago, you talked about the tremendous amount of sulfur that came out of Canadian stacks. Is that the same tall stack policy?

FLACKE: Canadians have done a lot since then. They backed off on their big nickel-copper industry. They take a lot of credit for it, but, of course, the whole copper industry went down the tube in the last ten years, so they involuntarily cut their emission in half, because they didn't have the copper to smelt.

QUESTION: Since this problem has been building up for 50 to 75 years, is it going to take another 50 to 75 years to turn it around?

FLACKE: I would say it would take another 25 years to straighten itself out. We have reached the crisis. I think New York did a good job of bringing national recognition to the problem. New York was the leader in bringing this thing to where it is today. In Congress, it is a big fight. Reagan couldn't get his changes in the Clean Air Act approved. I think, ultimately, we were responsible for that. We were the ones who gave the impetus to the national consensus on acid rain.

QUESTION: What are the problems you left for your successor?

FLACKE: Solid waste is a problem. The legislature is going to have to do something there. The fact is that we no longer can have landfills. If you want to protect ground water and you want to protect surface water, you really cannot continue dumping. When I was a town supervisor, we would have looked for a swamp away from everybody's house and fill it in. We would have ended up contaminating Lake George and contaminating ground water if we had persisted. Over the next ten-year period, you will not be able to use all the landfills in the standard metropolitan statistical areas that are around New York State. We are really at the point of no return. There is no place to put refuse. The inability to site resource recovery or use incineration is a "Catch 22." Mayor Koch is trying to put one in the least offensive place, in the Brooklyn Navy Yard. But the Orthodox Jews, who resettled in that area, don't want it. They've got enough votes in the City Council to defeat it. People on Staten Island are up in arms over Freshkills. The only community that has really been successful in siting a place was in Westchester County. Peekskill lost a big industry and the community welcomed the Resource Recovery Plant as an economic development. New York City and Long Island are absolutely in extremism on the issue of refuse. The governor's going to have some difficulties there, because he's made commitments to some constituency groups, and, in the last couple of weeks, has talked about putting a moratorium on incinerators. I don't think he realizes the consequences of that.

QUESTION: Well, is the problem that there are no real options?

FLACKE: The answer usually comes through crisis. Crisis and conflict bring resolution. Thus, one might say; "If I can hasten the conflict, I can hasten the resolution."

QUESTION: There has recently been stricter regulation of landfills. From that, one may deduce that landfills are out of favor. If you can project that ten years from now landfills will be very problematic, why hasn't the department just said to the state, "In ten years, we have to have a solution?"

FLACKE: We have.

QUESTION: Many county health departments seem to disagree. Is it a question of communicating to the local government clearly what they're going to have to do in the next ten years in order to cope with this?

FLACKE: I think I articulated what was necessary pretty well to the local governments throughout the state, both formally and informally, in travels and through the associations. You've got to remember, they don't know what to do about it either.

QUESTION: In looking at the budget, it appears that Encon was not one of the many agencies that collaborated on a proposal to establish a center for technological research at RPI, in Troy, New York. Yet, it seems that technological research is vital for environmental protection. It would seem that the common methods of disposal are going to be closed in ten years. This research would be imperative.

FLACKE: You have brought up one of the failures of my four years—the inability to utilize the universities. The academic community and the administrative agencies in the state don't work together at all. In many other states, they work closely together. I theorize that the origin of the problem was during the heyday of grantsmanship. The structure of the public and private universities in this state made them natural adversaries of state agencies in the competition for funds. Now it's very difficult to get all that talent working on a problem. And, the harder I tried, the worse it got. We made one attempt. We brought our senior management together and tried to instill faith in the academic community. They continue to think in terms of, "I got my money and you got your money."

QUESTION: You didn't succeed?

FLACKE: I really did try. If I had to do it over, I would do it a little bit differently. I would begin to form councils with some of them myself and would spend a lot of time working with them. A mutually beneficial relationship is possible; other states do it. Pennsylvania does a very good job. Massachusetts does a good job. Massachusetts has an excellent structure to coordinate academics and agencies.

If you honestly want to reduce the conflict, I suppose you ought to structure our system the way the Massachusetts people did theirs. A recommendation to seriously consider would be splitting DEC into two sections. One section would be the natural resource management side and its constituency—those who use the natural resources—Lands and Forests and Conservation. The other section would be environment quality and its constituency—the Sierra Club and the like.

QUESTION: What you're suggesting is a very old public administration principle that you don't mix advocacy and regulation?

FLACKE: Yes. I think the Massachusetts system seems to work a little bit better. Of course, that may just be "The grass is greener on the other side." They put their policy on the environment in the governor's office. I might add that they have a fairly weak environmental quality branch. They don't give them much money. Their

Fish and Game and Conservation people are off in a separate agency, and are seldom involved in environmental regulations.

Combining the two sections in this agency gives environmental quality in New York State an edge over most other states. Fish and Wildlife are the first people to sense environmental problems. So, if you have a strong conservation group with a strong wildlife biologist and strong laboratories, they will trigger the need for improved environmental regulation. If they're off in another department, they won't do it. But the problem with having the sections together is that although it functions better, it naturally brings out the conflict between being the regulator and the protector. You have this terrible constituency problem.

QUESTION: Hasn't the department had a pretty good relationship with the State College of Forestry at Syracuse? Isn't that one link with the academic community that's been quite successful?

FLACKE: Yes, but it's limited to the natural resource side, and it's zealously guarded. They have not made inroads into the environmental quality area.

I think the biggest step towards resolution is what the Rockefeller Institute is doing with the development of public administration in Albany. I hope it will do more over the next decade. I would certainly develop a better, closer alliance with the academic communities than we have in this state. We're losing out on some expertise that we don't have in the agencies. Top level professionals just can't accumulate the information and think into problems as the universities can.

I think the Rockefeller Institute has a great opportunity. I spoke to the New Jersey Institute of Technology down in Newark. That institute is very good. New Jersey is probably three years ahead of us in hazardous waste. They've just taken the whole engineering school and created a hazardous and toxic waste section to analyze the state problems. They have a whole group of students analyzing their problems. We don't have that. Any mature industry in the private sector is eventually going to link up with academia.

QUESTION: Could the problem be that the major university centers want to be all things for all people?

FLACKE: It could be.

QUESTION: Who would you turn to? Would you turn to Clif Wharton (chancellor, State University of New York)? Would you turn to Vince O'Leary (president, State University of New York at Albany)?

FLACKE: I made an attempt. The attitude that we received from the academic community was, "We'll be glad to do it, if you pay us to do it." I thought the academic people got off on a tangent. They said they got no reward for helping. They felt they were censured for doing public service. So, I went to Chancellor Wharton and said, "This is the way your professors feel." He said he didn't think that was true. Maybe the group dynamics worked against us at that meeting. The consensus that came out of that session was that a group of professors felt they received no reward for participating in the public sector, and, in fact, were looked down upon.

They were unhappy with the reward structure in the University. They received no brownie points, nothing at all for working in the public sector. It was the argument of the day.

That's what came out. The Rockefeller Institute should do a lot to break down the barriers between the agencies and the academic community.

At this time you have to force the professionals together. It's like pushing them into a type of narrow structure, and demanding that they come out with something. They don't even communicate. DEC needs ideas and conceptual thinking and they're not really getting them from the university resources we have in the state. We're not seeking them out. We spent a lot of money for consultants that might have been better spent in a university-agency structure for future thinking. I found the environmental movement very sterile in conceptual thinking—their leadership very poor.

QUESTION: Could the State University or private institutions have been of any assistance to you in developing your annual legislative program?

FLACKE: Of course they could have. I believe the commissioner should have a council of four or five people that would meet frequently as a kitchen cabinet. If I had to do it over again, I would create something of a Roosevelt-type brain trust for environmental management.

QUESTION: Does the legislature employ any specialists from any of the institutions that you might work with? For example, is there not a technical research office in the Assembly?

FLACKE: The legislators do not generally cooperate with the administrators. They have their own agenda and their agenda is not the same as ours. They have vote-getting agendas which, many times, conflict with problem-solving.

QUESTION: What are your chief conclusions regarding how to make the New York State system of government work? Would you like to comment specifically on legislative-executive relations?

FLACKE: Well, legislative-executive relations rely a lot upon the governor's strategy. Certainly, during Governor Carey's years, they could have been a lot better. It seemed to me his goal was a reduction in government spending which, to implement, required a very cool relationship with the legislative body.

QUESTION: Did the status of the relationships between the legislature and chief executive adversely affect your relationships with the legislature?

FLACKE: Programmatically they did, but individually they didn't. They said, "We don't like Carey, he is very difficult to work with, but we need you. You work well with us." We were responsive to everyone, Republican and Democrat alike. Our agency serves the Republican areas and it serves the Democrat areas, too. And so, we had to establish a rapport with everyone. We did a good job of it.

QUESTION: Were people like Assemblyman Maurice Hinchey satisfied that you were a vigorous enough advocator, or did you have trouble with legislators who tend to be advocates?

FLACKE: Maurice was a newcomer when Oliver Koppell and Bernie Smith were leaving, and there was some question as to what Maurice was going to be like when he took over. He took over a year after I came. Senator Fred Eckert was an anti-environmentalist. His goal in life was to deregulate. He was saying, "I'm going to get rid of this and I'm going to get rid of that." So, I had a long talk with him in the beginning. I worked very hard to calm Fred down and stabilize him so that we wouldn't lose important legislation.[9]

At the same time, Maurice was an unknown quantity. Over the last couple of years, Maurice developed his own strongly environmental agenda. However, in the beginning, he was not very environmental at all. He plays with the environmental oligarchy, and he is staying in the front of the environmentalists. He must do this. It is just a means to an end.

The end is re-election and promotion. I was a legislator. I was an elected official, and I know the methods required.

QUESTION: Would you change the party system in the legislature?

FLACKE: I wouldn't change it at all. I think that the dynamics of our political system are something that we all must adapt to. It's like the Adirondacks. I took the position that although there might be a lot of benefit in changing Article 14 (the "Forever Wild" provision of the New York State Constitution), it's been there a long time, so we might as well leave it there. The political system will adapt, but if its leaders are good, then it will eventually do all right.

QUESTION: With your emphasis on internal management, did you have much of a legislative program?

FLACKE: We developed a big legislative program. We had strategy meetings every Monday morning to discuss pending legislation. We pinpointed the projects and identified the constituencies. Very informally, we determined what was needed—what we were for, and what was not needed—what we were against. Traditionally, our agency operates with 500 bills a year.

QUESTION: Did your own managerial style tend to serve as an incentive to interest groups to pursue their own goals through the legislature?

FLACKE: Yes, it did. The legislature is entirely different than when I came in under Rockefeller's auspices. Truthfully, there are three groups. It takes three to tango down here. And when [Assembly Majority Leader] Stanley Steingut left and Stanley Fink came in, he decided that he was going to do his own thing. The Senate, the Assembly, and the administration are almost equal in power. They are all very, very powerful and independent. They have the money and the staff to be independent.

QUESTION: Do you find the legislative staff are progenitors of ideas? Do they come to you with ideas, or do they just react to ideas that you generate?

FLACKE: A combination of both those things. The legislative staff liked to work with the bureaus and the sections, developing interests. Our agency was so diverse that you must have groups working on various issues and programs. If you disagree with the legislature they will quickly form their own group to develop legislation.

QUESTION: Do you think Carey gave the leadership in the executive chamber? What was the relationship between your department and the executive chamber?

FLACKE: Personally, I found it easy to work with the governor. Perhaps I was an anomaly. I got along very well with him. I saw him as a man who really loved the environment. He didn't involve himself in technical matters, but he had a deep respect for them. My style of management was not to bother my boss, but to keep excellent lines of communication open. I always kept the executive well informed, so we never had a problem.

I always thought Hugh Carey respected and liked me, therefore, we did well together. He used to be tough with some people, but he never showed me a hostile day. Again, I consider myself a professional manager, and management is the knowledge and the ability to communicate with people the right way, which we did. We kept the governor out of trouble in environmental areas. We ran an honest ship and he respected that. He did not have an abiding interest in the day-to-day goals of the environmental movement. That does not mean he hated it. It's just that he never understood the radical left of the movement. He was urban-oriented.

We weren't really left alone, although we didn't have directive management from the executive chamber. Our good relationship was maintained, because we fully communicated. I insisted upon that.

Hugh Carey loved the natural resources of the state, especially the Adirondacks. His strength was in his ability to assimilate vast amounts of knowledge. There was not a program that he did not understand in great minutiae. Anything that we sent him, he knew. He retained every fact. He demonstrated that at the budget sessions. The governor had an unbelievably retentive memory. I would sit on an airplane with him and discuss very, very complex problems for 25 minutes, but when we'd land, it would just flow right out. He's an Irishman's Irishman!

QUESTION: What kind of problems would you take to the governor?

FLACKE: I would go to him with crisis problems, but always with a solution and alternatives. I discussed Love Canal, the Olympics, hazardous waste management, and so forth with him.

QUESTION: You thought that those problems might have had a negative political impact on the governor?

FLACKE: I thought we kept pretty much ahead of the game. We weren't faced with a large number of crisis problems. During the four years that I was there, we didn't have that many explosions. We could have had a tremendous number, if we didn't have the fine managers in place.

QUESTION: What would have happened if the governor drank that glass of PCBs?   [During a press conference concerning contamination in Binghamton, New York, Governor Carey offered to drink a glass of water containing PCB contaminants to prove that the level of PCBs was safe.]

FLACKE: I think he would have gotten sick, primarily because of the mineral oil that was in it. He meant well with that sentence; it was not a cruel statement.

One time ConEd wanted to burn a couple hundred thousand gallons of PCBs that they had accumulated in capacitors. Federal law allows them to be burned in an incinerator; they allowed it because it's a diluted PCB. That law still exists.

QUESTION: Have you any comments on your relationships with the executive agencies?

FLACKE: We had a lot of fights with the Budget people. I think everyone perennially has fights with the Budget people. Their job is to not spend money.

QUESTION: Even though you were fully authorized to do what you wanted to do, they delayed or did whatever was possible to limit the amount spent?

FLACKE: Sure, that was part of their game. They had their strategy. My biggest fights with the Budget people were with individuals. There were a few budget examiners who were incompetent. Eventually, I asked that they be replaced, and they were.

QUESTION: Who was DEC's budget examiner at the time?

FLACKE: There were three: Greg Smith, Mark Lawton, and Hugo Gentilerio, towards the end. He had been chief budget examiner for a long time. When Hugo left, we had a problem because they went through four or five chief budget examiners in a year. As a result, the people down below didn't have good direction.

QUESTION: Does that suggest then that the problem is primarily one of personnel? Is it one of the law? Is it one of the basic system?

FLACKE: I don't think the relationship with Budget is correctable in a retracting economy. Budget has to react by not spending money, and so they become spastic about doing it. It becomes a very cruel thing. How can you correct it? You probably could correct it or at least attempt to correct it by having a more open display of the budget process. That might not work though; it might even have the opposite effect.

QUESTION: The interest groups used to get pretty heavily involved in the budget process in the department. Is that still going on?

FLACKE: No, but they'd like to do that again. I cut that out. They would say to themselves, "We have one of our guys who works for the department; let's get him a raise," and that type of thing. That can be prevented with a good structure, and that's what we implemented. I'd love to manage the Budget Division for about six months. I'd restructure it. I would aim at better communication and better management. That's just an outsider looking in. By and large, we had enough leeway. The conflict was with this one budget examiner, primarily. Eventually, I went down and asked Mark Lawton if he had been relieved, and the problem went away.

QUESTION: Would it be any improvement if, once funds were appropriated for the various purposes within the department, you had the major discretion with respect to the use of them?

FLACKE: Truthfully, I didn't have much of a problem in that regard. We began to develop the ability to evaluate whether or not a program was succeeding. In the beginning, the professionals didn't like that. We used the management-by-objective system when we planned the program. Then, it was matched with time and activity so that you could know what your resources were at the end of the year. The final question which we were beginning to approach was: Did you really achieve what you were going to do with the money that had been allocated? Budget knew what we were doing in that regard. Therefore, Budget could cut them 25 or 30 percent and know they would survive. A system of communicating up and down at all agency levels, whether you really achieve it or not, is very important. Therefore, you must ask: Did you really do what you allocated the money for? Now, that never happens to state agencies. First you spend a year in the process of getting this year's money. Then you spend a year in the process of getting next year's money. But you never really spend time determining whether or not you actually achieved what you set out to do.

QUESTION: How were your relationships with the other agencies?

FLACKE: Very good. I refused to fight with any agency, although any bureaucratic organization will come into conflict with others, whether it is on a town level, a county level, or whatever level. It was difficult to work with other agencies, where we had conflicts. The fight with the Health Department will live forever.

QUESTION: Was that caused by internal problems?

FLACKE: I established a very, very strong personal relationship with [Health Commissioner] Dave Axelrod, and we insisted that our bureaucrats not fight. When I came into the agency, they refused to talk with the people from the Health Department. They wouldn't go into the same room. They wouldn't meet with Health. Institutionally, it was very important that DEC bureaucrats not meet with Health, because each one was looking for the other agency's money. It took Dave Axelrod and me about six months to straighten that out.

QUESTION: Do you think you had a good record in upward and downward communication and lateral relations with other states?

FLACKE: We did a very good job developing intergovernmental relationships. I established the Atlantic Alliance with Connecticut and New Jersey, which was a formalized process of getting the professional staffs to work together. It was very simple. There were two elements to it: the political side and the professional side. The professional side ran the agendas and did the work. The political side would come in and determine the goals.

There's built-in conflict with the federal government. New York State will not be able to get along with the Environmental Protection Agency for a long period of time. EPA has become very political. We get along well with our neighbors in Canada; we did form all those good relationships. I personally got along with local governments very well, but again, I empathize with them. Sewer aid is being cut back, but they don't really blame us. They know the problem is with Budget and the legislature.

QUESTION: Do you think there is competence enough in local government to deal with the problem?

FLACKE: There is great competence in local government. If there's a fault with state workers and state professionals, it's the fact that they believe they can do it better than local governments. That's entirely false. It's analogous to when I taught in the junior high school, and the senior high teachers thought they were better than the junior high teachers. Local government has more expertise than anybody. Local government can perform much more quickly than the State of New York on a daily basis.

When I was in local government, any time you got the heat you always blamed the state or the feds to get the heat off yourselves. When you're in town government, you blame the county. When you're in county government, you blame the state. When you're in the state government, you blame the federal government.

We are intensely interested in government because it's been our lives for a number of years. And, so we read and we listen. But, the average person in Lake George can't spell "Cuomo" or "Carey," and could care less about politics. Yet, he's very much interested in the result.

An example of that occurred when I served in the Adirondack Park Agency. I thought the people in my town would raise hell because I took that job, but no one ever said a word. But they were quite angry when the snow wasn't plowed and the potholes weren't fixed. There's a distinct difference between town and village government and all other levels of government. People are elected at the local level on the basis of themselves and their family. In small towns, they know what church you go to, how your kids act, whether your mother-in-law drinks, and everything about you. At the next level, the media begins to be much more sophisticated and is much more influential.

QUESTION: Was your relationship with the media friendly?

FLACKE: Yes, by and large.

QUESTION: Did you make systematic attempts to engage them or formally educate them? Or did you ignore them?

FLACKE: You must work very hard. The media is as important a part of government as the three branches. You have to really work with the press. But what is the press but editorial boards, reporters, young people? It's very difficult to capture the press. They zealously guard their independence and rightfully so. The press tends to regard environmental problems in the context of the Sierra Club.

So the best thing you can hope from the press is to make them objective by giving them all the facts. We did that through two or three seminars we held. We usually held a statewide seminar for the press on anything that was a major issue. These seminars were not media events. They were good and the press appreciated them, particularly the written press. For example: "What is Hazardous Waste?" We would spend a week with them in Albany in a classroom explaining it so they would understand the terminology. We did a good job there.

QUESTION: Did the press come to the seminars?

FLACKE: Oh, they came. They were very suspicious of the first one we held. They thought it was just a snow job.

We had a week seminar, which is really three days of work. They came, and they stayed, and they enjoyed it. My strategy was to keep myself and the major political people in the agency out of the seminars. Let the press work with the section heads and the bureaucrats and the technicians. It was not a propaganda thing. We brought all the technical experts in. We structured the program so that they could talk with the technical people. You can always do better with the press; it depends on what you want to do. I had fair, but not excellent relations with the press, in my own evaluation.

FOOTNOTES

[1] Robert Morgado, Secretary to the Governor (1977-1982).

[2] Harris Kerr, management consulting firm specializing in hotel work.

[3] Stanley Legg, a New York career civil servant, who held high level posts in several state departments. Between 1971 and 1974 he was Deputy Commissioner for Management and Field Administration in the Department of Environmental Conservation.

[4] Victor Glider, career civil servant who headed the Office of Parks and Recreation in the Department of Conservation before it was reorganized.

[5] Love Canal was a national environmental cause celebre in western New York. It resulted from the careless disposal of carcinogenic industrial wastes by the Hooker Chemical Company and the later residential development of the disposal site.

[6] The Minnewaska project was a proposal by the Marriott Corporation to build a major hotel and condominium complex at Lake Minnewaska in Ulster County. The project was delayed for years in litigation by environmental groups and ultimately abandoned by the company.

[7] James Biggane, New York State Commissioner of Environmental Conservation (1973-1974); Henry L. Diamond, New York State Commissioner of Environmental Conservation (1970-1973); Ogden Reid, New York State Commissioner of Environmental Conservation (1975-1976); and Peter A. A. Berle, New York State Commissioner of Environmental Conservation (1976-1979).

[8] Henry Williams, New York State Commissioner of Environmental Conservation (1983-present).

[9] Oliver Koppell, New York State Assemblyman (1970-present), formerly Chairman, Environmental Conservation Committee; Bernard Smith, New York State Senator (1966-1978), formerly Chairman, Environmental Conservation Committee.

Photo courtesy of
Fred Riccard

Governor Carey greets David Rockefeller at an economic forum held in the executive mansion. S. Robert Bennett, executive mansion superintendent and Robert Morgado, secretary to the governor, look on.

C. Mark Lawton, Director of the New York State Division of the Budget, (center) is joined by Meyer (Sandy) Frucher, (far left) at the annual dinner meeting with New York State Publishers to discuss the New York State budget.

Photo courtesy of Fred Riccard

Meyer Frucher, director of the Office of Employee Relations, discusses New York State employee contract negotiations with Governor Carey.

Photo courtesy of NYS
Department of Social
Services

New York State Commissioner of Environmental Conservation, Robert Flacke, introduces Governor Carey at a press conference to announce the signing of the Hunting and Fishing License Fee Increase and Moderinzation Bill.

Photo courtesy of John Goerg, NYS Department of Environmental Conservation

Photo courtesy of Fred Riccard

Assembly Speaker Stanley Fink makes a point at a joint news conference with the Governor and then Lieutenant Governor, Mario Cuomo, later Governor of New York State.

Photo courtesy of the NYS Commerce Department

Governor Carey and daughter Nancy welcome New York State Senate Majority Leader Warren Anderson to a legislative reception at the executive mansion.

Photo courtesy of NYS Commerce Department

The governor delivering the "State of the State" address before joint houses of the legislature in the New York State Assembly Chamber, at the beginning of his second term.

Photo courtesy of Fred Riccard

*New York City Mayor Ed Koch declares Governor Carey an "official good egg,"
to the amusement of Assembly Speaker Stanley Fink and Richard Ravitch, of the
Metropolitan Transit Authority.*

Photo courtesy of NYS Commerce Department

Governor Carey applauds the world athletes at the opening ceremonies of the 1980 Winter Olympic Games at Lake Placid. He is joined by U.S. Senator Daniel Patrick Moynihan.

Governor and Mrs. Carey are introduced to youngsters during one of their neighborhood get-acquainted tours.

Photo courtesy of Fred Riccard

Photo courtesy of
NYS Department of
Social Services

Governor Carey drops in at a New York City day care center, accompanied by Mary Burke Nicholas, director of the Women's Division and Barbara Blum, commissioner of the New York State Department of Social Services.

Governor Carey explains the impact of 1981 federal budget cuts upon New York at a press conference.

Photo courtesy of
Fred Riccard

Four governors, almost forty years of service: Governor Hugh Carey flanked by his immediate predecessors, Nelson A. Rockefeller and Malcolm Wilson, beneath a life-sized photograph of former Governor W. Averill Harriman.

Photo courtesy of
Fred Riccard

Photo courtesy of NYS Senate

Governor Carey joins with leaders of the New York State Legislature to sign a bill into law. (left to right) James Emery, speaker of the New York State Assembly, Warren Anderson, majority leader of the New York State Senate, Stanley Fink, former minority leader of the assembly, (now speaker) and Manfred Ohrenstein, minority leader of the senate.

New York State Department of Mental Health Commissioner, James Prevost, responds to a question at a public hearing.

Photo courtesy of
NYS Department of
Mental Hygiene

Governor Carey escorts special guests to one of the popular "I Love New York" festivals staged at the Governor Nelson A. Rockefeller Empire State Plaza. (left to right) Kitty Carlisle Hart, chair of the New York State Council on the Arts; Albany Mayor Erastus Corning II and Joe Raposo, composer, well-known for creating musical scores for Sesame Street and Muppet characters.

Photo courtesy of NYS Office of General Services

Photo courtesy of Fred Riccard

The "I Love New York" campaign, launched during the Carey era, was one of the most copied promotional slogans in the world. It's success made New York one of the most popular travel destinations, and instilled New Yorkers with new pride.

The governor greets Bobby Short, popular song stylist from New York's famous Hotel Carlyle, who along with many of New York's famous performing artists, contributed his time and talent to make the "Harvest of Music" festivals a resounding success.

Photo courtesy of NYS Office of General Services

New York State Commissioner of Transportation William Hennessy officiates at the dedication of the new Northern Boulevard bridge in Albany, New York. Albany Mayor Erastus Corning II is at the far left.

Photo courtesy of NYS Transportation Department

Meyer S. (Sandy) Frucher was director of the Governor's Office of Employee Relations between 1978 and 1983. Earlier, he served four years as executive director of the New York State Commission on Management and Productivity.

Meyer S. (Sandy) Frucher

Director of the Governor's Office
of Employee Relations

FRUCHER: I entered the Office of Employee Relations (OER) in Governor Carey's second term. I think his first term was marred by an atmosphere of hostility between public employees and the governor. That environment was caused by two major factors. The first was unavoidable circumstances. When Governor Carey came into office in January of 1975, he found himself with a severe budget crisis. The Urban Development Corporation (UDC) was on the verge of default (it later did default). Therefore, it was necessary to take various types of drastic actions that had never been taken before. For example, the governor negotiated a contract covering the first two years of his administration which gave the public employees a zero salary increase. That zero increase did not sit well with many people, particularly at a time when they viewed other government employees in similar circumstances, such as those in New York City, getting increases that exceeded theirs, through various mechanisms, such as cost of living adjustments.

The second problem was that the first Carey administration did not do a particularly good job in communicating with state employees. The Carey administration came into office after 16 years of Republican party rule, and felt that the bureaucracy in the various institutions of government was alien and hostile to the governor. Indeed, the state public employee unions were hostile. Their political demographics were not the traditional demographics of most unions. In fact, the Civil Service Employees Association (CSEA), the principal union that represents state employees, was not, at that time, a part of the AFL-CIO, but was an independent entity. So, they were somewhat hostile, somewhat alien. This new bunch of folks coming into office really did not have their communications worked out well.

I think one of the accomplishments, if not the primary accomplishment of my tenure, was that I opened up dialogue between the executive branch of government and the public employee unions. That led, I believe, to some very good things. They fall into some generic categories, such as: joint labor management efforts to improve the quality of working life, change in direction in such things as employee training, and the introduction of programs like the employee orientation program, which is in the process of being institutionalized across the entire government through funds that were negotiated in the last contract.

Let me cite one example of an accomplishment resulting from the new dialogue. The establishment of day care centers had been put into the state contract in 1972, but was never implemented. Then, three or four years ago, we opened up the first day care center at the Empire State Plaza. By the end of my tenure we had either actually functioning, or in process, somewhere between 16 and 20 day care centers in various locations around the state. Those programs, which opened up a joint labor-management dialogue dealing with the issues of quality of working life, were very, very significant and have the potential to be significant in the future.

One should generally not take credit for successes that are jointly negotiated in a collective bargaining agreement. However, when I look at the agreements, if I have to list certain areas that I am proud of having been associated with, I would include several articles as opposed to programs. I think that our restructuring of the grievance procedure and the disciplinary procedure will serve the state well. When I came into office there was a backlog of over 500 arbitration cases. Not only is there no backlog today, but we reduced the number of these cases in which the state is engaged by over 50 percent. We negotiated an entire restructuring of the way the state deals with time and attendance cases, and we now have an expedited procedure in the three CSEA units. Sixty percent of all our arbitrations relate to time and attendance matters. Now, within two weeks of a charge of tardiness, we have an arbitration and a bench decision given by the arbitrator. We have specific penalties, that are given literally on the spot, that will have a major impact on time and attendance cases throughout the state.

I look at the general disciplinary area as it relates to cases involving patient abuse as something of which I can be extremely proud. Before I was director of Employee Relations, there was not a three-to-six-month period that went by without having at least one or two so-called "messy cases" involving patient abuse. One of the major issues was that the state and the union had diametrically opposed viewpoints on what constituted patient abuse.

In order to deal with this, we created a special, select panel of arbitrators on patient abuse, which has now been recognized nationally as a model. The panel was jointly picked by labor and management, and was trained by funds that we put in the contract. As a result, both labor and management could present their points of view. We have only had one recent "messy case" on the issue of patient abuse. In that case, a member of the panel ruled that a CSEA employee who had sex with a 22 year-old mentally retarded woman should only be suspended for 30 days. Because the employee gave the woman money, and she accepted, the arbitrator concluded it constituted consensual sex.

I thought the decision was an outrage and unilaterally moved in my last week of office to strike the arbitrator from the panel. Interestingly, while I acted in a unilateral way, striking an arbitrator and attacking an arbitrator's decision, which is generally not within the rules of the game, the union didn't say a word because they knew that we were right. They felt, as I did, that if the integrity of the process was to be maintained, and if we were to retain this select panel on patient abuse, a decision like that just couldn't remain unchallenged. The decision stood, but somehow we had to make the point.

The other major change, which I believe was a result of the open communication that we developed in the last four years, was the ability of the state to negotiate in an area where any restructuring had traditionally been taboo. That is the area of health benefits. The ability to sit down and discuss mutual problems with the state unions for the first time enabled us to restructure the entire health package. While I believe we have one of the most comprehensive health benefit packages in the country, we now have employees making ten percent of the contributions towards their health benefits. Although this will save us $140 million over three years of projected increases, it is significant not just as a way to recapture some of the dollars. It is also a way to move the state to the forefront in medical cost containment, which is, if one talks about collective bargaining or employee relations, the single largest cost increase in the country. In my former life at Blue Cross—Blue Shield, there wasn't a day going by that we didn't encounter companies that were petrified of health insurance cost increases and inflation spirals. Major companies are beginning to feel that by 1987-1990, health benefit costs will wipe out their profits. It's spiraling that greatly. So what we're talking about is that the state employees are in the forefront in the country, because they negotiated a major restructuring with us. We hope it will bring a balance between benefits and contributions, and between legitimate expenditures and cost containment.

Sometimes, to the frustration of the Budget Division and the legislature, I changed the rules of the game in collective bargaining. In the past, collective bargaining was viewed in a very narrow way. I expanded what was put on the table. I did it with malice and forethought because I believe that there were certain areas that would never get funded if left to the traditional executive and legislative budget processes. Those areas, which I think were critical, are the quality of working life and training.

During my own tenure in government (not just state government) I watched an erosion of the resources being dedicated to the area of training; I also watched the over-institutionalization of training in state government. I decided that I was going to tackle this through the negotiating process. Thus, we expanded a contractual process, the collective bargaining process, to include, in effect, appropriation dollars for areas not traditionally funded.

We had watched the executive chamber cut funds for training and we had watched the legislature cut funds for training. When you view the world in a one-year cycle instead of a long-term cycle, training becomes very inconsequential. To battle the erosion of training programs, we stuck them into the contract, to the frustration, I believe, of both branches and certain individuals in government. I consider that to be one of our accomplishments. The Senate complained that they had twice, in separate legislation, turned down the concept of on-site day care centers, which was true. But we stuck on-site day care centers right in the contract. For the first time, we were negotiating programs as well as benefits, programs that would benefit not only the employees, but also the state. Yes, it had an increased cost in terms of the collective bargaining process, because it added things that were traditionally not part of collective bargaining. I believe, however, this approach will continue to produce long-term benefits to the state.

When we created joint labor-management committees, the so-called Webb/Klepp committees, one of the commitments I gave the union was that we would use these funds in an experimental way. We should be willing to fail, because if you aren't willing to fail, then you don't have the ability to go out and do creative kinds of ventures. I said to the unions, "As long as I'm here, if the programs succeed, I will allow you (which is a big hint) to present demands at the table which institutionalize some of the programs started in this joint labor-management process, and then put them into the contract as specific clauses."

Day care was one of these programs. We started day care centers through the joint labor-management committee. The union came to the table (I was shocked) demanding that we appropriate separate dollars for the expansion of day care. Well, they beat us down. In fact, we put in about a half million dollars a year so that we had a specific contract item for day care centers. The same thing happened with various kinds of training programs such as the apprenticeship training program—a program that I think will be very, very important as the state starts to look clearly at its work force and sees that it will have to start to make adjustments.

Nor did I take traditional management positions at the table. During my first negotiation, the union came in with a demand to have a union representative present at all counseling sessions, and I categorically denied it. I said, "Absolutely not." And they said, "Why? Counseling is being used to lay the paper trail for discipline. They'll bring in a person two or three times, not for real counseling but only to put in the record that this person was counseled, so that they can succeed when they bring a disciplinary action."

I suspended counseling for nine months. I said, "I will not agree to having someone in the room for counseling. It is not an adversary relationship. It's a training thing. It's part of what a supervisor should do. I will not agree to turn that into a courtroom. I will, however, suspend counseling for nine months." The offices of Mental Health and Mental Retardation went crazy!

During that nine-month period in 1979, we trained supervisors throughout the state. In the last round of bargaining, we didn't have a demand on counseling—not one demand. Nor did we have any grievances filed in the three years since then. Counseling was no longer an issue. So, I developed a credibility.

I don't think my accomplishments will evaporate, because we've institutionalized them in a couple of ways. One, we put them in the contract. There is nothing like sticking something in the contract to institutionalize it. It will stay for a while. Two, in the Carey-Cuomo transition, my office went unscathed. My deputy, someone who I recommended very highly, became the director of the office. He believes in the same things I believe in. Not a single person in my office has been changed or removed, and I consider that to be a major accomplishment. The integrity of that office has been maintained. The personnel, I think, are all committed to the same objectives and goals to which I was committed. Perhaps their thrusts may change to a certain extent, but I think inevitably they will follow the same course in terms of labor/management relations; they will work to expand the programs, and, hopefully, have the integrity to ditch programs that haven't worked.

QUESTION: In light of all your remarks about the absence of focus on management, the need for orientation, and so forth, to what do you attribute your own success in some of the areas that you identified earlier? Of particular interest is what you have referred to as your success in promoting dialogue between labor and management. What prepared you to do something like that?

FRUCHER: Well, I'm in the process now of trying to sell my autobiography, so I can tell you just how I ended up as director of Employee Relations. It involved an intellectual evolution. I started out working in the social services area. I can trace my own career through the afflictions of man. I started out in the poverty program. I then went into the manpower stuff, unemployment, and later found myself in addiction services. I went from poverty to unemployment to despair. In the end, I found myself personally in despair. After working through the poverty program, the various precursors to the Comprehensive Education and Training Act

151

(CETA), and the New York City Addiction Services Agency all by 1972, I thought that, at a relatively tender age, I was already burnt out.

I pulled out for a year, went to school, and started to think about my involvements. I began to think that I would be better off and be able to achieve more if I focused on the mechanics of the machinery. I found myself gravitating to programs relating to management of the bureaucracy and moving away from the on-line social service types of programs. The process interested me and engaged me. When I finished the Kennedy School, I did some consulting for a year. My wife was offered a job here in Albany and I came. The job that I ultimately got was to run the Commission on Management and Productivity.

I had started to focus mostly on the area of the personnel system and its various aspects. I came to the conclusion that the personnel system in this state was, and continues to be, a disaster—a total, absolute, unmitigated disaster. It's so scattered that it doesn't exist as a cohesive entity. I started to look at civil service reform and issues associated with it. The two years that enabled me to consider that process and to learn the issues were very useful. I was then one of the more fortunate public administrators, because I had a chance to do that, and then come in and be given a job where I could impact on that system. I didn't succeed in changing it completely, but I think I sure as hell shook it up.

QUESTION: So ultimately, you think your success can be attributed to your knowledge of that machinery and of the issues, rather than your personality or your authority?

FRUCHER: That is not for me to say. (Of course, in the privacy of my own room, when I'm shaving in the morning, I do occasionally wink.) The effect of my personality on the bargaining process is a difficult thing to discuss. I know I developed an incredible relationship with the people at the other side of the table. There are few people in the collective bargaining process who get a standing ovation from the other side. In fact, I was asked for an autograph by the entire CSEA team when we finished.

QUESTION: That was the eight percent raise?

FRUCHER: That was before the eight percent raise, and it was really a very touching experience. I was able to develop a real rapport and a real trust with the other side. We were able to achieve movement—changing of the structure—because they knew that we were sincere. I think they knew that I was sincere in trying to solve problems as opposed to sticking it to them.

I say what I think. It gets me in trouble in some ways. Once, I stood up in front of all the affirmative action officers and said, "Hey look, you know affirmative action has nothing to do with affirmative action officers. This is silly. They shouldn't exist, the job shouldn't exist. It's an affront. It's tokenism."

Saying it the way I did, I was almost lynched. They went crazy; some of them have been saying that "Frucher is a racist." That doesn't help me. In fact, I've had some confrontations with the Black and Puerto Rican Caucus on the issue. I wrote a memo to the new governor on my views on affirmative action. I said, "First of all, I think affirmative action officers should be abolished. The commissioner is the affirmative action officer and the appointments office should be the monitor. (What is this notion of a Grade 23 civil servant monitoring a commissioner?)"

It is the tradition of new governors, even when succession is within the same party, to bring in new people during a transition. Many of those people have not had governmental experience. Others have had governmental experience at other levels of government or in other governments. One of the things that strikes me as significantly absent, is that there is no orientation process for people who come into state government or into any other government. While you might have generalized analogies about how things operate, you don't have specific education.

Particularly in a transition process, such as the State of New York's, where you have a transition of personnel occurring simultaneously with the constitutional responsibilities of the governor to introduce a budget, you find new people who are in a total wilderness for many months. They have no communication with, for example, the second floor executive chamber because the governor and his senior people are engrossed by the annual writing of the budget. During transition periods in the past, many of the processes and institutions of state government were not made known to people who came into government. There was no set of documents, no set of instruments, only the permanent civil service existed to orient a commissioner to his new environment and his new job. That is a tremendous deficiency.

QUESTION: Would you comment on the Council on State Priorities activities in the Carey administration as a method of preparing for an incoming administration. Did you participate in that process of collecting data, preparing studies, and so on? And, how can you make preparation for training acceptable to the incoming people?

FRUCHER: I think the Council on State Priorities documents were useful, and the process was useful. However, it seemed to me to be more useful to the outgoing Carey administration than to the incoming Cuomo administration. It was a process by which the people from the Carey administration had a chance to list their accomplishments, but I don't think anybody in the Cuomo administration necessarily looked at it.

During all transitions, the outgoing administration prepares a series of documents for the new, incoming administration. (Curiously, the Cuomo administration did not have the traditional panels doing all the traditional white papers that are traditionally put on the shelf.) I'm not talking about the high policy issues. That's way above the level that I'm talking about. What we need is a single map, i.e., a schematic of the state government, that says: This is how the government that you are about to enter is structured. This is how this agency relates to that agency. Welcome to the civil service system. We know you want to bring in 50 people, but we have a surprise for you: you can't. This is the Division of the Budget. You think you're the commissioner. Wrong! The budget examiners are the commissioners.

There are two basic management tools that one needs to have in one's little kit in order to implement the findings of the Council on State Priorities or to implement the promises that the candidate for governor made while he or she was running. They are very, very rudimentary, but they are very difficult to learn. Some people come and go in commissioner-level positions without ever mastering them. They are the personnel and the budget systems of the state. In the final analysis, it is very costly for the state. Rather than restructuring and reshaping, what generally happens during the days of wine and roses is that you expand. It is easier that way.

I think that there are a lot of things that could or should have been done by me to prepare for the transition. I never quite was able to do them because of the rush of time. I think that somewhere in the government, somebody should have prepared something as simple as a manual to explain how the budget works and how the personnel system works, in relatively simple terms. It doesn't exist. When a commissioner comes in, there is nothing that you can give him or her, not even a little brochure saying: "Welcome to Albany—this is how you get to Cohoes."

I was absolutely appalled, and still am, that New York State, with a work force that is somewhere between (depending on how well Chrysler is doing) the 9th and 11th largest employer in the United States, has no real integrated personnel system. It's nuts! (I'll get into that when I talk about my failures.) Therefore, when a new employee comes to work, there is no system in place in terms of how to greet that new employee. There are no contacts for that employee when he or she enters the system.

When I arrived, new employee orientation was done agency by agency, or worse, location by location. There was no set packet of material or orientation to state service. One of the things that I hope will become institutionalized is the orientation program that we put into effect. It has a set of audio-visual aids that say, "Welcome to state service. This is what your agency does."

There are also checklists for supervisors. (Some of this may sound silly, but it's absolutely necessary.) It says: "A new employee should be taken to his or her desk, and should be introduced to the supervisor and to his or her colleagues. He or she should get the following materials..." For the first time, we put that together. Can you imagine the 9th or 10th largest employer in the United States not even having a simple, basic, rudimentary orientation package for new employees? Forget the commissioners, I'm talking about a grade three sweeper or maintenance person. It didn't exist. We're in the process of developing it now. The process takes a lot longer than one would have hoped. We've been at it for two years. Hopefully, by the end of this contract, which is in 1985, every agency will have an orientation program, and hopefully, it will get up to the commissioner level by the end of this administration.

It is very, very important to be able to make an assessment of what works and what doesn't work and to get rid of what doesn't work. One of the big problems is that we constantly add on and don't pull the plug when we should. Among the smartest things Mayor Koch ever did was to get on television and say, "I made a mistake. These bicycle lanes are stupid. Off they go. All right, we spent whatever, but it was a mistake."

I think it's the obligation of both the outgoing and the incoming governors to have in mind the management needs of his/her commissioners. A major failing of the civil service system is that there is no reward structure associated with the actual management of an agency. There is little or no ability to reward for performance. The whole system is based on external factors other than your job, for example, your ability to take an examination.

The reward structure of governors and even commissioners isn't really based on management of agencies either. Perhaps it is based on the visibility of one or two particular programs, in the positive sense, or on the gross disasters that occasionally happen. (They are really occasional compared to the ongoing functions of government.) In that whole big mass of the government, 99 percent of what goes on is never covered, never given any exposure, never given any real attention.

My predecessor Don Wallach, who I don't want to attack or criticize because he was a terrific guy, was brilliant.[1] He was one of the top people in the profession. However, his reward structure was somewhere other than in the management of the division. It was in writing articles and books and talking to a whole group of different people—not the union people, but the world beyond. In fact, when he accomplished something at the bargaining table, he destroyed himself because he went out and gave a speech about it, how he one-upped the union, and then he was never able to come back to the bargaining table again. The rewards, in most cases, are not internal

155

to the process. Part of the reason is the way the press covers government and the way government presents itself.

I had lunch today with two reporters. They asked, "How can we cover state government better? How can we understand the budget process better?" I said, "Well, in order to understand the state budget a little bit better, the important thing is to get the heck off the third floor!"[2]

You can manipulate an entire administration for four years by talking about new programs and new initiatives, capturing the press with big headlines and, all the while, never do a damn thing because nobody is watching what happens day in and day out. Legislators ask to talk about a new program and the press runs around excited about this new program, but nobody ever follows it past the day it is signed. They have a big ceremony when you announce the program, and you have a lot of stories about who is doing what to whom during the negotiations in the legislature. The governor signs the bill and it's a big media event. And then what happens? Nobody knows.

Fundamentally, if I had to give any advice to any high governmental official, I would say, "First of all, you should never lie to the media. If you get caught lying once, you're dead." Basically, I think that the public has a right to know. It is really the exception that government should hold back information. It doesn't take you long, once you're in, to understand that the public media is a very effective vehicle to facilitate a public-sector entrepreneur's achievement of his or her goals. One should be very happy to expose the deficiencies of the system, because, in the end, it is through that kind of exposure that you can reform the system. Self-criticism is very, very important to the public sector. A lot of bureaucrats are afraid of that kind of public exposure, and that's a mistake.

QUESTION: It would seem that a good administrator, a good manager, is going to have every incentive to perform. He will not only be able to go out and speak about what he has done, or write books about it, or be commended to the governor, but he will have the satisfaction that comes from having done a good job within his own organization. Isn't that a powerful incentive?

FRUCHER: If someone asked me right now, what was the single biggest mistake in public management of New York State in the last quarter of a century, I would say that it was the structure of the Taylor Law that allowed 95 percent of the workforce to be covered by collective bargaining so that there are no independent supervisors, except for a very narrow spectrum of employees called "management confidential." That was a disaster and a tragedy that can never be reversed in our lifetime, because the institutionalization of the unions and the agency shop are so great. It makes our work very,

very difficult. It makes the state a very particular and peculiar workplace, with no analogy anywhere in the private sector.

If you look at the most labor intensive industries in the private sector, you'll find that 55 or 60 percent, but not 95 percent of the workforce is organized. Of the five percent of the state workforce which is managerial and confidential, half is covered under Civil Service and more than half of the remaining two percent is confidential. In the classical sense, this means that the managers in this system are limited to such a minute few, that it is virtually impossible for them to actually manage.

The non-civil servant can be removed. A civil servant cannot be removed. It is inherent in the concept of measuring performance, by whatever standard you want to use (a good standard would be real performance as opposed to political performance), that a person would be removable for mediocrity—not venality or incompetence, but just mediocrity. You can't do that in this system. You can move people around, or whatever, but even that is somewhat limited in most circumstances. The notion of accountability, the notion of performance, the notion of judging somebody on performance and being able to do something about it is really limited to a very narrow spectrum. I don't think anybody has tried to implement an overall comprehensive performance evaluation program before.

I think one of the accomplishments of my tenure and the Carey administration's was that we tried to focus a lot of the workforce objectives toward a notion of performance and performance evaluation. While we succeeded in pushing through the notion of performance evaluation, we failed in our method of doing it. I think that is where my rotten personality came into play. I tried to push it too far too fast, and that was a mistake. I did not have the infrastructure in place to implement the program.

I never really cared about the specifics of the program. I gave that away. I said to groups of permanent employees (almost the union), "You figure out the mechanism." All I cared about were two basic objectives. The first was the absolute necessity in the workplace for a supervisor and an employee to communicate on the issues of goals, objectives, and accomplishments. That has been institutionalized to a certain extent—not one hundred percent, but to a certain extent. The second objective was relating compensation to the notion of performance. That failed because we didn't, and still do not, have a trained supervisory work force. So I put the cart before the bull. I made a strategic decision which was wrong. I was wrong because it failed; I would have been a genius, of course, if it worked. The decision was to hardball it, and I got my comeuppance. I figured I had a limited life in the job and, therefore, a limited time span in which to implement it. It seemed that if I didn't have the program up and going and institutionalized by the end of that particular contract period, which was the three years from 1979 to 1982, the opportunity would be gone, and I would never have the chance, or the system would never have the chance, to do it again. Frankly, I never had any support, other than a "good try," a "why don't you do that?" or a "do you really want to do that? Well, okay, why don't you go ahead and do it?" I never found any institutional support for the concept of performance evaluation because nobody really gave a hoot, and they still don't. So, I figured that the way to do it was to ram it through. Just take the football and run through the line.

Well, the bureaucracy stuck it to me on two levels. First, there are a lot of people who just resist change in general. However, a more important point lay beyond my own martyrdom on the issue. I was trying to graft on a management ethic to a system that did not have an infrastructure to do management.

You have people who are supervisors in the system who aren't supervisors. They happen to be supervisors because they can take an examination or, for whatever reason of fate, they end up being a supervisor. The difference between a supervisor in a mental institution and the Mental Hygiene therapy aide is the ability to take an exam, not the ability to manage. Nobody has ever taught these people any kind of management. Nobody gives the managers in the state system any tools to manage. We tried to do that with performance evaluation. The tools of the manager, in the classic sense, are the ability to reward and the ability to punish, and our system just isn't ready to handle these. You have to train people. (It is like giving freedom to a colony.) You need certain levels of skills in order to administer and manage. We don't have that in the work force. We've never trained people in how to set goals, how to discipline, and so on. I like to think that I started this process of developing some of those tools.

In the CSEA contract that I negotiated as I was going out the door, funds were earmarked for the first time for various kinds of management training, not necessarily related to performance evaluation, but to train people how to be supervisors. There is $1.5 million to be expended for management training of supervisors within that unit and outside of that unit. That money is going outside of the state civil service system to Cornell. Cornell is going to be doing supervisory training. By the end of this contract period, all the supervisors will have had at least a rudimentary course in supervision. We are trying to do this in some of the other areas as well.

QUESTION: The Achilles heel of performance evaluation is that a significant percentage of supervisors, perhaps the majority, cannot ever be trained to be effective evaluators of their subordinates. That is a very depressing thought. If it is true, then no performance evaluation system can truly succeed in improving productivity and producing the correct outcomes.

FRUCHER: Perhaps that is correct as it relates to blue collar employees. The CSEA has a very legitimate point that an MHTA is an MHTA is an MHTA.[3] There is really very little that one can do to measure the effectiveness of one MHTA versus another MHTA, or one secretary versus another secretary.

Perhaps another mistake I made on performance evaluation is that I tried to implement it from top to bottom. I should have put it in incrementally, starting with the managers and working down as far as the system had validity.

The preceding question remains very important. Regardless of whether or not the system has performance evaluations, how do you motivate a group of people whose reward structure is predicated on external factors, such as an examination, as opposed to achievement in the workplace? You can be the best damned employee in the workplace, but have limited ability to advance. The system is so constrained by its structure, which is basically an examination structure and a rigid kind of examination structure at that, that you have no place to go. Your time on the job might be better spent studying the ARCO series for the next civil service exam rather than doing your job.[4] That is the first problem.

The second problem is that you may be the best damned worker in the world, but you have been in the system for five years and you are capped out on your increments. Your only possible reward is the annual cost of living increase negotiated by your union. So, it is the union contract and an examination structure which dictates the financial rewards, particularly when dealing with people at the lower end of the socio-economic ladder. Those are external to the job. That's a tragedy. That is an absolute tragedy.

The specific issue that I tried to address in the performance evaluation system with CSEA was to give employees who were at the end of the increment structure a reward, to give them a bonus for the first time. That's the place where the union was absolutely ripped asunder. Another mistake I made was to co-opt the union into joining me in this performance evaluation effort, as opposed to saying, "This is management; you are labor." The union got killed because I co-opted them in the process. They had to sit there and be part of a process that started to choose among the employees. What I forgot, and what I've learned, or re-learned, or should have known, is that a union is an oligarchy. That is the fundamental rule: "All for one." I forgot it, and more important, they forgot it. And they got creamed.

As a consequence of my approach, performance evaluation won't be the full-blown system that I hoped it would be. I think I slowed it down by trying to push it through in 1979. That was a strategic mistake. In 1982, I tried strategically to pull back, so that New York State could develop the expertise to administer that kind of system, or any other kind of system that is performance-oriented. Whether or not it will be accomplished, I don't know. I will be standing on the outside or on the perimeter yelling in, "These are things that should not be lost."

There's no easy solution. There are a lot of different things that need to be developed, one of which is a commitment to public management in a very real sense. I've always felt that the two primary areas of focus and concern should be in the area of budget/management and in personnel. Structurally, the state is not set up to function well in these areas. There's no locus of responsibility for management in the state government. You have a Division of the Budget that really does not have an identity as a manager. It focuses on line-item issues rather than management issues. There is no management focus in this state. It really is a catch-as-catch-can process. There is no place in the state where a commissioner can say, "You know my agency is floundering; I really need a management team to come in here." There is no internal structure.

What has been a personal as well as a professional quest is to consolidate the personnel structure in this state so that it is more cohesive. That is basically what I consider civil service reform and it is, as yet, undone. The "rule of three" has always been secondary to me to having a cohesive piece of machinery.

We have a civil service system operated by a board which is not directly responsible to the governor. It is in a conflict of interest with itself. It should be strictly a judicial or an appellate body. There should be a personnel director who is responsible to the governor just like the Budget director. That personnel director should be part of whatever process exists in terms of discussion of layoffs or other issues, and should also be responsible for collective bargaining.

There should be a cohesive and single personnel structure in the state. Every single report that I've seen, going back to 1923 and including the Ronan Report, have all recommended some sort of separation of the Civil Service Commission and the creation of a personnel management office. Those reports preceded collective bargaining.

Now you have collective bargaining, and also the Civil Service Department with its Commission. In addition, you have the Budget Division doing personnel action, and OER directing policy which, in fact, can supersede the civil service law through its collective bargaining process. All are involved in personnel. In answer to the question, who's on first: who knows? There is no definite answer.

In some ways, I was "on first" because I had the ear of the governor. I had access and was able to drive personnel policy more than my predecessor was. I don't know, but I anticipate that my successor won't have that kind of access. Of course, that is situational or accidental.

QUESTION: You are talking about something similar to what was intended in the federal legislation.

FRUCHER: The federal legislation doesn't have collective bargaining. Their system was even more cohesive than ours. Ours is totally nuts because we have collective bargaining. Collective bargaining now drives it. In fact, a mistake made during the Rockefeller years was that they didn't understand (or maybe they did) that collective bargaining would ultimately drive the process, and they made absolutely no accommodation for it.

The fact of the matter is that we can change laws in collective bargaining. The legislature ratifies the results, and they supersede the civil service law. Why the heck do you then have a civil service law sitting there? Why shouldn't the whole thing be subject to negotiation? What is left not to negotiate? Why do you have the OER with collective bargaining sitting over here with limited resources, and the one agency with all the resources—the Civil Service Department—out on the State Office Campus, never brought into the budgetary or the political process? I hope that one of the things that can be accomplished is consolidation of the Civil Service structure. It is absolutely necessary.

Let me also say, for the record, that I think that the New York Civil Service is, or was, one of the best. I think it is deteriorating just as all civil services around the country are clearly deteriorating for a whole lot of reasons. I want to make it clear that I think that there are good managers in the system, but I think that they are probably accidents, as opposed to anything the system has nurtured. It is, perhaps, a question of timing. A lot of the good managers are the older people in the system. The brain drain in government is acute and is made worse as people get three years retirement credit as opposed to a cash payment. I have to tell you that I developed that concept. When I advanced the idea, one of the things that struck me was that we were going to be losing a lot of first-rate career people that we were not going to be able to replace.

One of the areas in which attrition scares me the most is Corrections. I've spent a lot of time with the Corrections people. We don't have a lot of the same quality folks coming along behind the wardens.

In general, we are not getting the same quality of person to come into the civil service. A lot of people are shying away from the traumas associated with public service, including the new concerns related to job security and the limitations on income. Also, the lack of a role model in the last decade (of course, before Mario Cuomo and Hugh Carey) for young people to look up to, and the inflated salaries for certain professions, are having an effect. When a kid just out of law school can walk into a New York law firm and make $40,000–$50,000 walking through the door, it is very tough for government to compete.

This trend is exacerbated by our lack of expansion of governmental programs and the constricting nature of the civil service system, as opposed to the former expansion of the system. We must remember that the civil service system on the state and local levels had an upward spiral. In fact, it was almost a spike upward starting with Roosevelt and going through Nelson Rockefeller. But recently, both the state and the nation have had either a flattening of that curve or a downward trend, so that there is no room for any expansion.

Can you imagine, while discussing whatever the number of lay-offs we are ultimately going to have, a commissioner or a Sandy Frucher going to the governor and saying, "Hey, you know, I think we ought to be setting up booths at the Harvard Business School, the Harvard Law School, and SUNY's Rockefeller College. Let's have a very active program to recruit the best and the brightest?" He'd say, "What, are you crazy? What do you mean, recruit? We are laying off 8,000 people!"

All these things have tremendous negative impact. I tried to address this in the last round of bargaining. I think we have put in money to start to retool people within the system, and to start to retrain them. I was almost obsessed with this in my last year—particularly in the professional areas. One of the things most likely to wear down a good, solid, hard-working human being, is the civil service system and the management system in the state. You take an individual who comes out of a professional school, and say, "Welcome to New York State government." Then, 20 years later, interview that person and ask him or her what kind of upgrading training, what kind of legal interaction, what kind of professional growth experiences he or she has had. Basically, they will tell you they have been working on the job for all those years. About eight years into their governmental service, their supervisors realized that they were one or two generations behind in the technology. Thus, they find that they are sitting at their desks, waiting for the bell to ring for them to go home. All the exciting stuff is being handled either by people who are coming in to exempt positions or by outside consultants, such as engineers or data processing people, because, obviously, we don't have the skills in the system.

It is true that we don't have the skills in the system. Not because the people intrinsically don't have the ability to develop the skills, but because we haven't given them the opportunity to perfect, hone, and keep up their professional education. The training isn't available for shrinks or engineers or data processing people. It's right across the board. There is no way within the public service for people to have ongoing continuing education and training.

I had some people do a report comparing the amount invested by the private sector in training and the amount invested by the public sector, and the difference was so vast that it was almost a joke. One of my accomplishments was that I increased the amount of money for management confidential training from $8.00 to $32.50 per employee. The increase is incredible, but the amount is preposterously small.

I think, too, that we have to take a long, hard look at the whole area of compensation, particularly as it concerns executives. You just can't allow the limited managerial salaries you have to be driven by the collective bargaining process. That's crazy. We fall into that all the time.

Also, in the area of compensation, a unique problem for the State of New York that must be addressed is the geographical vastness of the state and the fact that there are six standard metropolitan areas in the state. To try to find a number that cuts across all of them is impossible. A state salary goes a heck of a lot further in Watertown than it does in Manhattan. This is a very, very difficult problem.

I wrote a memo to Governor Carey on that issue as an objective of my last round of negotiation. I said, "I would like to try to find or look at some way of devising some sort of formula that deals with those sorts of geographical differences." Obviously, I could not get to it in that round of negotiations. We were, in fact, in lame duck session and we were dealing with limited dollars. From the unions' point of view it was: "Let's start with this base and go up." To them it was never a question of reallocating dollars. I chose as my own objective the restructuring of the health insurance, but I think that somebody is going to have to deal with that geographic issue and put it in graphic dollar terms.

The geographic difference of $200 for downstate and Monroe County costs the state $15 million. So if you are going to bring it up to $1,000 as an average differential, which would not be an unreasonable differential for downstate versus upstate, you're looking at an astronomical number—$100 million. It is a very difficult question, but I will tell you that unless we deal with that issue, you are going to find that the state institutions downstate are just going to crumble before our very eyes. The quality of service in the downstate institutions just does not compare to the quality of the institutions upstate. Don Sherill, who runs Downstate Medical, said to me, "I can't run a hospital. I would almost rather close Downstate Medical." His problem was not only the cost of living differential between upstate and downstate, but also that he was even paying less for a sweeper, let alone a physician, in his institution than the city was paying across the street at Kings County. He said, "The quality of my institution is deteriorating. I can't keep the halls clean. I can't get sweepers, because they are paying more money across the street."

On the Willowbrook campus, we have an outside entity called United Cerebral Palsy paying more to a mental hygiene therapy aid than the state is paying to a civil servant.[5] These are very difficult, $200 million issues that are left unresolved.

QUESTION: Would you comment on this unresolved issue of paying for the results of this last round of salary negotiations? These are enormous financial commitments, in terms of raises, in a declining inflationary situation.

FRUCHER: To me, the contract negotiation is not an unresolved issue. That is a commitment on the part of the state, the cost of which was factored into the state's projection. This was not brought out as clearly in the public debate as at the bargaining table. I said to the unions, "This year we are going to take the four percent lag and the next year you are going to have big layoffs." The layoffs were factored into our calculations, and I said that as openly as one can say it, not only at the bargaining table, but in the public media. When I settled those contracts, I said, "There are going to be layoffs next year. There's a lag this year, then there will be layoffs next year."

I believe that the contracts that we negotiated last year were fair, even with declining inflation. We knew that there would be declining inflation at least in year two. It is hard to project three years ahead in this volatile economy, but even if we did, we felt this year was the catch-up year. We were hoping for the declining inflation for the employee's sake. Thanks to Jerry Schrauf, we created the most comprehensive analysis ever of the state compensation structure and the collective bargaining agreements from 1975.[6] We found that the state employees had fallen behind inflation by something in the area of 40 to 41 percent, and that our settlements were literally half of the double digit private sector settlements in the preceding years. So I personally have no regrets over the size of those settlements.

In addition, there was a major give-back, to the tune of about $140 million in the health insurance areas, that no other employer was able to negotiate. Nobody negotiated that kind of restructuring within the context of collective bargaining, and no major employer had the guts to do that kind of restructuring outside of collective bargaining. General Motors played a little game to influence its collective bargaining by restructuring health insurance for managers, but they didn't get into collective bargaining. They gave all those benefits to the managers. It was a very cynical game.

164

Our contracts are still not competitive with those of other public employers. I looked at New York City increases. I looked at school board increases. I looked at local government increases. We found that even with this raise, state employee increases are behind those given to the other levels of government.

That is another major problem of New York State government on the delivery side. New York State government is a unique entity as an employer. We are the 9th or 10th largest employer in the United States, public or private, yet we have a relatively small percentage of our budget going to personnel costs. All of the focus is on layoffs or personnel costs, but they only comprise about $3 billion in a $30 billion budget. That's preposterous! In New York City, about 60 percent of the public budget goes for direct personnel costs. Personnel costs as a major obligation of the state pales in comparison to the total dimension of the budget.

The fact of the matter is that the service part of New York State government is being eroded by external political forces. Those forces really work with the legislature, which does not represent state government or state governmental services. Legislators represent, as they probably should, local governmental services. Therefore, the thrust of the legislative assistance process is to local governments, to school board systems, and to constituencies' assistance. The only state service that has flourished up until now, in this context, is the State University, which has very cleverly identified itself with local interests. It has almost made itself a local government entity in terms of how it lobbies. This is to its credit, but it's a major problem.

Though not an employee relations problem per se, it is important for the director of Employee Relations to keep the political realities in mind as he or she goes and fights with the governor or the legislature to try to get resources for the state employees.

I might add that I fought like a son-of-a-bitch to get a three-year contract that would exceed the rate of inflation in a lame duck administration. We did that consciously, not to pay off the unions, but to sustain the state workforce. I fought until I was blue in the face. I fought with Mark Lawton and I fought with Mike Finnerty. I didn't have to fight with Robert Morgado, because I think he ultimately understood the point.[7]

We knew what was coming in the budget. We said there are going to be two years of crisis, and we, with absolute premeditation, negotiated a three-year contract to protect the state workers so that they would get a fair shake at the bargaining table, despite the fact that they are a miniscule part of the state budget, and despite the fact that the other levels of government have gotten more money. We knew that whatever money we "saved" on collective bargaining would go into school aid and local government assistance to pay for somebody else's collective bargaining settlement. So, I don't consider those contracts a negative; I consider those contracts a positive.

Still, for the record, I also feel very, very strongly that the state work force has to be reduced either through attrition, early retirement, or layoffs. I believe this, not because I don't think that everyone out there is doing a terrific job, but rather because of the political dynamics. I cannot foresee that we will be able to sustain this bureaucracy over time. We are not going to be able to provide direct services with 180,000 people in state government; it is just not going to be able to be maintained.

QUESTION: Your sweeping goals would really require a massive revolution (and I think that word is an accurate word) in the systems of government, whether it is the civil service system, the collective bargaining system, the government structures, budget and management, you name it. To accomplish all that within a limited time frame is a virtual impossibility. So, you have to settle upon some priority. Go back to the subject of performance evaluation. To begin again so that it will succeed, you have to first build up the infrastructure, to commit it to work. That, in and of itself, might take beyond the time frame available. An effective performance evaluation process might be several years down the road.

FRUCHER: You have to pick and choose. A good public administrator has to be a special kind of entrepreneur, and has to articulate globally.

QUESTION: It would seem that there is a general flow of power. The creative use of power exists at the very top, at the commissioner level, and everything else down below, according to your own analysis, just cannot be relied upon either to implement programs or to do all the sorts of things that public servants should be able to do.

FRUCHER: I'm an optimist. I think these things can be reversed. The commitment to management has to be at the top. The education in good management has to begin at the top. The permanent civil service can have a major role in focusing a governor's attention on a management issue. But before the permanent government can do that, I believe a governor has to commit himself to the development of a management structure within the state.

It is absolutely critical for part of the budget process to be expanded into the Division of Management and Budget. I worked on some of this stuff with the Commission of Management and Productivity. Budgeting has to be geared towards specific program objectives—almost performance contracting between a governor or Budget Division and a commissioner to begin to articulate specific measures by which a commissioner is evaluated by the end of the year. It is very dangerous politically, I might add, but I think it is worth developing management goals, not personnel targets, for a particular agency.

With regard to management, the Carey administration got off to a difficult start. It was forced very early into very heavy kinds of crisis management issues. It is very difficult to come down and get involved in very parochial issues when you've been, as Governor Carey was, to the top of the mountain, flying to the White House to bail out the state, the city, and all the rest.

QUESTION: Do you think that the fiscal crisis had an impact on the way the Carey administration looked at management? During the Harriman regime, with Paul Appleby, and during the Rockefeller years under T. Norman Hurd and Richard Dunham, the Budget Division was used to a greater degree as a managerial arm of the governor; a greater sense of community existed between the chamber and the Budget.

FRUCHER: Circumstances may have forced the Carey administration to be more narrowly fiscally oriented and to deal with the Budget in a macro as opposed to a micro management sense. That doesn't mean, however, that I agree with the statement that the previous administrations were more interested in management issues. Indeed, I would argue that in the past, with the ability to expand (i.e., the ability to spend money) with significantly less constraints on a relative basis, there existed only a limited interest and focus on management. If an agency didn't work, you simply created another agency or authority. And, I don't think I'm being facile.

That is not a criticism that I am leveling at the Rockefeller administration, or the Lindsay administration, or the Johnson administration. It was just part of the times.

Let's look at the Johnson administration for a second. Nelson Rockefeller and Lyndon Johnson had very similar kinds of aspirations. They were both very grandiose, and I like grandiose public managers. I think dreams and aspirations and goals are good things and important in the public sector. Lyndon Johnson had a war on poverty, which I think was terrific. However, the whole basis for the war on poverty was to create parallel institutions to existing institutions, not to make the institutions that we had work better. Rather than have a focus on fixing up the public schools so that they could deal with the educational deficiencies of children coming into the system from poor backgrounds, they created the Headstart program external to the public school system. Rather than deal with the vocational education system that existed, they went out and created the Job Corps.

QUESTION: Would you comment on the source of difficulties between the governor and the legislature during the Carey years?

FRUCHER: I think legislative-executive relationships are going through an evolution. We are still in the transition from Nelson Rockefeller and we are two gubernatorial terms away from him. He dominated the process so much that the legislature is still reacting to that kind of executive domination.

I think Hugh Carey's personality may have had something to do with his difficulty with the legislature. Yet, his personality is not the sole reason the legislature started to exercise its own will simultaneously with Carey's entrance. It was a national trend, but it was exacerbated here. There was Watergate, and there was the growth of legislative staffs around the country. Here, you also had had one-party rule, and a very dominant personality.

Carey had a two-year hiatus because of the state and the city fiscal crisis, but once that was addressed, the legislature began to exert itself in a lot of ways. Competition for resources began that did not exist during those growth years, which simply means that the legislature is now battered directly by local constituency groups that are fighting for every dollar.

By and large, there is no real constituency for state service. Therefore, the tension between the executive and the legislative branches is going to continue to grow. This budget year is a good example. Because the legislature got caught with its hand in the cookie jar in the previous year's revenue projections, it was somewhat tempered and willing to negotiate in 1983. But that was not a normal year. It will return to what it has been as time goes on, simply because this incredible tension between the constituencies for the dollars is going to continue.

Potentially, this tension is good if the machinery is geared up to do what needs to be done—to, in effect, do more with less. Government could become more responsive. We really need a process to determine what government should be providing. We should have programs or studies gearing the manpower needs of the state to what the programmatic goals of the state will or should be. We should be looking at how to effectively harness new technology and how to improve our use of existing technology.

One of the programs that I started and I hope continues is an effort to provide incentive for employees in the administrative unit. For example, we would pay secretaries more to go into word processing, but then be very hard-nosed about reducing the number of employees in that unit. Obviously, there are a lot of problems. For instance, a supervisor is not happy to share one person and a word processor, because the technology has not figured out how to handle his or her phone calls and get the coffee.

Clearly, from the state's point of view, we have to look at manpower planning, the use of technology, and how to reduce the work force through attrition and technology, as opposed to layoff. We have to determine how much we want to do in-house and how much we want to contract out. In addition, when we contract out, we have to develop the mechanisms to monitor and regulate those services in a positive way.

One of the things that I did in the area of training was to consciously blow up the training unit of the Department of Civil Service. I just felt that it was antiquated. The only way to get real training was to put it into SUNY, CUNY, and Cornell—to go into the public education sector. To do this, I had an absolute battle royal in the last contract.

One of the things I said at the SUNY Board of Trustee's meeting was, "Hey, you know, your state agency has to serve the state. You have all these resources; there is no reason why state agencies, the state government, and the state personnel system should not be plugged into the State University system, where you can provide ongoing education and training. You have professional schools of every stripe in the state system; why isn't this somehow married to the state work force and to work force planning and training?"

The fight I had internally and externally to use the resources at SUNY was one of the most incredible fights. It blew my mind. I knew that there were hard feelings, but, boy, I'll tell you, I didn't realize how deep they ran. You can ask Mark Lawton, if he's willing. He and I had a shouting match about putting money in the contract for SUNY to do ongoing training. It got very tough.

QUESTION: You talked of large-scale executive-legislature issues. How about some of the structural things? How important is the fact that we have a Legislative Office Building built by Rockefeller and the fact that we gave district offices to the legislators?

FRUCHER: What has made even a greater impact than the staff and all the other structural reforms is the xerox machines.

QUESTION: But the Rules Committee consists of the speaker walking down the hall alone. That didn't change much!

FRUCHER: The Rules Committee is still the speaker walking down the hall alone, but the various party caucuses are not what they used to be. Your question can be broadened into a much larger question: whether or not benevolent dictatorship is a more efficient way of government than a democracy. What you are in effect saying or implying by the question is, "Wasn't it a hell of a lot easier when you just had two people to deal with, the majority leader and the speaker, and all these other folks were kept out in the wilderness? They didn't have staffs and didn't have pencils. They couldn't make telephone calls. It was a lot easier to cut a deal."

Absolutely. It was a lot easier to nominate people when the decision was made by five guys in a room who smoked cigars. They could walk out of that room with a candidate for President. Some very good candidates for President were nominated that way. Whether we were better off with the bosses than we are with reform, depends on where you sit.

QUESTION: Theoretically, the vast increase in staff should have facilitated the increase in work. The legislature should be better informed, better equipped to make intelligent decisions and to deal more realistically with the problems that are important.

FRUCHER: That's what it says in the textbook. Certainly, the net result is a prolonging of the legislative session. As opposed to 60 days or 90 days, it now goes on for six months or nine months. They never adjourn now, and always come back for a special session. Those sorts of advancements in staff and analytic capabilities are necessary because, somehow, the complexity of the issues is a lot greater.

QUESTION: One of the blessings that the legislative bureaucracy created is to be available so that the executive bureaucracy can cut deals with it. Then both bureaucracies sell the deals they have cut at the bar to their principals.

FRUCHER: Just so long as it is not a bar in a private club that discriminates! By the way, we ought to add that—policy on clubs that discriminate—to the accomplishment list.

QUESTION: During the time when you were with the temporary commission, we sensed that you were a new kid on the block. You had almost as many problems with the existing structure of the legislative fiscal committees as you did with the executive.

FRUCHER: I inherited something called the Joint Legislative Committee on Management and Productivity. God only knows why it was set up, but it was a joint legislative committee with no direction. I was given the job and they said, "OK, do something with it." I started to look at how one could make the government more efficient. I looked at all the literature, all the things done in New York State, and all the efforts to quantify the output of this or that. Finally, I began to think that all of this was silly. If you want to deal with the issues of management and productivity, then you have to start looking at the machinery, so that ultimately you can start looking at output.

Some of the hostility that was generated towards me in the later incarnation as director of Employee Relations emanated from the fact that I started to take on the issue of budgetary reform in the legislative process. That is the private preserve of a very few.

In New York State government, legislative oversight responsibilities are splintered. There is no cohesive legislative oversight process. You have the fiscal committees, the Legislative Commission on Expenditure Review, the Productivity Commission and its successor, and the Committee on Economy and Efficiency. There is no real focus. There is a difference between pluralism and a process that is just totally incoherent. A pluralistic process that forces resolution, even if it is through conflict, is one thing, but those legislative people, with the Committee on Expenditure Review in left field and the Committee on Management Efficiency in right field, never interact.

They never communicate with one another and certainly don't relate at all to the way the budget is ultimately put together. It just doesn't make sense.

The federal government found that out; it has a very clear, really structured post-audit function in the General Accounting Office, and it has created a highly professional legislative budget process staffed by the Congressional Budget Office. The feds don't go through the same kind of nonsense, be it split control or one party rule, that the state goes through almost every year on revenue projections and all the rest. The Congressional Budget Office is basically non-partisan, and highly respected. The federal budget process works a hell of a lot better after budget reform than the state budget process. A joint professional legislative budget office in New York State would not require many more resources, if you just put together what is spent on the Legislative Commission on Expenditure Review and the Commission on Management Efficiency, and reallocated some of the Ways and Means and Finance money.

There are, also, some very good things in our process that the feds could adopt.

QUESTION: Do you feel that you were given adequate support by the governor's office and Governor Carey personally?

FRUCHER: I had all the support in the world from the governor; I was allowed to do what I wanted to do. That was one of the joys of being a commissioner in the Carey administration. To the extent that a commissioner was riding the right wave, the governor's ability to delegate to people and give them the flexibility and the leeway to do what they have to do was a big plus.

Was I successful, for example, in getting the governor to address the commissioners on the importance of performance evaluation? No, I was not. So I didn't have that kind of support. In a lot of ways, I was out there on my own. In certain areas, it was very good, and in other areas it was not. When I had his support, I could do pretty much anything I wanted, including, in that last year, winning what I considered to be my single, biggest, internal fight, which was to get the approval for the size and the length of those contracts, which I believe with all my heart and soul was necessary to sustain the work force.

One of the few, if not the only, nice personal thing that happened while I was in office was when the governor said to my wife that he appreciated all of the fights I had with him to get him to do the right things in some of these areas. I had a lot of support from the governor. We had some tough times, such as a 16-day corrections strike, and a lot of brickbats on things like performance evaluation. It was an interactive kind of relationship.

One of the things that I believe I did well for the governor during my tenure was to insulate him from whatever brickbats there were in the area of collective bargaining. I took all the heat from the unions. They never went after the governor. That was my job. I paid a price, but it is an important part of the job to be out there taking the heat.

As a matter of fact, I talked recently to Tom Hartnett and I said to him and to Governor Cuomo that one of the governor's mistakes in this early round was that he was too far out front on the layoff issue.[8] Hartnett and Finnerty should have been out there, and they should have been taking all the heat. The governor should have come in at the end and said, "Here I am."

Look at government as a series of concentric circles. The person in the middle, the governor, is supposed to be protected by the outer layers. I think Governor Carey appreciated the fact that I did that very well. The downside of that is that he may have thought that I did it so well that I didn't need his personal help from time to time.

They weren't deliberate refusals. There just weren't focused efforts to help. He met with the union leaders when I asked him to. That happened. Interestingly enough, I don't think during my tenure he had more than two or three meetings with the union leaders, because it was absolutely unnecessary. If he talked to the union leaders, they felt that they had all the access in the world to the governor. Then they didn't have to talk to me. (It is interesting that during the layoff period there have been parades in and out of Governor Cuomo's office. The union leaders are mad.)

I don't think that Governor Carey, for a whole set of reasons, focused on the internal management issues. It is ironic that in a conversation that I had in Massachusetts with Peter Goldmark, his first Budget director, in April of 1975, he told me that one of his frustrations with Carey was that the governor was obsessed with the details of everything. It is fascinating how Carey moved away from that because he was swept up by the fiscal crisis and other things that took him somewhere else, never to return.

I think part of that has to do, too, with the lure of the big city and the isolation of Albany, which is an issue in New York State government. I don't believe it is an avoidable issue. I have finally come to the conclusion that if I were governor I would demand a residency requirement in Albany. This is the most transient and the most Balkanized government I have ever seen. During the transition, I did headspins. At one point, I literally was pounding the table with the governor, saying that he must insist that his commissioners reside in Albany. And he agreed. Mario Cuomo isn't in New York City. He'll spend a lot more time here, but I don't think his commissioners necessarily will.

It is difficult to recruit competent people who are willing to spend seven days a week here and move their families here. It is a lot easier to move your family to Washington, D.C., or to New York City, than it is to move your family to Albany, New York. That is a major problem associated with management of New York State government.

QUESTION: With respect to legislative-executive relationships, is the basic system sound, recognizing that personalities are going to change from time to time?

FRUCHER: I think it's sound. We live in a pluralistic society, and I don't know of any better society. Despite all the problems (we can go on and on and on about management problems, about turnover as a result of the four-year cycle and some of the difficulties associated with that, and the inability to have long-term plans), I still think the system works. It can work a hell of a lot better. Those problems cannot or should not be ignored. Basically, the tension between the levels of government and forcing the focus of debate on governmental priorities is a very good process, provided that some resolution is ultimately reached.

One of the frustrations in state government is that there haven't been any resolutions. The system works, but it is in a transition. There are some real challenges ahead. The Cuomo administration, if it is sincere in doing more with less, making the machinery work, and not having a major impact on the delivery of services when you have a reduction in work force, has a hell of a lot of work to do. To the extent that I can, I will deliver the message that there is now a major responsibility that this administration has assumed in trying to improve the machinery of government—to concentrate and focus on these very real managerial issues. And the extent to which the Rockefeller Institute, SUNY, and whatever other associations and individuals who care about government speak up is very, very important.

FOOTNOTES

[1]Donald Wallach, Director, Governor's Office of Employee Relations (1975-1978).

[2]The third floor refers to the third floor of the New York State Capitol where the legislative correspondents offices are located.

[3]MHTA, Mental Health Therapy Aide.

[4]ARCO series, a series of books used by people to prepare for Civil Service tests.

[5]Willowbrook, located on Staten Island in New York City, is a major State facility serving the mentally retarded. A highly publicized series of revelations in the media about shocking conditions at the institution led to the signing, early in the Carey years, of a consent decree that stipulated improvement of services for the retarded in State facilities, under the supervision of the federal courts.

[6]Jerry Schrauf, Deputy Director of Research, Governor's Office of Employee Relations.

[7]Mark Lawton, Director, New York State Division of the Budget; Michael Finnerty, Deputy Director, New York State Division of the Budget; and Robert Morgado, Secretary to the Governor.

[8]Thomas Hartnett, Director, Governor's Office of Employee Relations (1983 to present), formerly Deputy Director.

A career public servant, William C. Hennessy rose through the ranks in the Department of Transportation. He became commissioner in 1977 and served in that capacity until 1982.

William C. Hennessy

Commissioner of Transportation

HENNESSY: When one becomes a commissioner, it is a lot better to have had a head start. I was assistant commissioner and executive deputy commissioner for five years, before I was commissioner. Some of the things that I wanted to do as assistant commissioner and executive deputy commissioner I was able to complete as commissioner, because I had already begun them or was able to do them as a result of my earlier experience.

My work, during the five years I was the chairman of the Disaster Preparedness Commission, was a very important part of my life. It was also an important part of my life during the previous five years, since Governor Rockefeller sent me to Elmira during the Agnes flood. After that time, I stayed with all the disasters in the state: the floods, the snowstorms, whatever they happened to be. It ended up with a Disaster Preparedness Commission established by Senator Bernard Smith from Long Island, after Long Island was completely bottled up by a snowstorm that lasted three days.[1]

Governor Carey appointed me as chairman of that Commission, and its work was extremely important. The commission not only coordinated emergency action after particular disasters, but it also developed disaster plans for any eventuality, be it a flood or even a nuclear disaster.

My role was to develop the plans so that local government could respond to whatever disaster occurred. That was a very important accomplishment in my life because it hadn't been done before. That is a job that has to be continued. Commissioner of Health David Axelrod is now the chairman of the commission. He worked with me during the five years that I was commissioner, so he has all of the knowledge that he has accumulated over those years.

The federal role makes disaster preparedness work very complicated. To learn it takes a lot of time and experience. I was especially trained for it. The government pays 75 percent or 100 percent of the cost depending on the type and extent of the disaster. We developed plans for evacuation of the nuclear plants in the state. The governor is now involved with the problem at Shoreham. We don't have satisfactory evacuation plans for our nuclear sites. As the former chairman of that commission, it's regrettable. It's something that, try as we did, we were not able to resolve.

Is it possible to develop an adequate evacuation plan? I'm not sure. That's an unresolved issue that David Axelrod is working on right now. There are models in Europe, and we have our own models, but we have no confidence in them. We have developed plans, but not to our own or to anyone else's satisfaction. We've done the best we could. How do you get two million people out of Long Island? How do you get a million people out of Westchester County? We've got the plan. We have the traffic patterns. Everything is set up to do it, but there is no question in the minds of those of us who have been dealing with it, that complete chaos is going to reign. It is something that the state has got to focus on for the next few years to develop some sort of a satisfactory plan.

QUESTION: One gets the impression that this Disaster Commission was to a large extent a reflection of your own interest. Dr. Axelrod was an integral member, and he has now picked it up. Suppose there had been a complete change of administration. Was there the impetus or was there a built-in mechanism to address this problem and to continue interest?

HENNESSY: Yes, the Disaster Commission itself consists of about 20 commissioners, with an executive committee of about six of us, including representatives from DEC (New York State Department of Environmental Conservation), DOT (New York State Department of Transportation), Health, and the State Police. It would have regenerated itself through the Office Of Disaster Preparedness and would have had to be reestablished by law. It's a fact, so I don't have any qualms about that, as I do about the impossibility of their task.

It is frightening. It was frightening for me to live with it. If you are in that capacity, you know that any day one of those things might go, and you are going to be sitting there with that awesome responsibility. I am awfully glad to be rid of it.

QUESTION: These are low-incidence, very high-cost events. How does one decide what kind of priority to put on preparing for these sorts of things? Essentially, don't we just hope that we never have to spend a single dollar?

HENNESSY: Actually, we do not have much choice because the federal agencies—FEMA (Federal Emergency Management Agency) or NRC (Nuclear Regulatory Commission) are very demanding in what they require before they continue a license or provide a new license. They are constantly at us to do better. At the state level, it is not a choice. I do not think it should be a choice, because, God knows, if it ever happens it is going to be just the God-awfullest thing ever imagined.

QUESTION: On the other hand, considering the facilities and the resources that were available, it seems that a remarkable job has been done to prepare for possible emergencies. I monitored one of the practice drills last August at the Hornell Center, where an imaginary alert was called at the Oswego nuclear plant. From seven in the

176

morning to seven at night, we watched the representatives of the 20 departments that you just mentioned handle the work that was necessary: getting word out, arranging for bus transportation, and many other things. I had no idea that this kind of thing had taken place and that the preparation had gone as far as it had.

HENNESSY: We have worked on it for five years. We have actually tested every site, and some of them two or three times. It is not that I am dissatisfied with the work we have done. We've done the best that the scientists working on this could come up with. It is not Hennessy or Axelrod. It is hundreds of brilliant people who are working on these plans. It is the impossibility of it.

COMMENT: There is another perspective to this. It is by chance that we are at the stage that you describe, because in one of the budget cuts years ago the Civil Defense Commission was essentially dismantled. Only by chance did it end up in Transportation and possibly your predecessors saw the need for such an organization to be resurrected.

HENNESSY: You are right. A lot of it is just natural instinct that took us down certain roads.

That completes the tale of the Disaster Preparedness Commission, which was a very important part of my life from the time I went to Agnes in 1962 to 1982—20 years of disaster work.

Within the Department of Transportation, I consider the creation of the Capital Programming Division an accomplishment. When I was assistant commissioner of the Operations Division, we may have had 500 projects going on at the same time. My jurisdiction was Maintenance, Construction, Design, Traffic, and Safety. I had a system of little cards just to keep it straight. The first thing I did, when I became commissioner, was to break up that organization, make an Engineering Division out of it and take out all of that other stuff. It worked a lot better.

It had been impossible with all those projects. We did not have them on computer; we did not have a management system. So I went to Commissioner Schuler and brought to his attention that we needed such a system.[2] I had seen something done in the University where they had a system, and the South Mall had programming of their contracts.

The Capital Programming Division has been a godsend in the department. We now have everything computerized. It is a marvelous management system. Now our Planning Division has a group within it that has a condition report on roads. Road condition is determined through physical inspection and by employing geometrics with a little device we have. They then program where we are going to spend our money out of our needs. There is no political game played at DOT with money—not in my experience. Now, as chairman of the Democratic party, I'm going to try to change all

177

that. It took 20 years to get away from it.

When we developed this capital program and put it into our computers, we also did another thing: we moved our existing systems from our planning sections into a design group. By doing this, we literally saved months and dollars, because we got away from planned roads and into reconditioned roads. You would be surprised how much money that saves. When you plan and engineer something to death, you can really do a number on it.

We got into the reconstruction and preservation (R & P) way of life. Ray Schuler was the person who developed that program. We got away from the planned highway and got into preserving what we already had, and we literally saved millions and millions by doing it. Thus this capital programming resulted in changing the department around.

In my years as commissioner, one of the things that was always predominant in my thinking was our local transportation system. I don't know exactly why. Perhaps it is because I came up through the ranks, beginning as a 20-year old working on the local roads and state highways. I have always thought that the local road system and local transportation needs were never treated fairly in the financing process. Our local systems were falling apart even more rapidly than the state systems. So, as I progressed at DOT and when I was assistant commissioner of Operations, I developed an attitude that I wanted as many of the federal dollars that were coming to New York State as possible (and this is heresy to my dear friends in Budget) to go to the local systems.

I began to testify in Washington when I was assistant commissioner of Operations, and then when I got to be a chairman of one of the commissions in the Association of State Highways Officials. My counterparts in different states used to think that I was absolutely mad, to want to give up our trust fund dollars to local governments. However, after I first testified and they heard the response from the Congressmen, I had a lot more people that went with me the next year. After three years of that, we made our first dent in that category in the Highway Act of 1974, which allowed us to spin off as much as 35 percent of our special bridge replacement money for local bridges.

Since then, we were able to develop our local roads participation to a point where two years ago, the Consolidated Highway Improvement Program (CHIPs) was passed in our legislature. That program took the place of the Donovan Program and the old Irwin Plan with which we funded town roads. Under those plans, we told towns exactly how to spend every dollar. We told them that their town road had to be a specific width and even specified the width of the shoulders. It was just not the right thing to do, to impose our standards on town roads.

As a result of that Consolidated Highway Improvement Program, we now have a dedicated fund. Revenues are going into that fund and directly out into the local road system. That is an accomplishment, because I could see the end of the trail with the legislation. The dedicated fund was a result of a lot of advanced planning, and you rarely see a lot of agencies and a lot of people go to work together to try to accomplish something of that nature. I know that county officials and town highway superintendents are just pleased as punch with that whole CHIPs program.

That is what I tried to do, more than anything else, as a commissioner. If I wanted to leave a mark, it would be that local road systems were going to be given a bit more attention than they had ever been given before.

QUESTION: You alluded several times to the need for localities to take a major role. What is your opinion of the capacity of localities, especially in those where elected officials are responsible for highways and are not chosen on the basis of their expertise?

HENNESSY: If you are talking about the City of New York, their capacity is just as good as the state's. If you are talking about Suffolk County, it is very good. If you're talking about rural counties, forget it; they have little capacity, yet they have as many miles of town roads as there are anywhere. How on earth are we ever going to get it back together again? There has to be a concentrated effort either to find a way to reinforce the local capacity or else the state has to do it themselves.

QUESTION: Is there any prospect of moving in the direction of a single state-administered transportation system, where the county and town highways are part of the state system?

HENNESSY: There is no state with a single administrative program. There are states that have mixtures, combinations. I do not think it is a bad idea to at least take a look at it. I mentioned before that I am a local government person basically. It is the level of government that works best. If we could devise a maintenance system for county and town, I think it would work just as well as the state's maintenance system. That would be heresy at DOT, but the fact of the matter is, that you are only talking about imaginary lines in the road when you are plowing snow. Whether or not it will ever come to that, I don't know. It would require a great deal of study to do it in an orderly manner. But it could happen, and it would not be all bad.

QUESTION: Is there any sort of thinking along these lines going on at the department now?

HENNESSY: No, I don't think they even want to think about something like that. One of the things you have to keep in mind is that your men have to work in the winter as well as the summer. When the state has men waiting for a snowstorm, the county workers and the town workers are also sitting around in the same geographic area waiting for the same snowstorm. So you have three different levels of government waiting for the next snowstorm. You would probably need the same number of men waiting for the same snowstorm with an integrated system, but maybe you would not need the same number of management people, pieces of equipment, or anything else, if you had an integrated maintenance system within every county. I also doubt if you could ever bring about a system that would include cities. But, I know it could be better. The only reason it is being done this way today is because it has been done this way for 200 years.

QUESTION: If you were to begin your official responsibility again, how might you change your course? What would you do differently?

HENNESSY: Oh, I probably would have started off in Budget.

Seriously, somehow, as DOT commissioner, I would have relied more heavily on a non-regulatory role. I got caught up in the regulation processes, the myriad of permits, and the bureaucracy. I began to believe that government was the cure for all things.

As I got into the commissioner roles, I could see the frustrations that go with the red tape. If you look very carefully at localities, you can see that the future lies in local governments. The sooner we recognize that we are going the wrong way in increasing state government and federal government, the better off we will be. We ought to be enhancing local governments. Our health problems, our transit problems, our safety problems, and our environmental problems— all of those can be just as easily handled locally, if you look at it from outside.

I was inside and I got caught up in the process of state government. If I had my druthers, I would rather see much, much less state regulation. All a state government is, is a regulator. It is constantly regulating something or other, or auditing, or overseeing. When one starts compounding those regulations in each one of those agencies, it is mind-boggling.

In retrospect, for example, I believe that if there was a capable local or county health association, they would have been better suited to have handled Love Canal. But it wasn't there. So, naturally the state had to assume it. We weren't wrong in assuming it; the mistake is that there was no adequate local government agency.

QUESTION: How do you achieve that?

HENNESSY: Somehow or other, a governor or a legislature is going to have to demand it boldly enough. I am sure that government leaders today would agree with me that there is too much government.

QUESTION: You almost suggest a major constitutional issue ahead in terms of the distribution of funds.

180

HENNESSY: It probably will never happen, because those in government are not prone to change.

QUESTION: Does the high proportion of the budget that goes to state aid contribute to the problem, or does that help ease the burden of the local governments?

HENNESSY: I don't know. That is a very, very complex question: whether or not you ought to be collecting at the state level and trickling it down afterwards. That is for somebody smarter than I to handle. Most of the regulatory roles of state government are unnecessary, including our permit process for driveways and our permit process for weights. Is it necessary for me to give a permit to a moving company in New York City? Is it necessary for us to have variable truck rates for goods?

QUESTION: Haven't you had proposals for a certain amount of deregulation?

HENNESSY: Yes, we have had several deregulation bills go in, but they do not get out of the legislature. In the last couple of years, I really did try to deregulate somewhat. It's necessary. It's tough, but perhaps one year you surface a bill, and the next year it takes on a little validity, and one day it happens. There has to be a concentrated effort from some unknown source to make it happen. It will not happen just from a governor. He is too busy to make it happen. Budget directors can't do it. It has to come from, maybe, you guys in this institute.

QUESTION: Is there anything else you'd do differently?

HENNESSY: No, I think that if it were possible to bring about a good local government system, that we would all be quite happy. Commissioner Schuler left me with a state system of roads that was not as good as when he became commissioner. When I left the commissioner's office, I left a system that was not as good as when I became commissioner, and that's too bad. As hard as we worked and as dedicated as we were, there was not much we could do about the deterioration of the road system, because the dollars just were not there and personnel had been cut back. Yet neither of those alibis is the ultimate reason for the falling-apart of our infrastructure. It is because there was no public knowledge of the condition of the system.

I think that the legislature and the public would have responded if they had knowledge of that system. Commissioner Schuler first started developing public awareness of the fact that we ought to take care of the system that we have, before we go into any more expressways and interstates. He made me cognizant of that. I have always thanked him very much for that, because as I came to know the system better and see for myself the problems that we had, I realized that it is a good thing that we started sounding the alarm back then.

Speaker Fink is the first legislator who really understood the problem.[3] Three years ago, I had a briefing with him, and he responded to this problem. Perhaps he did so, because it had a good flavor for statewide campaign material as well as being a genuine need. I have always felt that he wanted to do something about the problem. Two years ago, he conducted hearings throughout the state. I attended as many of those as I could. I believe that bringing about the awareness of our infrastructure difficulties was the thing that has now triggered this five-cent per gallon gasoline tax. The rest of the states were not even talking about infrastructure three or four years ago. New York State was first to start blowing the whistle about our bridges and things like that. When the speaker got involved with the program, it took off. Of course, that was very helpful.

In terms of accomplishments, it has not yet happened. However, bringing the thing in and putting it out on the table for people to see and look at was important for a lot of our programs. Sometimes, in the agencies, we have a tendency to squirrel away problems. I know that I was that way often; I would rather try to solve something than bring it out and let everybody take a look at it and work at it.

The infrastructure problem is now going to be addressed with our five-cent federal tax, and the bonding that's programmed for this year for our matching share. We may be able to do it in ten years if the plan that Speaker Fink developed and we took up works. That's high in rank of what we've accomplished in terms of public awareness programs.

QUESTION: Is it significant that Speaker Fink was the one with whom you had this liaison? Where was the chamber? Where was the executive role?

HENNESSY: I don't know. I think that sometimes it just happens that way. The Legislature responds sooner than the executive. That is not unusual in many of the program areas. This time it just happened to be the speaker. I think the executive was trying to balance a budget and could not or did not want to go into such an infrastructure program as we were talking about. One of the sidelights of it was that Governor Carey tried to obtain the dedicated tax with his license registration fee two years ago, and he did not get the support in the legislature to do that. We were not calling it infrastructure at the time; Speaker Fink came up with that jargon. But Governor Carey had attempted to put another $135 million in that dedicated fund for infrastructure programs.

QUESTION: Who is responsible, in your estimation, in New York State for the erosion of the infrastructure? Why, for example, was there no attempt long ago to develop a maintenance program?

HENNESSY: Rather than to deal with who was responsible, I will deal with what was responsible. I know when we started to concentrate on the interstate problem and all of the federal monies were going to build the new interstates, states had a tendency to focus on using that money, because it was money that was at hand to create jobs. The economy was stimulated through the development of the interstate. Each corridor was another economic developer. As we put literally billions of dollars into the interstate program, we stopped addressing our local needs and our state highways and concentrated on completing those expressways. In response to your question, there really is no 'who' because it happened over so long a period of time.

QUESTION: Is it true that infrastructure maintenance is not the sort of issue that politicians like to take by the tail, because it means raising taxes and doing other things that are unpopular? Maintenance programs require a sort of focus and a kind of investment that are different from developing infrastructure further. Ultimately the burden falls upon the ordinary citizens' shoulders, and politically that can be fatal.

HENNESSY: You are saying, I think, that the political process did not want to put the money where it was needed the most. A Budget director has choices to make, not that I ever agreed with him, but he went ahead and made them anyway. When you're dealing with the choices between your operating dollars and your capital dollars, those are difficult decisions. However, one cannot quit providing operating dollars for the maintenance program. They can be limited, but not given up. Capital dollars may be given up. Build nothing for two years, if you wish. We did that from 1970 through 1972. We even canceled all of our consultant engineering contracts, some of them 80 percent done. We did not have the money to complete them. Those choices had to be made and they were made— rightfully or wrongfully. Perhaps we had to finish up the University or perhaps we had to finish up a hospital someplace else, or a jail. (Our jails are falling apart.) So, we had to give up something to do that. I never complained; I would challenge and fight for every dollar I could get, and not blush at all if I took it out of Mental Hygiene. But the fact of the matter is, when you're dealing with capital and operating dollars, those choices are just plain tough.

QUESTION: You think this can become very popular politically? If we stop building in large measure and make use of this public education which alters the climate at the pinnacle, this could be a very politically popular program. You can spread the money around; indeed, you have to spread the money around.

HENNESSY: Really, it is not popular until you cut the ribbon. The jobs are the key to it all.

QUESTION: You can't really cut the ribbon on a repaving job.

HENNESSY: No, that's the problem. In an election year we do, though. The real issue keeps going back to the condition of the system—jobs are the spinoff of it. The pressing question is: Is the system going to be improved now that the public awareness is there? If it spins off into a vote for an assemblyman, that's fine, but I don't think there is much of that in it. I think it is more of something that the government just has to do. There is no credit—nobody wins on deferred maintenance.

QUESTION: Wasn't there also an effective capacity in the department's program, and the interstate sopped up a large amount of it?

HENNESSY: Yes. The limited engineering capacity to build and to inspect had a lot to do with it. We were running at capacity for ten years—1960 to 1970. The work forces of the DOT were fully extended. We had no capacity to address the issue of maintenance.

QUESTION: To what extent has the newly developed interest in bus, rail, and air transportation had some indirect, if not direct, influence on the neglect of the highway infrastructure?

HENNESSY: Somewhere between 1965 and 1970, the state started to concentrate to a great extent on MTA (Metropolitan Transit Authority) and the transit systems in New York City. When you talk about buses and trains, you are talking about New York City. Ninety-five percent of our transit problems are there. In 1973, we had zero budget in operating dollars for MTA. I think Governor Wilson was the first to promote such a thing. It came into being under Governor Carey. Today, we are talking about $300 or $400 million a year that go to subsidize the fare. In 1973, they didn't do that. You might say that that's $300 or $400 million a year that might have gone into highways or might have gone into bridges that are falling down. So, in a sense you're correct—transit has taken away a lot of money. Back in '65-'70, we sent a lot of capital money down that way to build the Second Avenue subway. I see you are familiar with it? It is still a hole in the ground.

QUESTION: How much of the decision to build is based simply on the Federal Highway's formula of '90-10'?

HENNESSY: We had to use 90-10 money for interstates. You use your interstate money first because the State of New York made money on that. We get 90 percent of the project back. After you take out your state taxes and in-house work, the state actually made money. So, the one thing we always did was use our interstate dollars first. That was for new construction, by definition. I blame the construction of the interstate for the neglect of the highway infrastructure. I don't say it was wrong. I am glad we got our interstate done, but now we are going to pay for it in this other fashion.

QUESTION: The question, about bleeding highway construction because of the needs of mass transit, triggers in my mind a question about the reorganization that created the DOT. The goal, as I

184

recall, was to create an overall department that would weigh mass transit needs against highway needs and create some balance in the transportation system of the state. I wonder whether you think that that was an error, given where we are now?

HENNESSY: No, not at all, because I do not know what the alternative would be. I broke up this big division I once headed (I figured if I couldn't do it, no one could) and created an Office of Public Transportation, an Office of Engineering, and an Office of Maintenance and Operations. Those are the only three offices in the department; they are the line. So, you see, Public Transportation has the same weight to it as Engineering, which includes the construction division.

When we go for our budget, public transportation in all of the cities of the state has the same fighting chance as highways. You are dealing with capital dollars which are in the same account. I must say that the New York State Division of the Budget (DOB) and DOT work very closely, even with the MTA budgets. We are very much involved.

QUESTION: To what extent did integrated transportation planning (i.e., a tradeoff between highways and mass transit) emerge under your aegis?

HENNESSY: In so far as financing is concerned, I think it was done mostly by Budget people dealing with our submissions. We sent it to DOB, and what came back might bear close resemblance to what we presented, or they might have taken our whole capital spending program and shifted it.

As far as an integrated planning process is concerned, there really is no planning going on today with railroads. They are there, but we are not building new railroads. We are not building new expressways. The building we knew 20 or 30 years ago, new expressways, I-88, even the Buffalo Transit Line, is not going on. The kind of planning that's going on now is financial planning—where to put your dollars next. It's a little more sophisticated than it ever was before.

The first on the hit list is dollars for transit. I don't know where it's all going to end as far as parity for transit is concerned. Two years ago we started a fair fare policy. When we said fair fare, we meant the customer would pay 50 percent and the state would pay 50 percent in a subsidy for a bus ride or a transit ride. The New York City transit system is just about at that level right now.

There are those who think that transit shouldn't be subsidized, that if somebody takes a bus ride, they ought to pay the cost. I don't believe that, anymore than I believe that elsewhere in this state they should have to pay for their canal ride or train ride or anything else. There's a legitimacy to subsidy. Raising the kind of dollars that are necessary to subsidize mass transit is the other side of the coin and is a more difficult question.

185

There are thus two unresolved issues: first, how to bring about that fair fare, and second, if you do bring it about, then how do you pay for it in the future.

QUESTION: Do you think the state should play a major role in that?

HENNESSY: Yes, or else it won't get done. It's the antithesis of everything I believe. I believe that the state should get out of the business of building roads in counties and towns and leave it up to them. Unfortunately, it doesn't get done because their needs seem to be always someplace else. And, it won't get done unless we force them to do it in some fashion or another, but no one wants that. It's a very, very critical issue in the days ahead. It's not enough that we've recognized the problem. The conditional problems of the system are much worse in the local system. The condition of the local bridges is much worse than the state bridges, even though our problems are bad because the bridges are bigger.

QUESTION: One might be able to argue that one of the primary beneficiaries of infrastructure is industry, especially the aspects of infrastructure that you've been coming up with. In a certain sense, this is a cost that has always been socialized. In your opinion, should it be the responsibility of industry in the future to play a greater role in subsidizing the infrastructure?

HENNESSY: Practically speaking, I don't know how it would work. You would have to do it in some fashion that would tax industries generally throughout the state for this purpose. You couldn't just say to a single industry, "You're responsible for all the infrastructure in your county."

QUESTION: Even if it was localized?

HENNESSY: How would you force General Electric to fix up all the roads in Schenectady County? I don't even know how industry might be defined for such a program. It would be just too complicated. It bothers me, from a builder's point of view, that industry is not building more themselves. It bothers me that industry today is "paperizing" their profits and losses, instead of reaching out and building more and making more products. In this country, industry would be well advised to expand on their own programs and do more themselves, rather than to go out into communities and build bridges. It bothers me that they're taking their money and buying more property, instead of putting it back into building.

QUESTION: Where does something like the highway or the transportation program fit into job creation and retention?

HENNESSY: I think it has just a tremendous impact on jobs and employment. Mostly, it feeds on itself. When a $100 million capital program is put together, probably 60 percent of that money goes to salaries, and most of the products are purchased within the general region. That $100 million is going to be working in that region and turning over and over.

There's a billion dollar construction program going on at DOT right now, and there has been for the past few years. (The capital program has invested maybe $300 or $400 million a year, and it takes two or three years to build, so you're turning over that kind of money all the time.) When you're dealing with that kind of money, you're dealing with a lot of jobs. The money is going out into the community and, when it turns over, it keeps turning and turning until it's building new commerce and opening up new corners for development. There's no end to what new construction does. It not only enhances the community, but it enhances the economy as well. I believe, with every fiber in me, that building is very important. We must have a constant rebuilding program. Maybe I shouldn't have gotten on that industrial kick, but I feel very strongly that industry isn't keeping up with their end of investing in this country of ours. They have to resume building.

QUESTION: What was your relationship to the contractors and the suppliers? In what way did they help put this package together?

HENNESSY: As a commissioner, I was not involved in obtaining materials. However, as a rule we used local products. For instance, the concrete and blacktop were normally local products. The lumber was usually purchased locally by the contractor.

QUESTION: Does the public come out and lobby for your programs in any way? Will they just sit by and disappear when the contracts are up?

HENNESSY: We've never had too much help. Contractors' associations are tied up in their own selfish interests and involved in their associations' activities. Their lobbying is not very effective. I think that labor unions are much more effective in lobbying for highways and bridges. The AFL-CIO is very effective. They can put the clout of the whole building trade in back of the capital dollars, and I'm sure that budget people felt it in terms of labor support in the budget process.

QUESTION: We would be remiss if we didn't ask you about Westway.[4]

HENNESSY: Westway is a very good jobs program. I say that not only for the construction itself, but also for what it would do for regenerative activity on the west side. But Westway has been bogged down in legal problems for ten years. I don't see that as overwhelming though, because most major projects are bogged down that long these days. Persistence is the only thing that matters, until the court tells you "No."

QUESTION: Did you expect Westway to be well under way while you were still commissioner?

HENNESSY: I was hopeful. I promised Governor Carey in 1978, when we were campaigning, that it would be under way in the next year. It didn't happen. I promised in 1979 that he could say it would be under way in 1980. Every year I had to renew my vows to Governor Carey that it was still a "go" project. I couldn't say right now whether Westway will ever be built.

QUESTION: Do you regard as a problem the fact that most major projects are bogged down for ten years? Do you see any way of resolving it?

HENNESSY: No, I don't. Because I don't find any fault with the system. I was in the other system, you see. I was one of those people who would send a bulldozer up to a front door and scare the hell out of the inhabitants. I condemned property that perhaps should not have been condemned.

Think of what we did on the South Mall project. We had survey parties that were surveying in both valleys. We called them north malls and south malls. (That's what I always understood to be the genesis of the name. It was a decoy that we had working at that time.) I was secluded in a little office at 103 Washington Avenue, across the street from the State Office Building, and was in charge of making the map. The plan was to file this map in the county clerk's office pursuant to eminent domain. The filing of that map gave the people of the State of New York title to everything within it. It included 40 square blocks of the City of Albany. You talk about a surprise one morning; that's exactly how it happened. And it wasn't all abandoned houses. There was a big Italian community right in the center of it.

We shouldn't do that again, today. We did it then, but we shouldn't have. In today's environment, it would be the wrong thing to do. We did it at Stewart Airport, too. Governor Rockefeller also wanted to do it at the West Valley nuclear waste disposal site. I got to be quite an expert at massive condemnations.

There were no planning or environmental impact statements and things like that. I don't fault the system. I fault the players, like myself, who have made mistakes. Perhaps if we had done our work a little more carefully, we wouldn't be in the situation we're in today. Perhaps we'd have ended up with a judge with whom it was a little easier to deal.

The fact of the matter is that we're here, and so far the courts have not found cause to detract from the original concept of Westway at all. The problems that we've had are environmental considerations. The only thing that's holding up Westway today is a mitigation plan for the striped bass. It behooves us to try to resolve that single issue. Perhaps there'll be another issue tomorrow.

I can give you many examples of situations where we were in the same scenario. We were in a hopeless situation on I-88 ten years ago when the Rotterdam people stopped the whole project. We were actually in construction of the south end of I-88. We had to stop construction and pay off the contractors, and it cost us $30 million in lost money. Only fools like myself would go ahead and try to build a job after we got stopped like that. There wasn't anyone who thought that we'd ever get going again. We did the environmental impact statement all over again, and had our hearings all over again. It took us four years to restart, but I-88 is done now, and I'd hate to be without it.

In Rochester, the outer loop goes through a park, and we knew we were going through a park. We knew we were going to get hung up in our environmental work. We knew we would get lawsuits. Nevertheless, it was the right thing to do because we were going to rebuild the park, substitute land, and do the things the law requires. Everything happened the way we expected, and more, but the outer loop is all done now. Transportation would be very difficult in Rochester without that outer loop. In Troy, the Hoosick Street Bridge was going all the way to the Supreme Court. Every project is the same way.

QUESTION: You have the perspective of a person who's done this for a long time. One cost is that politicians have problems investing in things that require a long time to pay off. The other cost is, of course, financial. That's troubling to me. People hesitate to undertake projects, knowing that these political and financial costs are inevitably there and are going to escalate, or that the political benefits will accrue to somebody else who's not now known.

HENNESSY: That's a very good thought, because it's something that a technician like myself might not deal with realistically. I might say, "I'm going to build Westway. I'm going to do it." Somebody smarter than I has to turn me off, like Governor Cuomo or Carey. Perhaps I should have been turned off and not pursued I-88 to that extent. The cost was high. It would have been realistic to stop at that point, but somebody in government higher than I would have had to order the project killed. I haven't really thought much about this. But it's very real. We may have built some of those interstates when the price was too high. Perhaps we should have backed off.

A perfect example is the Rye-Oyster Bay Bridge. We have backed off a lot of projects like the Rye-Oyster Bay Bridge. John Cammerer went to his grave hoping it would be built one day.[5] In every community there are projects that are passed on. The interchange under Washington Park in Albany isn't dead. It hasn't quite matured ten years yet!

QUESTION: Who made the decisions on these individual projects? To what extent, for example, did it come out of the governor's office? To what extent was a program of the department based on their studies alone? Where was the relationship in deciding which projects had to be cleared with the governor's office and which didn't have to be cleared?

HENNESSY: In my ten years of responsibility in DOT, I don't believe that I ever cleared a job with the governor's office. It doesn't work that way. They may be involved in a larger concept. The governor may be out on the southern tier and make a commitment to complete a southern tier expressway. He may be in a speaking situation in a community. (We always prepared briefing papers so that when he went to a community he might make commitments to projects.) Then, in turn, the operation's officer of the governor's office keeps us informed of whatever commitments were made. We would deal with those in a programmatic sense, never in a political sense.

In my career—and I was just a laborer under Governor Dewey— I've never experienced any political types of decisions being made on a highway budget. It just never happened in my experience at DOT, and that's pretty good.

QUESTION: You seem to give the impression that your department is fairly autonomous. As far as initiating and implementing projects is concerned, it appears that not only was it not necessary to clear them first with the governor's office, but that you had the same latitude in legislative relations. Is that also true with regards to constituencies outside the state government?

HENNESSY: If you're talking about a reconstruction or a rehabilitation job, the department is pretty much autonomous. However, legislation is required if you're on a new location. You always have the new budget which must be approved by the legislature and developed by the Division of Budget. I don't blush or shy away, however, from saying that the department is pretty much autonomous.

QUESTION: Did you find that legislative support for new projects was there when you required it?

HENNESSY: Yes, and it was pretty much perfunctory. Whenever we initiated a new project, it came from the planning process and the environmental impact statement. When that was the case, we pretty much precluded the governor's office and the legislature, because it's an entirely different process. It's in the public arena already, really. The public is going to decide whether the road goes there or not. Lately, the public decides whether you're going to widen the road and take down trees. It's gotten to that point. It's a public process these days.

QUESTION: How would you compare the autonomy of state agencies under the Carey administration with prior administrations with which you were familiar?

HENNESSY: Cabinet responsibility is a very, very important part of the whole government process. Governor Carey relied upon cabinet responsibility more so than Governor Rockefeller. Governor

Rockefeller had strong program associates. He ran a stronger liaison with agencies. They were stronger people than were Governor Carey's people. Governor Carey had a stronger secretary and operational office. There was more firmness and more control in the Carey administration than I had known before. I didn't know the Rockefeller organization all that well. I was an assistant commissioner and a director at that time. I knew it well enough, however, to know that they had a very strong program associate role. I can't speak for the other agencies, but I can speak for DOT. Governor Carey gave me as much responsibility as I wanted or ever needed, and authority to do my job. The constraint came from Budget, as I've learned through the years; it didn't come from the executive. Accessibility was never a problem with either the governor or his secretary as far as I personally was concerned. Governor Carey was a person who did not shy away from delegating responsibility and authority.

QUESTION: Was that overt or more by default?

HENNESSY: I think it was overt. I think that he wanted it that way and had confidence in his cabinet. There's no way to say this unashamedly, but I believe that Governor Carey had a very good cabinet. I was just a mistake. I just happened to be there, but the rest of the commissioners were just very, very fine hard-working people. As I go down the list of commissioners, I don't know a single one that I wasn't very proud to work with. Governor Carey was well advised to give those people that responsibility.

QUESTION: Is there a difference here between what could be called the basic system and the individuals who were operating? In other words, was the system basically sound? Could it have functioned properly or are changes necessary? On the other hand, were the problems primarily with respect to personnel? Was there a combination of both?

HENNESSY: My problem with your premise is that I don't think there was a problem with the system. It was a good cabinet and a good system. I don't think that the Carey executive chamber operated as efficiently or was coordinated as well as the Rockefeller-Wilson chambers were, only because there was too much control in one place rather than sending it out into more functional areas. I knew most of the program associates in the Rockefeller organization and worked with them to a great extent in my South Mall days and my real estate days. They worked very closely with the agencies, talked to the commissioners regularly, and carried programs and administrative functions to the agencies so that there was strong executive leadership, rather than strong agencies carrying out their missions. I don't know which is best. I liked the way we did it.

QUESTION: Perhaps you were being a little too modest a

moment ago when asked about the autonomy of your agency. You seemed to suggest that it was a result of the fact that the governor was willing to delegate power in general and to leave it to you and also to the other commissioners. Certainly that's an important factor; if he wasn't going to do that, the whole issue of autonomy would have been much more controversial. But, once delegation was accomplished, to what extent were you as an individual responsible for carving out that autonomy for the agency?

HENNESSY: I wouldn't characterize it that way. We had a group of commissioners who were in sort of a cabal. It included Barbara Blum, Orin Lehman, Robert Flacke, David Axelrod, John Egan, and me.[6] As a matter of fact, I have a plaque inscribed "to the mischievous group." Every one in that group is a strong person. They all ran their departments very well. And so, I don't think it was the Hennessy personality, or the Blum personality, or the Flacke personality. However, it was the governor's personality that allowed him to cope with spinning off that kind of responsibility. It's not dissimilar from the responsibility that the President spins off to his cabinet at the national level. It works if you have the right kind of people. If you have a cabinet of misfits, you're going to have problems.

QUESTION: Did you find it a problem that the structure had one principal strong assistant on the second floor?

HENNESSY: It wasn't a source of difficulty for me. I was never turned aside from conversation with Bob Morgado or the governor. I can't speak for the other commissioners. I think I had a little different situation in that regard, in that I may have developed a better relationship with the governor than some of the other commissioners because of campaigning and working with him more closely.

I had no problem with that singular pivotal person. The Rockefeller methodology was more appropriate for government, that is, to have more wide-spread functional people: a strong budget person, a strong appointments person, a strong operations person, and a strong secretary. It's very important that you spread that out a little more. Once again, the Carey method worked perfectly all right with me.

QUESTION: In retrospect, would you have done anything significantly different with respect to your relationship with the overhead in control agencies with whom you worked? Is the system satisfactory? Are there changes or improvements that might be made?

HENNESSY: Once again, I say that it is a lot easier for an agency head to deal with other agencies under the Rockefeller system. We had a club and got together for lunch. We had a camaraderie among us as commissioners. As commissioner of Transportation I would have to develop a good relationship with Vic Bayler in Civil Service and Howard Miller in Budget.

In contrast, under the Carey administration, you carried your

192

own water to the agencies and you fought your own budget fights. I'm not sure it's the best way, but it was our way. If I had my druthers, I would rather have had someone out of the governor's office that I could ask to intercede on my behalf.

COMMENT: It seems that the increase in government has forced the multiplication of programs and has forced the greater autonomy that you mentioned for the agencies, but the staff structure has not kept pace with it. The Division of the Budget is the best example of this. Staff agencies are still living as if it were 20 years ago when the individual budget examiners could influence programs. The system may not be keeping pace with the evolution that's going on. All the things that we were going to delegate to the agencies, the agencies picked up but they weren't relinquished. Budget and others still feel they have to get into that extreme degree of detail. It is counter-influencing the role of the agency.

HENNESSY: It's counter-productive. An example of it is that the Budget Division has increased three-fold since 1975 and DOT is operating with 2,500 fewer people.

COMMENT: To carry that one step further, the antidote to the role of the Budget is probably the rise of the legislative budgeting function. It's the same, but now it's got a competitor.

HENNESSY: And your national picture is in exactly the same focus.

QUESTION: If you want to reclassify a clerk to a senior clerk in the Hornel office, it takes how long? And how many people have to act on it.

HENNESSY: Oh, I wouldn't have the foggiest notion. I wouldn't even have time to deal with something like that. You have to go through a complete process.

QUESTION: That's the point. To some of us it would seem to be a rather technical thing that could easily be handled within the department on the basis of a very, very quick review of the situation.

HENNESSY: Yes, but that's traditional; it's never changed in the history of time. It would take a whole new administrative approach for that to happen. Even in Rockefeller days and way back to Dewey, there was never a Budget director that gave up that right.

QUESTION: If you wanted to shift $500 worth of money from travel to fuel in the Hornell office, it would take you weeks to get it done.

HENNESSY: No, it would be done that week. I could do that, but I could not put on a new clerk. If I wanted to have five laborers in a particular residency, they would not let me fill those five someplace else. If there is a legislative mandate to institute a program and the director of the Budget doesn't agree with the program, then the funds aren't allocated. It gets down to the program basis, and gets away from the nickel and dime personnel.

QUESTION: Has the role of the Budget gotten too strong, and are they too out of touch with reality in terms of what the state needs?

HENNESSY: Yes, yes, to both of them.

QUESTION: Another interviewee said that while there are professional people working in public service in New York, there is not a professional public service.

HENNESSY: He's full of baloney. I don't know who it was, but that's not true.

QUESTION: He said there's no sense of career.

HENNESSY: That's absolutely untrue, and that upsets me. About a third of DOT's people are engineers and career people who have spent their lives designing roads and inspecting construction. In my 35 years, there has never been a tinge of scandal in New York State or DOT. That can be attributed to the professionalism and the spirit of the people who have a sense of security in their jobs, and the pride that goes with building and constructing roads. The competition within the system itself breeds a spirit and a fairness into the professional ladder that makes people want to stay with it. There isn't a great deal of turnover in that engineering division.

That's only one side of it. I can go to a completely different side of it and look at the maintenance. Maintenance workers are working for $11,000 or $12,000 per year, and they are called out at two or three o'clock in the morning into the worst kind of snow storms. These snowplow people can't even see ahead of them. That kind of job is not professionalism per se, but there's a very, very good attitude on the part of the public servant.

At DOT, we have an engineer who gave 25 years of service in Public Transit, and a 30-year engineer in Operations. The head of the Engineering Division has been there 25 years; he came to us out of college. To say there wasn't professionalism in state service is just not right.

QUESTION: Does the system recognize performance adequately?

HENNESSY: Yes, it recognizes performance, because I got to be a commissioner! It recognizes performance because the Civil Service system works. Performance is attached to knowledge in civil service, because you must pick one out of three candidates. In my own case, I started at a grade five, or something like that, as a surveyor and inspector, and I went right through the whole system of taking exams. I never had a provisional appointment or anything like that until I got to be assistant commissioner. Anybody can do that. I didn't even have a college education. So the system works. You can go into any department and if they have a genuine career ladder, not some spooky arrangement for political purpose, it works.

QUESTION: Are you encouraged by the people who are getting on at the bottom rung now? Do you think there are problems with the kind of people who are being attracted to state service now, compared to when you began in the state?

HENNESSY: Right now, it's very difficult to attract people because of the freezes and layoffs and things like that. People are not attracted to the state service today. I don't know what their recruitment problems are today, but traditionally we have always been able to compete, not well, but sufficiently.

I think the problems are not the attractions, but the departures. The people who leave get discouraged by such little fiascoes as the current layoffs.

QUESTION: One of the things that characterizes what you describe is that you were willing to move from location to location.

HENNESSY: Well, you have to. You have to be willing to compete—that very word "competition" is the key to the whole Civil Service process. You have to be willing to do something more than what you're classified to do. If you're inspecting on a road, you have to also be willing to go in the office and reduce notes. If you're in real estate and you're negotiating, you have to be willing to do some appraisal work too, and learn. The whole secret to the Civil Service process is competition; if you don't compete, you're going to stay right where you are. That's the key to it all.

QUESTION: Do you see any good reason now for any important change in what could be called the basic personnel system?

HENNESSY: No, and I'm a dangerous person to ask because I was in the system for 36 years. I believe very strongly that this Civil Service system is the right and proper thing. I believe very strongly in CSEA (Civil Service Employees Association) and PEF (Public Employees Federation) and the union capabilities that go with this system. I believe very strongly that politics doesn't have a role in certain levels of government, and that professionals should not be tampered with.

FOOTNOTES

[1]Bernard Smith, formerly a New York State Senator (1966-1978) and Chairman, Senate Environmental Conservation Committee.

[2]Raymond Schuler, New York State Commissioner of Transportation (1972-1980).

[3]Stanley Fink, Member, New York State Assembly (1968-present), Mr. Fink assumed the Speakership in 1979.

[4]Westway is an extremely controversial project to build a multi-billion dollar highway on the west side of Manhattan. It has been delayed for many years by environmental litigation.

[5]John Cammerer, New York State Senator (1966-1982).

[6]Barbara Blum, Commissioner of Social Services (1978-1982); Orin Lehman, Commissioner, Office of Parks and Recreation (1975-present); Robert Flacke, Commissioner, Department of Environmental Conservation (1977-1982); David Axelrod, Commissioner, Department of Health (1979-present); John Egan, Commissioner, Office of General Services (1983-present).

*James A. Prevost served as commissioner of Mental Health from
1978 to 1982. Previously, he had been director of Hutchings
Psychiatric Center in Syracuse, New York.*

James A. Prevost

Commissioner of Mental Health

PREVOST: Mental health practice in this country, and in fact in all of western culture, has been undergoing a rapid transition. These changes affected my tenure as the state commissioner of Mental Health both at its beginning and throughout my five years.

The first major historical antecedent is the two-class system of care for the mentally ill in this country, greater in mental health than any other health care disability, a system which has resulted in the segregation of the indigent and severely mentally ill, frequently involuntarily committed into large state institutions. This was an outgrowth of the moral treatment era of the last century, which unfortunately resulted in the warehousing of those chronically impaired by mental disability. Those patients who were less severely ill and could pay for their treatment, on the other hand, were cared for in the private sector. One consequence of this two-class system was the training of American professionals in the mental health field for the treatment of those patients served in the fee-for-service, free enterprise, private sector. Unfortunately, this legacy continues even today and service for the poor all too often means poor service.

The second major antecedent relates to the rapid expansion after World War II of the mental health professions and the range of treatment modalities, frequently without an empirical basis, resulting in an amorphous conceptualization of mental illness and the inability of the field to deliver on its promises. The subsequent loss of credibility with the public was a very real concern when I began my tenure as state commissioner.

This was the context in which this country and New York State responded to the federally initiated policy of deinstitutionalization in the 1960's. Therefore, in 1978, the primary issue confronting the new Office of Mental Health was the inadequate support of the long-term mentally ill discharged from the institutions in the preceding ten years. The most significant accomplishment of my time in office began in 1978 with the initiation of the Community Support System (CSS) for the chronically mentally ill. This program, which each year received increasing support from the legislature, grew to $75 million and the enrollment of some 40,000 patients formerly treated in state institutions. Subsequent research proved that it was successful, and other states have now followed New York's lead. Even so, this program will need to be twice its size if New

York's growing problem of the mentally ill on the streets is to be ameliorated.

The CSS not only was responsive to the mentally ill discharged from state institutions, but also seemed to change the attitude of professionals concerning the care of this type of patient. Because it was a program provided through contracts, it brought in other providers previously uninterested in the care of the chronically mentally ill.

There were several other accomplishments by the Office of Mental Health during my tenure that I would like to mention. Over the five years, the Office of Mental Health became an agency that did what it said it would do. The ensuing credibility within the halls of government in Albany resulted in further support from the legislature and the control agencies within the executive. That increased credibility allowed us to enforce state policy, not only with the state institutions but with local government. For example, early on, the County of Oneida refused to include programs for the chronically mentally ill, as required in their plans. After several warnings, we withheld the matching state dollars to this county; this resulted in a court suit brought by the county. We eventually won that suit and the message went out across the state that we were very serious about our planning guidelines.

Another accomplishment involved improving the quality of care in state operations by reorganizing state facilities to include a Division of Quality Assurance in each. By the end of 1982, this resulted in the greatest number of fully accredited state hospitals in the history of New York State. Complementing this reorganization was the development of an agreement with the Joint Commission of Accreditation of Hospitals in Chicago, establishing a multi-year plan for complete compliance of the facilities' physical plant. The ensuing assessment procedure gave us the information necessary to discontinue several building programs and focus upon those physical structures that had long-term utility. The legislature, in turn, responded to this planning precision in 1982 by doubling our capital budget from the previous year.

A major gap in the provision of services for mentally disabled children was the absence of a supervised residential treatment program between the usual group setting within State Social Services and State Education and that provided by hospital care within the Office of Mental Health. We conceptualized the residential treatment facilities for children and provided the leadership with these other agencies over a two-year period. This resulted in the passage of legislation with funding establishing this new program.

One last endeavor that promised to assist the routinization of these changes was the development of an organized constituency.

Legislation passed in 1982 established the first Mental Health Review and Planning Council which went into effect in April of 1983. Differing from other councils, this body will share in the authority of the commissioner, by advising on all policies and regulations before they are signed into operation.

QUESTION: How does the existing Planning Council fit into the organization, and is this change just for Mental Health?

PREVOST: The new Mental Health Review and Planning Council will work within the overall goals of the now existing Mental Hygiene Planning Council and yet, will do so with more authority, in that it will be able to review all regulations, objectives, and specific plans. Furthermore, the new law requires that members from the old Planning Council form part of the new Review Council and thus provide a bridge of communication between the two.

The second bridging structure was established in 1978, when the old Mental Hygiene Department was divided into several offices. This structure is called the Interoffice Coordinating Council, a group that continues to meet every few months, serving more as a basis for communication than mutual policy development. Apparently some felt that this last group should serve as a type of umbrella agency in Mental Hygiene. However, the interests of the separate offices and their constituencies are considerably different, and therefore the Interoffice Coordinating Council never became a Mental Hygiene Department in new clothing.

QUESTION: Would you list some of the agency's internal management achievements?

PREVOST: Up until 1978 the allocation of resources to the individual state facilities frequently occurred through the intercession of legislators "looking after their own." Since there was not an acceptable methodology for the allocation of funds, those staff in the field that caused the most noise got the most attention. It was as though the squeaky gate got most of the oil. I was quite familiar with this strategy, since, as director of the Hutchings Psychiatric Center in Syracuse, I had learned how to protect one's hospital and how to secure the most resources possible. Now in Albany my concern was for the entire system and the inequity of allocation among the state facilities. We therefore set about developing a method that would assess patient need and then allocate personal service funds against that patient work load. Since 80 percent of our budget is given to funding staff, this seemed a reasonable way to proceed. Futhermore, this methodology allowed us to establish staffing standards and report a profile for each facility to all those concerned. When we started in 1978, the variation between state facilities against this ideal standard was from a low of 65 percent to a high of 130 percent. By the end of 1982 this variation was reduced to 94 percent at the low end and 97 percent at the high end. While initially a concern of the legislature, this form of equity eventually won their support. They allowed us to hold onto staff resources, despite a declining patient census because of the natural death rate. This, then, caused an improvement in the overall staff-patient ratio throughout the state.

A second internal organizational change involved altering in a major way the composition of the senior staff in the Albany central office. When I came to Albany, it was apparent that while there was a good deal of talent, many had just become too set in their ways. We had a form of bad bureaucracy in which the job became an end-point in itself rather than a means to an end. These were not bad people; they were people in need of a change. Over the ensuing two years, the majority of the senior staff in the central office were replaced, and a very active recruitment program brought in talented people, many of them new to state government. While this took time, as these new people became familiar with the ways of Albany government, I believe it was a major force in restoring vitality to the Office of Mental Health.

This revitalization also allowed us to take a close look at the economics of our system with the realization that a new program, if it was to occur at all, must be underwritten by new dollars. While the legislature might be kind to us, greater efficiency on our part was needed. Over the last three years of my tenure, this improved management resulted in doubling our revenues to $400 million. This in itself allowed program expansion, and permitted us to say publicly that the program expansion we requested was, in fact, paid for by money generated by our existing programs and was not a new cost to the public.

QUESTION: Was this money from the federal government?

PREVOST: Yes, this was federal money aggressively sought by us, not only in its collection, but in making sure that every possible dollar allowed us by law was, in fact, included in our rates. Initially, it seemed as though there couldn't be much more federal money forthcoming, because of the exclusion from Medicaid of in-patients between the ages of 21 and 64, residing in state institutions. But we were still able to find an additional $200 million between 1979 and 1982.

One further internal management change that occurred was in response to the legislature's request for long-range planning. Beginning in 1978 and every year thereafter, we published a five-year plan which not only informed our constituencies in the legislature, but allowed us to do more than just crisis management. Even if ten percent of your time is spent in long-range planning, it allows you to make all those other daily decisions in a way which fortifies the overall direction and vision of the agency. This also allowed us to develop a reinvestment policy, which meant that we could take existing resources within the facilities and redirect them to community program development.

QUESTION: Is it your experience that the priorities of the agency are shaped in some directions and not in others by the availability of federal funds?

PREVOST: The pacing and timing of the agency's priorities were certainly affected by federal funding. This does not mean, however, that directions not funded by federal dollars were excluded. For example, a major theme of the Community Support System was the establishment of partial hospitalization, usually poorly funded in this country. In fact, the number of treatment episodes provided through this service modality for the past ten years has remained at only three percent of all service provision. Through our CSS state funded program, however, New York increased its provision of partial hospitalization for the mentally ill by 56 percent in the past five years. One thing became clear. Without state subsidy there was no increase in partial hospitalization. In response to your question, then, I would have to say, that while we attempted to secure all federal dollars, it was a matter of fitting those dollars into the direction you had already established, and not merely being reactive to federal funding. Of course, we spent considerable time in Washington attempting to affect the development of regulations which, as much as the legislation itself, determined how dollars would flow. In fact, we established a full-time staff that did nothing else but work with Congress.

This entire matter of economics and program was a lesson well learned through my tenure. While policy must be based on the clinical technology available, this by itself is insufficient to drive the system changes needed for the mentally ill. One soon finds out that unless this clinical know-how is mated very closely with sound management, little will occur. I recall, when I first arrived, observing well-trained clinicians failing in their presentations before legislative fiscal committees and the State Division of the Budget, simply because they couldn't describe their clinical program endeavors in the economic language required by these control groups. Soon thereafter, I brought into the central office experienced managers and administrators and coupled them with the program people, in order to weave together these two threads into a single fabric. As I look back at the internal operations of the Office of Mental Health over my five years in office, I would have to say that it was managerial attitude closely combined with clinical program understanding that, more than anything else, gave us a strong agency.

QUESTION: What kind of things did you do to get more out of

your personnel? What did you inherit in terms of quality?

PREVOST: While I referred to this before as a problem of bad bureaucracy, there was another issue back in 1978. With everyone knowing that the old Department of Mental Hygiene was to be divided up into separate disability-oriented groups, others such as Tom Coughlin, who was to become the new commissioner of Mental Retardation and Developmental Disabilities, had already recruited the very best staff from the old department.

QUESTION: When you use the term 'staff,' do you mean just professional?

PREVOST: I have been using the term in that way, but do not wish to exclude paraprofessionals. There are 39,000 employees in the Office of Mental Health, which should give you some idea just how expensive it is to maintain people within institutions. This is especially true when one realizes that 20 percent of the patients now in our state hospitals would not need to be at that level of care if alternative programs and housing existed in the community.

I found that the most important factors for all personnel were good supervision and relevant and attainable incentives. Early in my professional career I found that both of these ingredients were necessary in working with paraprofessionals, just as they are with professionals. Training programs are absolutely necessary, since, if handled appropriately, they establish within the work force not only expertise in the preferred technology, but a sense of inquiry, discovery, and a desire for change. Performance evaluations, when handled appropriately and tied to salary increments are also a major incentive.

QUESTION: Were there also problems with personnel relating to the hiring of minorities?

PREVOST: Even though we initiated the agency's first affirmative action program that was acceptable to the State Human Rights Agency and the maintenance of a work force that today is made up of 32 percent minorities, problems still exist. For example, the lower grade positions are weighted with minorities much more than anyone could possibly justify. Attempts to change this, however, ran into issues of competitive salaries. Highly trained minority professionals could frequently find positions that would pay at least twice as much as those offered by the state.

QUESTION: Did these minority problems cause conflicts within your institutions?

PREVOST: While we were never pleased with the state of affairs, I do not recall any major problems within the institutions because of minority imbalances. Our policy was that a particular institution should not just mirror the ethnic composition of its environment, but that staffing should reflect the ethnic composition of the patients treated in that hospital. We were pretty successful with that policy. In fact, those hospitals where the minority is the majority in patient census are also hospitals in which the staff is composed of a minority which is the majority. When complaints did occur, it was always difficult to tell whether or not this was an issue of race or just poor management. What was needed for minority staff was the same that was needed for everyone else, i.e., career ladders, more training, and opportunities. That was why the state's attempt at performance evaluations with salary increments tied to these evaluations was so important, and why it was such a tragedy that this incentive was poorly implemented.

QUESTION: Would you please talk further about that interesting experiment, the performance evaluation effort?

PREVOST: There seemed to be two problems with the way New York implemented performance evaluation. One was that the unions understood that the money would be freely driven by the work force's performance. On the other hand, the State Division of the Budget, as I understand it, realized that there had to be a cap on the amount of money available for reward. The employees, at least in my agency, took their lead from the unions and were therefore extremely disappointed when evaluations had to be repeated with a ratcheting down of the number of positive evaluations. That this happened points out another problem with the way we implemented the new evaluation system. We just didn't take the time in this state to train the supervisors how to do a good job at rating their personnel.

QUESTION: We have found that when insufficient groundwork was provided, the outcome is predictable.

PREVOST: I thought it was a great managerial tool and it's a shame that we did not do better by it.

QUESTION: While we have been spending a good deal of time on management questions in relation to the legislature, may we now discuss your relationship with the executive office, particularly the unique relationship in Governor Carey's administration with an outside consultant. Did you have dealings with that?

PREVOST: Dr. Kevin Cahill was the one who hired me, in conjunction with Governor Carey.[1]

QUESTION: Were the policies that you talked about cleared with the governor, Dr. Cahill, or Bob Morgado?[2]

PREVOST: For the initial three years of my tenure, I cleared questions of policy with Dr. Cahill and after that with Bob Morgado. With Dr. Cahill, it was a matter of discussing ideas either on the phone, while riding in a car, or during weekly meetings in the capital. He would ask a few questions and then say: "Well, why don't you go ahead and let me know if you need any additional help."

Later, with Bob Morgado, it was a matter of making more formal presentations. These two individuals had different styles. Kevin had an amazing intuitive sense and Bob was more focused on accepted managerial practices. In both situations, I felt that they allowed a special friendly relationship, which gave me a sense of comfort. I felt I could call either one if needed. When Kevin left, there was a certain tension, because of the tension that existed between the two of them when Kevin was in government. Initially, I would have preferred a more direct relationship with the governor. After a while, however, I realized that with the direct access both had to the governor, I could, in a very real sense, see them as surrogates for the governor. Since both had many responsibilities, one had to be selective in the source of problems that would be brought to their attention. Frequent checking about policy attitudes and values was sufficient. Filling in the spaces on actual directions was a chore my senior staff and I gladly accepted. If I ran into obstructions, I always knew that I could contact either of these two gentlemen and obtain their support.

QUESTION: Would money follow these policy decisions?

PREVOST: Usually, if one ran into trouble you could count on either of them to intervene. One of the problems, however, of Dr. Cahill was the lack of structure in Albany supportive of his decisions.

QUESTION: You mean there was no way for him to follow up?

PREVOST: Every major policy direction established by Dr. Cahill in health matters would, of course, have multiple ripple effects upon other projects, requiring a well-connected Albany staff for appropriate management. At times this did not appear to be available, that is, the cross-agency relationships and, especially relationships with the Division of the Budget. Therefore, following through was difficult at times. This was not the case when Bob Morgado added health affairs to his responsibilities, since he already commanded an apparatus, especially with the control agencies, to insure implementation. One should realize, however, that the Office of Mental Health was able to accomplish its objectives under both Cahill and Morgado, albeit in different ways.

QUESTION: Did you ever deal with the governor?

PREVOST: Now and then at sub-cabinet meetings and at least monthly at governmental social affairs, especially at the Executive Mansion. There seemed to be a group of commissioners, at least when I was in office, invited more often than others to attend events at the mansion. This group included Tom Coughlin, Jim Introne, David Axelrod, Barbara Blum, Bill Hennessey, Bob Flacke, and me. This cadre, in conjunction with several of the governor's program associates, would frequently carry on business at these affairs.[3]

204

QUESTION: Did the governor, like Rockefeller, pay little attention to a department for a long period of time, and then take a very intense interest for a brief period of time?

PREVOST: In one way this was true, since I never knew just when I would see him. It was the sense that if he did not engage you, most likely things were going along all right. When Governor Carey did get involved directly, it was always a surprise to me that he was so well informed and capable of rapidly grasping the issues, clarifying the problems, and directing a solution. I also came to realize that his intermittent involvement with the Office of Mental Health did not mean that he was unaware of our problems. With Cahill and later with Morgado, he was regularly briefed. Because of his amazing memory, he could pull out details in a later conversation, thus providing a current problem with prior information.

QUESTION: Which of these two scenarios would Governor Carey be most comfortable with, the human services or the managerial or both?

PREVOST: I don't know. He certainly had an interest in human services and seemed comfortable using managerial techniques. My experience with Governor Carey and his second floor staff portrayed for me a very crisis-oriented type of leadership. All too often, it seemed as though the second floor staff was more oriented to instantaneous reactions to whatever appeared in *The New York Times*.[4] I believe that all of us, especially in conjunction with the governor's aides, could have formalized communication and therefore, problem-solving in a way that was not so reactive.

QUESTION: Are you saying that you would have liked some kind of regular forum?

PREVOST: Yes, along the lines of a formal structure that would in fact establish priorities. It should have been a disciplined process that was comprehensive in nature and lent itself to the development of a perspective across all agencies of the government. A greater sense of long-range planning would, I believe, have provided all of us a better sense of just how to handle the crises that are inevitable.

QUESTION: Could you describe in a little more detail just how meetings occurred? Who would take the initiative, the commissioner or the governor's office?

PREVOST: Usually, there would be a telephone call from a second floor program associate five minutes after they heard of a crisis, and they would demand a full response before lunch. Usually, this crisis would be an outgrowth of a larger problem that a commissioner had attempted to bring to the second floor's attention unsuccessfully.

A good example was the issue of the homeless in New York City. It was a predictable issue and part of the larger problem of housing and caring for marginally competent people. For several months I had been requesting in the strongest words the need for the second floor to bring together a number of state agencies to deal with this issue. It seemed to me that at least my contacts on the second floor understood the issue too narrowly. For them, it was just a matter of poor discharge policy from state institutions, and therefore my issue alone to handle. There was much evidence to the contrary. Studies indicated that only 20 percent of the homeless had any previous psychiatric hospitalization. In addition, it was the city's policy, through their J-51 tax abatement program, to decrease the number of single-room occupancy beds on the upper west side, moving them to luxury apartments. The city made no arrangements for the displaced poorer residents, preferring to describe the problem as just poor Mental Hygiene policy. Unfortunately, it wasn't until the horror stories began in the news media, making this issue a crisis, that effective work was coordinated by the second floor.

QUESTION: We haven't talked much about relationships with other agencies, although we did talk about the relationship to the Division of the Budget. Are there changes that could be made that could facilitate the work that you were doing and help with some of the problems which you faced?

PREVOST: While I understand the focus on accountability now in government and the energy-shortage-driven restraints on the economy, it did seem to me that the control agencies, especially the Division of the Budget, went well beyond any reasonable interface with a program agency and attempted to actually operate the agency. This was more a problem of middle management in the Division of Budget (DOB)—long-time bureaucrats who could not see the difference between fiscal and program management. Clarifying that interface would have been an assistance to us.

QUESTION: Could you have done more if you had greater flexibility with funds?

PREVOST: Oh, I certainly think so. However, that was not forthcoming. In fact, it got to be such a poor situation that we arranged to sign memoranda of understanding with the DOB as a way to confine them and clarify the leeway we needed in order to get the job done. We had to deal with them as though they were part of another government—an actual alien linkage—which no one controlled. Quite possibly, if we had a type of human service umbrella agency or a forum that would provide counterpoint, not DOB invasion, then more progress may have occurred. What I'm really talking about here is not a matter of personalities, but assuring a balance between roles within the creative tensions of government. Such balance allows program interest sufficient valence with a government that, at times, merely seems interested in a fiscal product.

QUESTION: How much of this experience do you think was a product of Willowbrook, which occurred before you came to Albany?[5] There was such complete concentration for a time on that event that everything in that department was judged against it.

PREVOST: I think you're probably right.

QUESTION: You don't know how well off you were. There was a time when a budget examiner would actually determine the number of gallons of paint to be allowed in an institution. I agree with your analysis of the problem you faced, but I also want you to know that the Budget traditionally assigned very detailed people to Mental Health.

PREVOST: While that history may be so, it does not change my views or my feelings about it. You should know that it was not my intention to always win. I just wanted a fair hearing. Nor am I trying to do away with the necessary tension that exists between fiscal controls and program. Program agencies should be able to justify their requests and to be accountable and to be efficient. I'm attempting to describe organizational changes that would allow operations in my former agency to reflect the best clinical judgment possible within economic constraints.

QUESTION: Are you saying that, because there was a vacuum in planning at the highest levels of the government, the direction of government was in essence determined by middle management in the Division of the Budget?

PREVOST: What I am saying is that, while planning was occurring within an agency, this planning was not sufficiently tied to other human service agencies so that priorities could be determined for the entire administration. In the absence of this, staff of the Division of the Budget provided the coordination and therefore made decisions in ways that inappropriately weighed fiscal concerns only.

QUESTION: Please comment on your relationship with the news media.

PREVOST: I guess it would be an understatement to say that the power of the news media is tremendous. No one argues with their responsibility to keep the public informed. I did think, however, that too often they focused on the cult of personality rather than the public policy issues at hand. For example, Governor Carey's opinions, philosophy, and type of leadership did very well for New York State. In the last couple of years of his tenure, however, the media seemed to focus more upon his personality than the issues he was attempting to resolve.

Another problem with the media was their focus upon individual events, such as a specific mental patient tragedy, while ignoring the overall program policy issue, which may have been the basis for the isolated event. This lack of balanced reporting had its effect upon members of the legislature. At times it seemed that some legislators would respond to a problem only from what they read in the news media, rather than taking the time to understand the larger systems issue. This could be a major problem, since it also seems to me that the legislature is growing in power in New York State. It is therefore important that their interest focus on overall goals and objectives and then the monitoring of an agency as they hold it accountable, rather than getting involved in an isolated event and attempting to pass legislation detailing just how the agency should deal with such an event. In other words, for example, they should require a thoughtful policy on discharge of patients, but not involve themselves in just how to perform a discharge assessment.

QUESTION: How do you deal with the problem of acceptance of the mentally ill in the community? One feeling is that the community is becoming increasingly more tolerant and accepting of the mentally ill. What is your perspective?

PREVOST: I think that the stigma of mental illness continues and, in fact, may have been increased by the mistakes of early deinstitutionalization. As the economy becomes worse, I also expect that tolerance for one's brother may decrease. Even with this though, I think we have had some success through our ten-fold increase in the number of community residence beds and the expansion of the Community Support System. We have learned how to work closely with neighborhoods regarding their fears and prejudices. Even so, one must realize that we are asking society to think differently about the mentally ill, a group of people that have been segregated into large institutions for the past century and now, because of advances in technology, are being treated in the community.

QUESTION: What are some of the unsolvable problems you've left your successors?

PREVOST: Oh, a good number. For example, I was never able to close a state hospital. We were not able to forge out new fiscal arrangements with local government, nor were we able to develop the kind of working relationship with New York City that I thought possible.

QUESTION: If it were 1978, when you were beginning your tenure as commissioner, what things might you have done differently if any?

PREVOST: While the Office of Mental Health required sound management early on, I think I would have focused more upon the leadership needs of the system. In the last several years of my tenure, this was my major concern. In order to get the job done, this meant the development of credibility across all levels of government, among the constituencies, and among mental health professionals. More could have been done at the boundaries with other human service agencies in New York. In other words, I would have attempted earlier in my administration to work with those crucial external linkages necessary for the support of the Office of Mental Health.

FOOTNOTES

[1]Dr. Kevin Cahill, Special Assistant to Governor Carey (1975-1980).
[2]Robert Morgado, Secretary to the Goveror (1977-1982).
[3]Thomas Coughlin, New York State Commissioner for Correctional Services; James Introne, Assistant Secretary to the governor (1975-1978), Deputy Budget Director (1978), and Commissioner, Office of Mental Retardation and Developmental Disabilities (1979-1982); David Axelrod, New York State Commissioner of Health; Barbara Blum, New York State Commissioner of Social Services; William Hennessy, New York State Commissioner of Transportation; Robert Flacke, New York State Commissioner of Environmental Conservation.
[4]"second floor" refers to the floor of the Capitol on which the governor and his staff have offices.
[5]Willowbrook, located on Staten Island in New York City, is a major state facility serving the mentally retarded. A highly publicized series of revelations in the media about shocking conditions at the institution led to the signing, early in the Carey years, of a consent decree that stipulated improvement of services for the retarded in state facilities, under the supervision of the federal courts.

Muriel Siebert was superintendent of banks from 1977 to 1982. Prior to entering state service, Ms. Siebert had spent 22 years on Wall Street. She became the first woman member of the New York Stock Exchange in 1967.

Muriel Siebert
Superintendent of Banks

SIEBERT: Our chief challenge was in confronting the problems that existed in the banking industry. Since the 1930's we had
not had problems of the magnitude present when I entered office. I
was in office a few months when the problem with the Municipal
Credit Union (MCU) came up. This was the credit union of the
employees of the City of New York and of the state employees working in the city. That was the first time that we took possession of an
institution to rehabilitate it, rather than liquidate it. Liquidation
would have been out of the question because it was larger than the
National Credit Union Association (NCUA) Insurance Fund. The
fund, I believe, was $90 million or $95 million and the MCU, when
we took possession, was $130 million. If we had turned it over to
the government, it would have been chaotic.

The MCU had not had an election in seven or eight years (the
Department of Banking is still in the courts with it). There has been
testimony that they actually used to put guns on the table. That was
the first major issue I faced. We never had anything like that before.

Then, one day, it was on the front page of *The Daily News* that the
MCU was in disarray. A run started and I sent in examiners. They
handed out letters from me to depositors saying their money was
safe. It didn't matter. People stood in line around the block. We
waited.

We waited until the MCU used up all of its liquidity. We even had a
drawer of requests that we could not honor. We waited until that
final minute, and then we took possession. I could then say at the
press conference that they had met all their withdrawals out of their
own liquidity, to calm people down. We knew by that time that we
were legally proper; we could not be overturned for taking possession. So, that was the first big problem we overcame. Examiners had
never been geared to rehabilitate an institution.

I think I was lucky to have had the challenges that I had; I saw
them as exciting. In the Iranian situation I was lucky too; I claim I
had a lucky little angel on my shoulder.

One election day I was home watching the morning news and I
saw the Iranians take the hostages. They gave election day off to the
state employees, probably to encourage them to vote. I called the
deputy superintendent in charge of examiners. It was the first time I

ever called him at home. I said, "Get examiners into the four Iranian agencies tomorrow morning." We were there one week before the assets froze, watching every telex in and every telex out.[1]

When the freeze came we had ten percent of our New York examining staff in those four places. We set up the channels for fresh money that came in from London. We could never really get up and publicly say that the Iranian government was a good citizen; otherwise, we probably would have been picketed. However, it did send money into the U.S. We set up a channel through which fresh money came in every day from London to pay Iranian students, to pay Iranians in this country who had medical bills, and to pay U.S. corporations that had shipped goods. The Treasury Department gave a special license. They paid U.S. corporations that had shipped goods before the freeze. They could have said, "Take this against the assets that are frozen," but they didn't.

They used to send the money into Bank Melli, the Iranian bank in London. We then sent it upstate. We started out using the Manufacturers Hanover Bank upstate, which nobody would think of attaching, and from there we brought it down to New York.

After a while people realized what we were doing. One of the Iranian banks, Saderat, I think it was, did not trust the United States banks. They sent money into Canada. They would not bring any fresh money into the U.S. That was something that had never been done before. Initially, the feds were not involved as closely as we were. They later oversaw the operation.

I think the savings bank problem was a unique problem. The Federal Reserve Board (FRB), but primarily Chairman Isaac of the Federal Depositors' Insurance Corporation (FDIC) wanted to put "discipline in the system." This would have meant that we would have had a closed bank with lines of depositors seeking their money. We opposed them and won. I think the meeting I had at the White House helped. It was arranged through Bill Casey, whom I knew through my Wall Street days, when he was head of the Securities and Exchange Commission (SEC).

Morgan Guaranty held a subordinated debt of about $30 million in the Greenwich Savings Bank. Morgan Guaranty had invested in three of the big banks. The FDIC said they would not recast the subordinated debt. The debt would then become worthless. Morgan then said they were going to have to sue. We were afraid that would become a closed bank with lawsuits—it would have been the first savings bank to go down. We won, and it showed the department that we were at least as good as the feds.

The deputies were in the room when Bill Isaac of FDIC said, "We're not going to pay." Roger Mealey, assistant treasurer to Don

Regan, said in the White House that we shouldn't pay the depositors with over $100,000 in the bank. I knew that this was something that would affect New York as a center of world finance. If I did anything which would influence the department in the future, it was in forcing the department to realize that, although the feds were bigger than we were and had more staff and money, they were not necessarily better. We won in a couple of cases.

Politically, I was a Republican appointed by a Democratic governor. However, people didn't look at me as a Republican, nor did they look at me as a Democrat. I think they looked at me as a professional person. This had not been the case with all superintendents. I had a deputy superintendent who told me that he used to keep track, for the superintendent, of how much banks were contributing to various campaigns. That never went on while I was there. I took pride in the fact that I was running the department on a non-political basis. I was trying to do the best job that I could do. That would be what I would consider to be my contribution.

I think the Marine Midland controversy was a case in point.[2] I did not feel that the Hong Kong-Shanghai Bank should own the bank that was either number one or number two in every upstate area. That was not a political decision vis-a-vis Republican versus Democrat, although it was regarded by some people as such. The decision was based on the fact that we could not get the same information from that bank as we were getting from banks that were chartered for 150 years in the state. Also, I did not know whether they would continue to serve upstate New York.

It was a fact that there was no central bank in Hong Kong (which is now being borne out with the problems in Hong Kong). The Hong Kong Bank is the de facto central bank of Hong Kong; they have been providing the liquidity for the other depository institutions.

Yet, it was taken by people as a political decision. I was told, in so many words, that I was doing it because I was a Republican. They said I was embarrassing the governor because I was a Republican. I was asked, "Why are you worried about those apple growers upstate?" My decision was not based on that. I would say that was the only time the fact that I was a Republican was brought home.

I saw politics when it was rumored or announced that I was in the group that was going to be fired. At that point, I know that Jack Haggarty, counsel to the Senate Majority, went in to see the governor's counsel and said, "If you fire her, then you are not going to get anyone else confirmed." I also know Democrats, Lillian Roberts and Victor Gottbaum, for example, who called the governor's office and told them I had saved their credit union.[3] At that point I was probably too emotionally involved. No one likes to hear on the radio every 15 minutes, that you are going to be fired. I had a three o'clock appointment with Bob Morgado on the Hong Kong deal.[4] I received a call from someone at *The New York Times* at two thirty who said that I was going to be fired at three. When I left the meeting, there was a reporter from another paper in the hall who asked me if I still had a job, so I turned around and went back to Bob and said, "I think you better talk to that guy." That was the only time there were partisan politics. People were rallying around me.

QUESTION: One of the points you emphasized, when you first started talking, was the extent to which your own agency was a non-political institution. What about your dealings with legislative leaders? Doesn't that require a different sort of involvement in politics?

SIEBERT: If I had had the experience or knowledge, I wouldn't have stepped on people's toes or made some of the mistakes I made initially. That would have held me in better stead. I would have known who Fred Ohrenstein was. The words "Minority Leader" didn't mean anything to me. If I had known the system, I might have had better results the first time around on the usury rate bill. In any case, it would have made it a lot easier.

At the end of my tenure, when I wanted something, I would just sit down with Warren Anderson and Stanley Fink, and the department would get what it wanted. I don't mean get what we wanted carte blanche, but we received support. One time, when I needed the emergency financing, Stanley Fink said, "My leadership trusts you, Mickey. You've got to come up." I was in his conference room with about 40 legislators. They went out and they passed the bill.[5]

It would have made my life a lot easier at the outset if somebody had given me a two-day course explaining who was who and why. You have to realize, I was a totally non-political person and I knew nothing about the legislature and its protocol. Somebody could have said; "If you go up and call on Senator Anderson, you should also go and call on Stanley Steingut," or "If you talk to Jay Rolison, you should also talk to George Cincotta."[6]

I explained this to the new superintendent when I had lunch with him. I advised him not to make the same mistakes I made just because no one took me aside. If there is one thing that would have made my life a lot easier, it's that someone would have taken me aside. Then, I would not have made some of the mistakes I made. I think that it took me a couple of years to get to know these people.

QUESTION: Did the new superintendent ask you, or did you volunteer to talk with him?

SIEBERT: We had some mutual friends and he had asked me. I was supposed to have lunch with him, but he canceled. I went up to the swearing in.

One of the joys of getting people into office who have been successful in business is that you don't go out with your own little petty jealousies and hope the next person falls flat on his or her face to make you look good. I think that is important.

QUESTION: Did you have a public hearing before you were confirmed?

SIEBERT: I had a public hearing before I was confirmed. It was before Jay Rolison's Banking Committee. I had had a fight with a newspaper reporter years before; he had written a nasty story, and Jay had it.

The reporter was Dan Dorfman and he used to write the "Abreast of the Market" column in the *Wall Street Journal*. At the time, my Wall Street firm did research on institutional selling, and my analyst Morton Sloan, who used to follow the electronics stocks, had given Dorfman some confidential information on one company's production figures. It was supposed to be confidential, but the next day it was published in the *Wall Street Journal*. I called Dorfman up and really blasted him, since the company was calling us and threatened to sue. Dan is known for having a long memory. He wrote a nasty story in the *New York Magazine* saying I did not have the character or quality to be commissioner. I had to explain all of this to Senator Rolison publicly.

QUESTION: How much help do you feel the fact that you had come from the financial community, started your own firm, and had experience with the Stock Exchange, provided? You didn't come out of the traditional mold.

SIEBERT: Since I had started as an analyst in research, I could study something and make a decision. Importantly, when there was a decision to be made, I didn't necessarily take the easy way. In the savings bank crisis, the governor said, "Well, the feds have a $20 billion problem, Mickey. We don't have the money." I just wasn't going to give up that easily.

That's when the governor and I started to be friends again. Morgan Guaranty called him out of a meeting and said, "You're going to hear that Mickey is in Washington fighting, but she is fighting for us and she is fighting for the safety of the banking system." I saw him at a luncheon and he said, "Is this true?" I said, "Yes, sir." And we became friendly again.

I think it was the fact that I had run something. Marty Mertz, who was the head banking partner at Peat Marwick, said, "You know, Mickey, you run the department like it's your own company." I ran it the way I had run my business. These places have to be run like that, otherwise the red tape and bureaucracy is overwhelming. It is a culture shock when you come from the real world.

QUESTION: Of course, you have a long experience in business, and you have referred to that during the entire conversation. Were there any unique and positive experiences that you had from government that you might not have had from business?

SIEBERT: If I were to use them, the contacts would be invaluable. I walked out of the office of the commissioner of Banking knowing Walter Wriston on a first name basis, whereas before, I was just the woman who made the Stock Exchange "coed." [7] Since I was able to switch from Wall Street and be successful in government, it gave me a broader acceptability. It showed that at least I was not just in a little niche downtown. I now know the way the country works, for better or for worse. My experience in office gave me a broadening and a working knowledge of the political process. Maybe I will use that in my own industry, maybe I won't.

I knew Bill Casey because he was SEC commissioner. During his tenure, they put in negotiated rates. We had a purely research firm geared to doing business with institutions for which they gave us the orders. If I recommended Emery Air Freight to them, and they bought 200,000 shares, then I would get the order. When they put in the negotiated rates, but did not make floor brokerage and clearance negotiable, it meant that the non-clearing, small research firms were going to become extinct. So, I went down to see the chairman of the SEC with all my records of those with whom we did business.

I now know how that process works from the other side, which I think is important. If they ever do anything that's really going to take a piece out of my business, it's sure I'll go down there and express my views. I now know how the thinking process works.

I also have a very strong feeling that successful business people have an obligation to be in government. It is not a one-way street; you cannot just be a taker in this world. My mother raised me, saying that if you are lucky or successful, then you owe; you have an obligation. There are a lot of people who, if given the opportunity, will dig in and do their best. I think a lot of people, at least a lot of people on Wall Street, feel strongly about this. Wall Street has, historically, produced people who go into government for a while, because they can go in and come back.

QUESTION: If we could step back from your personal experience, do you have a more or less favorable view of government than you did before you started in government?

SIEBERT: I have a more favorable view of government now. The people that are on top work like dogs. I think the public does not understand how hard the commissioners and the top people from various agencies work. That is very favorable.

When I was appointed, one of my friends said, "That's an honorary position, isn't it? How many days a week do you go to the office?" That person didn't understand, as I now understand, that the people with responsibility in government are hardworking.

Conversely, I now have disdain for some of the political figures who, the minute they are in office, only care about getting themselves re-elected. I have had experience with some of them; their word is no good. They should not let their own personal situation get in the way of doing what's right. Some of that game-playing leaves a lot to be desired. I think that anyone who is in the political or governmental process has to stand up. Otherwise, you shouldn't go into the process. There is an obligation to the public.

I can see a lot of things that are wrong in the country. New York, for example, should have more incentives to develop business. The structural unemployment that exists has taken 20 years to build; it didn't happen overnight. It happened the first time the Japanese cars hit our shores, and we've been doing nothing. It is not purely labor at fault, it is equally the fault of management and the lack of leadership coming out of Washington. So, I think that people who have been in Washington during this entire period should not be returned to office. If they have not recognized the problem and not tried in their own way to do something, then they should not be returned.

There are going to be a lot of people who are never going to work again in their careers. Observe Buffalo, New York and Cleveland, Ohio, my hometown. Those steel factories aren't going to produce anymore. Those auto factories won't be producing. We have major problems, and it is incumbent on us to face them. That is not being idealistic. Frankly, I think it is being hard-nosed. I intend to start giving speeches on the subject of structural unemployment.

QUESTION: When you entered office, did you find the internal management of the department in need of improvement? If you restructured things in any way, what things remain to be done on the management side?

SIEBERT: The bulk of the department's function is the examination process. We put in some innovations. Some of them we were forced to put in, and some of them are good. We used to examine banks every year, as did the federal bank authorities. We now examine alternately with the feds. They examine one year, we examine the next year. We did the same thing with the FDIC, except in troubled institutions. We found a way to make the same number of people go farther. We had to. In the regulated institutions, the assets went up by probably $300 billion to $500 billion when I was there.

We chartered 50 new foreign banks, so that there were 50 new institutions that had to be examined. Yet, our staff did not go up. We had to make it happen anyway. Every other year makes sense, but we were still having a hard time meeting our schedule. We always had a large number of examinations starting in December. Technically, we began them according to what was demanded of us. However, they wouldn't be finished until early the next year. We were always playing catch-up. Part of the reason for that was the fact that, at one point, we had examiners in the credit union, in the Iranian banks, and in something else simultaneously. You do that when you're reacting to emergencies; the site of an emergency is where the examiner should be used.

QUESTION: There is a theme that seems to run through a number of your answers—that in many areas you felt a mismatch between your responsibilities and your resources. Would you elaborate upon the greatest and least problem areas? Where did the biggest mismatch exist?

SIEBERT: The examination process was being done all right. We were as good as the feds, maybe a little better. When it came to the problems in the thrift industry, I shifted around the deputies and brought the best one, Alan Cohen, into the thrifts.[8] I then went to see Bob Morgado.

I would just move people around. If I had problems and I needed specific talent there, that's where I would move people. When we needed some of the top people at Bank Melli for awhile, we just put them there. Some of the people that we had to bring down from upstate threatened to sue us. They didn't want to work downstate. We had to pay per diem, but you just do what you have to do in an emergency. At least, that's my attitude.

New York is the equivalent of a small U.S.A. When you get upstate, they are totally different people. I was born in Cleveland, Ohio, so I understand these people and realize the way they think. Cleveland is a sister city of Buffalo.

When I was campaigning, it was them against us, upstate against downstate. This antagonism is a built-in problem which, unless the person who is elected makes a definite attempt to get key people from around the state, will only be intensified. It is something that any governor who comes in must work at, whether it is an upstate governor or a downstate governor. There was some resentment. If it was through any fault of mine, it was because I did not spend enough time going around to the various cities upstate. That is something that the commissioner should do. We had upstate offices, but I was rarely up there.

QUESTION: Did you find problems between upstate and downstate banks?

218

SIEBERT: I didn't have problems per se between the upstate and the downstate banks because our New York City banks had the right to branch. However, none of the city banks did particularly well upstate. Because of that, a lot of the banks in the city would have bought the Marine Midland bank.

We had good examiners around the state. In the Banking Department, we protect the consumer. However, the department could do more around the state in letting people know that there is a Banking Department that regulates their banks. We did it for the first time when the billboard people gave us free billboards around the State for the "Shopping for Credit" campaign after we increased the usury rate. I made a decided effort there. We put out three or four million brochures around the state.

QUESTION: Are there any things that were left undone?

SIEBERT: You always have a continuing agenda. We have one lawsuit that is still going on. It was us against the Greater New York Bank. We questioned their accounting and that is still there. Everybody knows that loans to Less Developed Countries (LDC's) are vulnerable.

If Congress had not passed that law late in December, there would have been major problems in additional savings banks. However, interest rates have also turned. We had one package which we presented to the FDIC which would have merged together about six or seven of those banks that were going to go under. If we had received $500 million worth of paper from the FDIC and not a penny in real money, the cash flow would have worked itself out in five years, and we would have closed half the offices.

We had presented a package where Bowery would have been the lead bank. Otherwise, there would have been another dozen banks going in the next year. I just felt the public wasn't going to take bank closure after bank closure. So, we put together a package after analyzing the problem, and we worked closely with the Bowery. We received resignations from all the Bowery people; it was not that we were out looking for their jobs. We presented the resignations to the FDIC but we did not have to use them. In an area that is as over-banked as New York, you don't need a savings bank on every corner. Some of that real estate is extremely valuable. I was sorry to leave that one. We had presented it, but I left, and now the head of the FDIC has given a speech saying that the FDIC even knows how to break up banks. If interest rates come down and stay down, the FDIC solution is good, because every bank will remain independent. Our approach would have cost the FDIC much less money.

We had the New York Bank for Savings broken up until both upstate and downstate banks complained. It ended up that they gave the whole thing to Buffalo. We put together teams in our office to do bidding for parts of the bank. We worked out how to divide them, since it was rumored that the New York Bank for Savings was going to go to a commercial bank. That would have meant a closed bank deal, with chances of having a bank with people standing in line for their money. I wasn't going to take that.

QUESTION: So, you changed your role from being a regulator to being a match-maker.

SIEBERT: Yes.

QUESTION: Can we go back to the savings banks for a moment? It has always been a mystery where you and the absorbing banks found the resources to take over those banks that were not in a liquid position.

SIEBERT: The FDIC temporarily provided the liquidity or the paper that was used as capital. The banks provide liquidity to the extent that depreciation allowed a flow of cash coming in. Here was an example of the cooperation that I got with the legislature. If they had not passed that emergency legislation that we had passed earlier for the savings banks, we never could have done the Greenwich Bank, because we couldn't have counted their paper as capital.

QUESTION: Was this Buffalo bank so phenomenally successful compared with others?

SIEBERT: No, but their bids were creative. Both of the Buffalo banks were stronger than New York (Erie opted for a federal charter). New York City depositors are more sophisticated. They took their money out of the five percent accounts first.

QUESTION: But the periodic reports on the savings banks in New York City, for example, left very little basis for optimism.

SIEBERT: Now, some New York City banks are in the black. Look, we created their problems. The legislature and the regulators did it to them. That's why I fought so hard for them. We did it to them. We had a seven to eight percent usury ceiling for years. We didn't allow them to do anything else. We forced them to loan at those low rates. I worked so hard, because I realized it was nothing that they had done; it was what we had done to them.

One of the things I did which I can take pride in, was to get a deputy in charge of the foreign banks. They used to be tucked under the commercial banks. The foreign banks said that they never used to feel welcome coming into the department, even though they were a major piece of business in the city. It is important to have a deputy who knows those institutions and their rules and regulations so they are not tucked in the same category as a Morgan Guaranty and a Manufacturers Hanover. They don't belong there.

The first year we got the deputy, but not one person for supporting staff. The next year we were able to move some people around.

These were frustrating things. We were chartering as many as two and three new banks a month. The department always had the policy that when banks opened, we would send the examiners so they got off on the right foot and obeyed our laws. In that respect, the examiners are good will ambassadors. It is a significant position because the foreign countries respect bank regulators much more than the American banks do. The chairmen of the largest world banks pay courtesy calls on our office out of respect. The ambassadors would also call on us.

This was because the foreign banks hold the banking examiners in high esteem. There, it is a lifetime career. When you go to the Bank of England, these people are revered and respected. Here, the ones that stay in government service are not the best. It is just a difference.

The foreign banks are also strangers in this land, which is another reason why they are more respectful. The division that deals with foreign banks is an important part of the department, because they have about $100 billion in assets. It was $80 billion and it probably is up to at least $100 billion, with the way the dollar has gone, and with the LDC countries. In any case, it is a big job market in the city, and that is important. For example, there are 26 Japanese banks that the department regulates. The department is like a good will ambassador.

QUESTION: Have you left any problems for your successor and, if so, are they resolvable? Is there anything in the field of interstate banking, international banking, or federal/state relationships on examination?

SIEBERT: The biggest problems are the LDC loans. Now, we have abdicated our authority there. The feds would never give us a vote on the LDC loans. In fact, when we started to request it, they took away our observer status. We had input in Congress. A lot of the International Banking Act was a result of testimony that we gave.

I think the competition between the federal bank regulators and the state bank regulators is disgraceful. When the federal comptroller was allowed to charter foreign banks, he said no reciprocity. We sued with other states and lost. We've had reciprocity in the banking law, and it made sense. Where our banks could do a whole business in a certain country, they can come to New York and do a full business. That makes sense. You don't give away what you can sell.

I went to China on vacation and spent time with the Bank of China. I wanted the Bank of China to become a state-chartered bank. I bartered with them. Just take one bank from New York in, it doesn't even have to be a state-chartered one, and we can say there is reciprocity. Instead, they said, "No reciprocity," and took out a federal charter.

All the Australian banks changed charters from state to federal, because that way they did not have to admit our banks. They could get full power in New York without giving our banks full power.

Reciprocity was successful in Spain. When the Spanish people came over and said they wanted to open up, not agencies, but branches, we said, "Look, just take one or two of our banks in; you don't have to take them all in." I can understand why a country like Spain doesn't want ten major banks going in. They initially took two of ours, Morgan Guaranty and Manufacturers Hanover, and we gave them all branches. In that respect, it works and it is the way it should be done.

Then the comptroller's office created a loophole, and we sued with other states. One of our problems was that the attorney general didn't have a capable staff. Louis Lefkowitz was easier to work with.[9] Whenever we had an institution to take over, we would call Louis and say, "Listen, I have to go out and hire outside counsel." The only time we needed outside counsel like that was when we were taking over an institution, or in something special. Louis would call every morning at eight o'clock and say, "What can I do to help you, Champ?"

Bob Abrams used to criticize us for using outside counsel.[10] He even mentioned it in his report. So, I gave him an opportunity to participate in the Argentine bank liquidation. The head of the Argentine Central Bank had been in our office one Wednesday and said, "Don't worry, the problems we're having with Bancambia International Regional (BIR) will be worked out." However, two days later, Ed Eustice, the deputy in charge of foreign banks, came in and said, "We have a problem; they're going to put BIR in liquidation tonight." In order to prevent that, I said, "Get examiners up there." He said, "They're out to lunch." I said, "Tell them to walk down from Bank Melli." So, all of our examiners at the Iranian Bank walked down three blocks to the Argentine bank.

We had to get outside counsel. We were turned down by four firms. I called Bob Abrams and said, "We've got to have papers tonight." He couldn't do it, but Simpson-Thatcher could, and did.

On things like that, we need flexibility. I think we have lost law cases that we should not have lost because of inflexibility. I think we might not have lost the case on reciprocity if we were better represented. We could not get a top grade lawyer. That is not the kind of a case the State should lose. You can't expect the attorney general to have people who are expert because these are specific laws. The department tells me that the guy who is handling the case that we have against one savings bank is really dedicated. He's doing a great job there. But you never know how lucky you will be. It depends on whom you draw. I think that is one weakness.

QUESTION: Is the multiplicity of federal bank examining agencies a serious problem?

SIEBERT: If it is a state chartered savings bank, the FDIC has a regulatory rule on it; if it is a federally chartered savings bank, it is under the auspices of Federal Home Loan. The FDIC and Federal Home Loan have different attitudes. If it is a state chartered commercial bank, you have the fed involvement, plus the FDIC which also gets involved in the act. So you always have an extra regulator, which some day Congress must do something about.

The other states depend on New York. New York carries the load for the states. Our largest bank is bigger than the banking system in most states, which is why they depend on New York.

QUESTION: The industry is changing and institutions are becoming more similar. If New York has the only truly professional competitive State Banking Commission, why have state banking regulations at all?

SIEBERT: In some states the superintendent must be a banker. There, the state banks do whatever they want to do. There are 14,000 banks and the bulk of them are state. These are little banks, but the states want it that way, and the banks want it that way, and they are very happy.

QUESTION: Would you regard this as a problem? If so, what is the solution for it?

SIEBERT: Some of the state banks change to federal charters; that's why we are losing the savings banks. They should also take away the regulatory powers of the fed. The fed has too many built-in conflicts to be a regulator. You cannot have the fed, which at times has literally bargained with countries to support the dollar, saying that you can't buy a bank. This should not be done. The fed is putting pressure on some of the banks, now, to increase their LDC loans. The fed is the lender of last resort, but should they have regulatory power too? There are built-in conflicts in that. I think the fed could very well be out of the examination business.

The two deposit insurance agencies could be merged. This has been talked about, and it will come up again. I sat in the room one day when the states almost went to Congress and asked them to repeal Title X, which created the Financial Examinations Council. They then agreed to try to work more closely with the states. It was at that point that we gave Allan Sullivan, who was my assistant, a leave of absence. He was down in Washington as the liaison between the Examination Council and the state for about a year and a half. I once sat in a meeting and looked around the room at the representatives from the five federal agencies, the governors from the fed, the people from the FDIC, Federal Home Loan, and the comptrollers office, and I realized that nobody there had ever met a payroll—a whole room full of people! Things should change a little bit down there.

QUESTION: When New York State was pressured to reindustrialize, industry's relationship with the banks was terribly important. What sort of relationships did you have with industry?

SIEBERT: From the way industry came to my defense when I was having problems, it was evident they respected the fact that I went out and fought for them on the usury rates.

The only problem where I really had pressure from anyone was with the Marine Midland. That was mammoth pressure; the people from the Hong Kong bank were really in there. One day, Morgado was on the phone and said, "Stop screwing around and approve the deal, period." I said to him, "Are you ordering me?" He said, "Yes." So I said, "Bob, you've got my job." That was the only time that I had pressures of that kind.

For the most part, they were my decisions to make. We had certain pressures on the usury bill, but I felt strongly about it. I knew that all the banks were calling the governor, they were calling Fink, and they were calling everyone else, but I knew that there would be no credit in the state if we didn't go ahead. So that was a case where I was on the same side as the pressure. I think the elected officials had more pressure on them than I had on me, because they had an election coming up. How do you tell people that you are going to raise their interest charges?

QUESTION: Did the elected officials pressure you?

SIEBERT: I can't say that I had pressure from any of the elected officials. I will say that it probably took me two years until I got to know these people.

QUESTION: Can you explain how the problem with Marine Midland was resolved?

SIEBERT: They switched charters. They took out a Federal charter. That's what Senator Proxmire calls "competition in laxity," and he's right.

I had four or five different indications that the Marine Midland tightened their lending criteria. When I was still with the state, one of Governor Carey's appointees on the Job Development Authority said that Marine had tightened. He said that you couldn't get loans out of them up there. Then Jay Rolison said to one of my depositors that in Poughkeepsie, the Marine had tightened their standards.

There were also two incidents when I was campaigning which indicated the Marine Bank had tightened. I lunched with five or six of the county chairmen up in Corning. The one from Chemung told me that Chemung County Trust had loaned the total amount which they could legally loan, and they needed more money. Marine said that they didn't have any more money. He said that he had to call Gene Mann, who is the number two man at Marine in Buffalo. I also heard the same in another county. I met a man up there who had a small loan company, and he said that his line had been eliminated by Marine.

I don't know if these are isolated cases, a general tightening, or if international loans are more profitable. The department doesn't get the figures anymore, so we will never know for sure. The bank was not a troubled bank at that time. They needed capital, but they were not troubled. They had recovered from their big losses.

QUESTION: I notice that in your comments about the Hong Kong Bank matter, you never mentioned that you had discussed it with the governor. Did you get direction from the governor?

SIEBERT: I got direction from Morgado. It took over a month to get in to see the governor.

QUESTION: What kind of relationship did you have with the governor?

SIEBERT: The Hong Kong deal was the first time that I ever talked to the governor on any banking matter.

QUESTION: He gave you and the agency very little direction?

SIEBERT: That is correct. If there was anything big coming up, however, we would call the governor's office because we felt they were entitled to avoid surprises. I called Morgado; sometimes he would call me back, sometimes he wouldn't. If it was important or if he didn't answer, I would talk to Del Guidice, or I would call the program associate.[11]

QUESTION: Did you sense that your department was neglected by the governor?

SIEBERT: I feel he did not realize the potential of the department to help in economic development.

QUESTION: Did you sense that it was a general pattern relating to all the departments?

SIEBERT: I think I was treated equally to all the other commissioners. I did go to Washington with the governor. Together, we saw the chairman of the fed concerning the international free zone. He viewed that as creative business-getting. We did get the free zone through. My department and I did a lot of work on that one. We occasionally passed banking laws with Morgado, but we were basically on our own.

QUESTION: Were there times when you felt you needed to see the governor, but couldn't, and didn't even get the indirect help you needed through Bob Morgado?

SIEBERT: Well, when I came in, I tried calling the governor a couple of times, and I discovered Morgado would call back.

I would say, in retrospect, it worked two ways. It had some positive effects because I was able to run the department. I was making the decisions. The one time that attention was lacking was when I realized the severity of the savings bank problems. I sent the governor (the first time I ever sent him something) a 40-page report marked "Confidential." There were four copies: one each for Morgado, the governor, Del Guidice, and our program associate. It identified the months in which the banks were going to go broke. Tony called me the following day and said that he had all four copies. I later got a smaller version of the memo to the governor.

At that time, I could have used some help. I got into the White House only because of my reputation for being the first woman member of the New York Stock Exchange. That's how I had those contacts. I know it is not an easy job, but at that time I could have used some muscle. It was not there for me.

QUESTION: Did you send the governor regular written reports on a weekly or monthly basis?

SIEBERT: We sent a report every month or so in which I listed public appearances, etc. I did not send the governor regular written reports, although we were in regular contact with the program office. We did have Banking Board meetings, and the governor's office would get copies of the schedule of the Banking Board.

I started the policy of telling the Banking Board in the executive session what we were working on, because I felt that they were entitled to no surprises and because they were extremely helpful to me. For example, when it was announced that I was going to be fired, they passed a resolution in my honor and sent it to Carey's office. They really went to bat for me, but that was because I treated them like a corporate board. I felt that they shouldn't leave a meeting one week and then be surprised when we took possession of an institution the next week. So, they were 100 percent on my side. I think the Banking Board is something that should be expanded. It is functional.

QUESTION: Did you have the feeling that anyone was reading the final reports you sent to the governor's office besides your program associates?

SIEBERT: I think that Tony was reading the final reports I sent to the governor's office, but I don't think anyone else was reading them.

QUESTION: Did the governor's office ever try to coordinate what you were doing in the Banking Department with what you were doing in some of the boards of which you were a member?

SIEBERT: No. I was partly responsible for State of New York Mortgage Agency (SONYMA) being twice shaken-up. The last time they were shaken-up I called Morgado and said, "I might be ex-officio, but I've got to get off this board or I'll ruin my reputation." Similarly, at Urban Development Corporation (UDC) board meetings, I asked them about the competitive bids on legal fees, for example, and they used to tell me they didn't have to get them.

QUESTION: When it came to the program, did you get support from the governor's office?

SIEBERT: On the major banking bill, I did not talk to the governor or Morgado. I did talk to Mike Del Guidice. He was pretty good. We did talk to the counsel. We always had a good relationship with the counsel. And Mike was pretty helpful. At least, we could go there and discuss it with him. That was good, however, because it gave me a sense of individual accomplishment and I did not have any undue political pressure of any kind.

QUESTION: Do you see any need for any change in the basic relationship between the executive branch and the legislative branch on such things as the budget? Does the Division of the Budget have an appropriate responsibility? Is there too much of a tendency in the legislature to cut whatever the governor recommends? Is there too much of a tendency on the part of the governor and his staff to cut to the absolute minimum, and, therefore, put you in an unfortunate position if the legislature cuts further?

SIEBERT: I think each governor would probably be different. When Rockefeller was governor, I'm told the Banking Department got whatever they wanted, but he obviously knew banking. We were never ill-treated; it was just a different direction. I did resent it when I was fighting the Hong Kong-Shanghai Bank deal, and then had that special survey from the Budget Division. That I resented. The newspapers played it up. Morgado sent them down and Tom Poster of the *New York Daily News* heard about it, and wrote it up. Ernie Kohn did the report which I resented.[12]

QUESTION: Did you ever appear before a legislative committee or hearing on your budget after the governor submitted his?

SIEBERT: No.

QUESTION: Each year, the legislature, the Senate Finance Committee, and the Assembly Ways and Means Committee jointly called in a number of the department heads.

SIEBERT: I was never called in. I think that they didn't bother with us because we were first instance.

QUESTION: I am interested in whether or not you feel the experience of joint conferences would have been beneficial. Was it the kind of thing that you would have hoped for each year?

SIEBERT: No, not in most situations. The only time that it would have been helpful during my tenure was when we tried to get our examiners upgraded. We were losing them to the feds. Budget objected to grade increases, and then the Civil Service commissioners overruled them. Then Morgado said "No," so it was "No." One of the Civil Service commissioners told me that Morgado later called and said, "You gave away the whole store."

We went up there with charts and graphs and comparisons

between the federal examiners' salaries and our salaries. We had the blessings of the banks, and they were even willing to pay for it. The Budget office said that if they upgraded our examiners, they would have to do it across the state agencies. We spent an awful lot of time and effort on that appeal.

Morgado said that if they upgraded our examiners, then they would have to do it for Insurance and for Agriculture, too. The Civil Service Commission had overruled the Budget staff, but then the governor's office said, "No way."

QUESTION: Is there a possibility of a judicial review in a situation where the department initiates the request?

SIEBERT: No, we just took that from the governor's office and folded our tent and went away.

QUESTION: Do you have trouble defending the existence of your London office in your budget? Was that a target?

SIEBERT: Yes and no. We always have to examine whether we have the office there, or whether we send examiners abroad. You should examine a clearinghouse bank in different cities at the same time as a discipline. When you don't do it, you run into problems. So, when they show that the assets in London of Morgan Guaranty are a certain dollar amount, you want to determine them in Tokyo and a few other places at the same time.

We would send examiners every other year to Tokyo, Hong Kong, and a couple of other places. There were countries we could get into; there were countries we couldn't get into. Knowledge of overseas operations can be very useful. For example, I entered into a deal with American Express. We saved them their full banking license in England, because London was not going to give it to them.

Now, American Express has an international bank. Our department regulates the American Express Foreign Agency, worth about $1.5 billion. The bank itself is about $6 billion—at least it was at the time. The Bank of England set new criteria for defining what a bank is. Since the American Express had no one regulator that was in charge of the entire operation, and since they were incorporated in Connecticut, the Bank of England was not going to recognize them as a full bank.

I felt that a New York company should not be disadvantaged. So, I went to the Banking Board and they gave me permission to examine the bank once a year, charging them the same fees that we charge the clearinghouse banks. The Bank of England recognized the examination reports, and gave them the designation of a bank so that they could compete. The Swiss authorities also recognized it. As a regulatory agency, we came out better because we knew the whole institution that way. No one had been examining the whole thing, and now, once a year, we examine American Express.

Should a regulator go on making deals like that? I say "Yes." The Banking Board said it was okay, as long as they paid the same amount of money. "You can't give it to them cheaper than you're charging us." This was fair enough. We examined American Express International Bank every year. Every regulator has to have a certain flexibility. This was a case where the Bank of England knew us well because we had examiners there.

We always have problems getting people from the banks on the Banking Board and the clearinghouse, because they have to live in New York State, and most of the clearinghouse bankers live in Connecticut or New Jersey. They have not been able to fill certain seats. People stay on to attempt to resolve this.

QUESTION: Before we began this interview, you made a comment on first instance budgeting, which led me to believe that you were not totally satisfied with the way in which budgeting was handled for the Department of Banking. Do you want to elaborate?

SIEBERT: We needed a flexibility that we didn't have, depending on what was going on in the industry. We were always borrowing examiner positions and classifying them into something else. The banks were aware of it. The banks said, "Please pay our examiners more. Please give them more money because we pay for it." We didn't have a gun to their heads to get them to say that.

When you run into problems of great magnitude, the kind of problems we had, it would be beneficial if there were more flexibility. There are times when you need expert lawyers. For example, we had a tremendous influx of foreign banks. We needed a group of people that knew those laws. The foreign banks' operations are totally different from a clearinghouse bank.

There should be flexibility. We made things happen, but if a major bank such as Mexico Loan collapsed, the department couldn't handle it. Sure, the fed would be there, but then we would be abdicating our responsibility. It would take determination. We hired attorneys at such low fees that they were basically useless until they got experience. We couldn't get quality people. When you have these emergencies, you need quality people. We couldn't pay them enough, so they would stay at the department two years and then go on. The ones that stay there are not the ones that you want to stay there. That's the problem.

We would lose the good people. I understand it. Once they get fully vested, they can take early retirement. It's almost normal for higher ranking officials to take an early retirement. They will go to a bank for ten years afterwards and make money. It is a normal extension of a civil service career. In a sense, it is good because it means that a 45-year-old person who has been in the department for 20 years can become a deputy. However, the lack of flexibility which caused people to leave because they felt dead-ended was bad.

QUESTION: Can regulation work when you have a flow of people leaving your department and going into the industry they regulate?

SIEBERT: I think that is accepted by all regulators. I think it is much more prevalent in the feds—that's one of the reasons they go to the feds. You can't expect somebody to keep working for the salary we pay. You know the salaries have been behind. We are way behind the federal examiners. We have examiners who leave and go over to the federal agency. They make more at the comptroller's office. We lose the bright ones who go over to the feds.

QUESTION: There are changes in banking with respect to such things as multiple types of deposits, computerization, and a few things of that sort, creating a demand for skills of the kind that many of your people don't have. Does this lead to minor crises with respect to doing a job?

SIEBERT: We couldn't keep good computer people. Yet that was one area where we should have had really skilled people because of the possibilities of planned robbery by computer. It has happened, yet we couldn't keep the people who could deal with it. We tried to get upgrades for the computer people and couldn't get them. That's going to happen more in the future because there are many opportunities to go elsewhere. Once we had to do a special project, and we were short of people. I think it was for the Senate. They found out that some of the bank computers were not recording enough interest for the people, and we had to make a study on all of them. We didn't have the people.

QUESTION: Does your location in New York make you particularly vulnerable to loss of personnel?

SIEBERT: Our advanced computer man maybe made $30,000 to $35,000—that's nothing. The work is in New York. If the computer people were in Albany and the banks had to pay them per diem to come down to New York to examine them, that would be worse. It is fighting one way or another, you are always fighting something. When it came to exotic kinds of trading, such as foreign exchange or futures, we did not have the skills.

Furthermore, I had no discretion with respect to hiring outside experts. We had no consultants in computers. Occasionally, we would hire somebody from outside to lead a specific course to train examiners. Other than that, it was all legal costs. We had been given money and thus were able to hire a couple of attorneys which we needed because we were given extra work with that last usury rate bill, and because we had to make certain reports. We brought down Barney Karol, who had been in the governor's office in Washington, who was knowledgeable about banking.

QUESTION: You made an analogy between running your own company and running the department. Of course, if you run your own company you can hire and fire the people who work for you. To what extent was that true in your department?

SIEBERT: I did have some control. I sent one deputy out to the field and he ended up taking early retirement. We had two deputies—one was in charge of examiners and one was in charge of the assorted financial institutions, like check cashers. We had not examined a check casher in two years because they were fighting over the new format of the report. I didn't know this, although my first deputy knew it. By law, we had to examine them every three years.

When it was brougnt to my attention that we had to examine every check casher that we regulate in the next year, I said, "What happened?" I was told by Neal Soss, my first deputy, that they couldn't agree. They each wrote the blue "cover yourself" memos. We've put "unsatisfactory" or "below average" on both of their evaluations. Under the banking law, we can send a deputy back to the field. They can retain deputy salary, but not status. Every superintendent has wanted to send one deputy back to the field, but everybody was afraid to do it because of the time involved. I did that to one deputy. He then took early retirement and is now with a bank. It takes a positive effort where you realize you can get involved in hearings.

I was able to hire some of the people in the department. I made a deal with the governor's office. I would take one of theirs if I could go out and hire one of mine. I realize that is the way life is. So, I was able to bring in Sam Abrams, who was an outstanding deputy and secretary of the Banking Board. I was able to bring in Paul Lee, who was a great general counsel. But, it also meant that I had to hire some of their people. John would say, "Look, I've got somebody here—you've got an opening and we have some people," and I would have to take them.[13] But we cooperated well.

It would be good if there were more exempt spots, but that is the way life is. It would also be good if there were financial incentives that you could give people. A program was put in at the start of my tenure, but it wasn't enough. When you can give people an incentive, there will be some that will really work harder—you won't have this "nine-to-five" attitude. That's important, because there are some good people there, but after a while that civil service mentality gets to them. If you give them a financial incentive, you might bring out some entrepreneurial spirit.

QUESTION: With respect to the present system, you've mentioned at least one improvement that you would propose; namely, greater flexibility with respect to budget and civil service matters.

Are there other changes that you would suggest?

SIEBERT: I think it would have been beneficial if there had been some cabinet meetings where I actually knew what was going on. We might have had more of an overlap.

QUESTION: Did your department have many joint activities with other state departments, and if so, how did that work out?

SIEBERT: We worked closely with Insurance. We worked closely with Urban Development Corporation. We worked on SONYMA with the other agencies. We weren't the only agency on SONYMA. The Job Development Agency, the Labor Department, and the Commerce Department were also there. There are some good, talented people. On UDC it was we, Commerce, and Insurance. It is good to have several agencies on some of the boards, because I think we all can bring a lot to it.

QUESTION: Could you talk about the SONYMA a little bit?

SIEBERT: I understand the board of SONYMA has been redone again. When I was on it orginally, it had five people. I used to love the meetings; they were 15 minutes long. I realized, however, that it was an agency that really could do some good, and then I resented the fact that it was 15 minutes.

Gary Brodie had worked on that a lot. As red lining took hold, after the first usury rate increase, they expanded the role of SONYMA. They added Mildred Rosen as the comptroller's representative; Shirley Lans, a professor at Vassar; Frank Lugavina; and Bernie Charles to the board. It was probably the most political of any of the boards. It was also the only all-minority board consisting of blacks, women, and Hispanics.[14]

The agency just didn't do as much as it could have done. This was before the federal government put restraints on it. At that time, it could have been open-ended; we could have had a couple billion dollars worth of good paper out there. It was all good quality paper because it was backed by mortgages. We could have added much more liquidity to the New York Mortgage Market. Unfortunately, it became a dumping ground for a lot of political people who needed jobs. Some of the people that I looked at in the Banking Department and who didn't seem qualified ended up at SONYMA, which was pathetic. An agency which has recently been given added responsibilities is not the place for politically sensitive people.

I understand that a certain number of jobs have to be given to minorities, and in many cases, these people have not had related experience. If you had more exempt positions in the Banking Department, then you could hire a few in the Banking Department. The efficiency of the Banking Department would compensate and they would have an opportunity to learn. However, when you take people that don't have the experience or background and put them in an agency which has all new functions, it becomes the unknowledgeable leading the inexperienced. That is what I think happened at SONYMA. That is why they have had to redo it a couple of times.

When an agency like SONYMA is given an insuring and a reinsuring function, which is something new, you can't take people that are not experienced. You can't hire people just because they are minorities, unless you are lucky. If you do have these IOU's for jobs, then put them in existing agencies that are running well. They will get absorbed and they will learn. Michael Kenny and Tom Clarke are examples. Tom Clarke was the first black Deputy; he's in Consumer Affairs and he does an outstanding job. But he had background. He came in and he performed.

Michael Kenny was a young guy. Until he passed the bar exam he was assistant to the superintendent. Afterwards he went into Legal. He is now counsel for the black bank Freedom National. You had people there from whom he could learn and gain experience. In the real world, you wouldn't take a bunch of people who don't have the experience and give them a new function. And you shouldn't do that in government either.

I think the people there tried to make it work, but it would have been much better if they could have refused to take some of these people who had no experience. In some cases, it was their first job. It just became too political; it was an agency that grew wild. Recently they added somebody from the Budget. Now I understand they have redone it again.

QUESTION: Is there need for a mechanism to resolve the difficulties that arise between department heads or, based on your experience, can these normally be ironed out through discussions?

SIEBERT: We didn't have any serious problems. Sometimes we used to get angry at SONYMA; other than that we didn't have any problems. I had a problem with John Dyson when he said I should be fired for not approving the Marine takeover.[15] That was John, more than anything else. With that exception, we didn't have any problems. I think we could have worked more closely if there had been some cabinet meetings. Then, I might have known what other departments were doing, and we might have been able to get involved.

QUESTION: Is there need for a mechanism to get a disagreement to either the governor or one of his assistants? Is there any need for small, interdepartmental committees of related areas where these things might be prevented before they got serious?

SIEBERT: We worked closely with Al Lewis on things.[16] We worked closely in the Job Development Authority. There were three commissioners involved in it. We didn't need a mechanism because we didn't have any problems. But, I do think that, with so many agencies in the Trade Center, it might be a worthwhile function if, once a month, they took over a dining room to allow discussion.

FOOTNOTES

[1]As one response to the Iranian hostage crisis, the Carter administration in Washington froze all Iranian assets in the United States. Special steps were taken in New York to facilitate payments by Iranian banks to individuals and companies dependent on this source of funds in the state.

[2]The Marine Midland controversy arose from differences in New York State government over whether the state should permit one of its major banks to be taken over by a Hong Kong-based bank, which could not be effectively reached by state banking regulations.

[3]Lillian Roberts, Industrial Commissioner; and Victor Gottbaum, President, District Council 37, American Federation of City, County and Municipal Employees Union.

[4]Robert Morgado, Secretary to the Governor.

[5]Warren Anderson, Majority Leader, New York State Senate; and Stanley Fink, Speaker, New York State Assembly.

[6]Stanley Steingut, Speaker, New York State Assembly (1975-1978); Jay Rolison, New York State Senator (1966-present), and Chairman of the Senate Banking Committee; George Cincotta, Member, New York State Assembly (1959-1977), and Chairman, Assembly Banking Committee.

[7]Walter Wriston was then Chairman of the Board and Chief Executive Officer of Citibank.

[8]Alan Cohen, Deputy Secretary of Banks (1981-1982).

[9]Louis Lefkowitz, New York State Attorney General (1957-1978).

[10]Robert Abrams, New York State Attorney General (1978-present).

[11]Michael Del Guidice, Secretary to the Governor (1983-present).

[12]Ernie Kohn, First Deputy Superintendent of Banks (1979-present).

[13]John J. Burns, Appointments Officer to Governor Carey.

[14]Gary Brodie, Deputy Superintendent of Banks (1981-1982); Frank Lugavina, Member, New York State Banking Board; Bernie Charles, Chairman of the Board, State of New York Mortgage Agency (SONYMA).

[15]John Dyson, New York State Commissioner of Commerce (1975-1979).

[16]Al Lewis, Commissioner of Insurance (1978-1982).

The Carey Governorship

Gerald Benjamin

Just two years after his departure from office, Governor Hugh Carey was recalled by one political writer as a "forlorn, forgotten figure" on the New York political scene.[1] In contrast to his successor, Mario Cuomo, who immediately sought to seize personal command of the executive branch apparatus and yet to approach the state legislature with a careful regard for the prerogatives of its leaders and members, Governor Carey was remembered as a remote, barely interested chief executive who preferred to fight rather than negotiate with a legislature he disdained. It became common in New York in the mid-1980's to juxtapose Cuomo's early achievements—timely adoption of a balanced budget for two consecutive years, and a new spirit of cooperation in state government—against Carey's failures—constantly missed budget deadlines, and diminished gubernatorial power as a result of continuous executive-legislative contention.

Several factors contributed to these unfair first recollections of the Carey legacy in New York State. The governor's greatest achievements, overcoming the New York City fiscal crisis and, at the same time, preserving the fiscal integrity of the state, came early in his first term. (In commenting upon his less stellar second term, Carey once remarked: "What am I supposed to do, save New York City twice?")[2] In addition, the essentially conservative, tax-cutting record of Democrat Carey's later years was ignored or misrepresented by the Republican candidate for Governor in 1982, Lewis Lehrman, who in seeking to establish his conservative bona fides, ran a massive but unsuccessful media campaign that really attached the record of Nelson Rockefeller, not Hugh Carey. Furthermore, in its early days, Mario Cuomo's administration was served by the establishment of a stark Carey-Cuomo contrast, and deliberately sought to nurture it.[3] After all, the outgoing governor was extremely unpopular in 1981 and 1982, and there was political advantage for the incoming chief executive to distance himself from his predecessor in style, approach, and temperament.

In fact, when Governors Cuomo and Carey are compared, what emerges on several levels is not their differences but their similarities. Both are Catholics and lawyers, alumni indeed of the same law school, St. John's in Queens. Both are shaped by their ethnic roots and feel deeply about them. Both have large families and a commitment to family. Both succeeded as outsiders in the politics of New York City's outer boroughs, Carey in Brooklyn, Cuomo in Queens. Both demonstrate a propensity to be less reliant upon and trusting of others than upon their own private political judgment. Both even share a thinly veiled disdain for "ordinary" politicians, and a tendency, unusual among American leaders, toward a public preoccupation with death and "the meaning of it all."

The most important similarities between Carey and Cuomo, however, were their shared positions on many issues, and agreement that the overarching political task before the contemporary New York governor was the need to reconcile traditional liberal concerns with the new fiscal constraints of the 1970's and 1980's. Hugh Carey's comment in 1975, at the outset of his first term, that "there is no contradiction between having a liberal philosophy and a concern and compassion for people and at the same time being realistic enough to know you have to pay the bills or the people aren't going to get the programs," could easily serve as a summary of the theme of Mario Cuomo's widely hailed 1983 inaugural address.[4]

But the effect of political and governmental circumstance and of the actions of others notwithstanding, Hugh Carey must take considerable responsibility for the fact that his political epitaph did not read, as he once said he wished it would, "He did his best, and he had character."[5] His continual unpredictability and propensity toward startling extemporaneous comment on public issues regularly confirmed a reputation for "quirkiness." On one occasion, after a fire had released carcinogenic PCBs throughout the Binghamton state office building and caused its evacuation, the governor said that he would "walk into Binghamton into any part of that building, and swallow an entire glass of PCBs, and walk a mile afterwards."[6] Of course, he never did this, but the comment did produce an editorial in the *Binghamton Sun,* entitled "Carey's Gone Cracker Dog." Even at the press conference held on the eve of his leaving office, the governor could not resist causing an uproar. There he described state legislators as "small boys," suggested that the December 1982 New York City subway fare crisis had been faked, and remarked that he had directed the use of State Commerce Department "I Love New York" funds during the gubernatorial campaign to offset political advertising by Lew Lehrman.[7]

In his remarks in this volume, as elsewhere, Hugh Carey has urged that those interested in his record look at substance, not style. "Take out the personal stuff," he told Richard Meislin of the *New York Times,* "and what you have left is a government that works."[8] In truth, when this distinction was made during his tenure, Carey generally came out well. *The Economist* commented, as his 1978 election campaign got under way, that though the governor's personality was "difficult" his accomplishments were "substantial."[9] And, in October of 1981, when pondering whether to run in a primary against his chief, the incumbent governor, Lieutenant Governor Mario Cuomo wrote in his diary:

> Carey is generally perceived as weak, but analysis reveals it's mostly attributable to a perception of him personally as unlikeable and distracted from the business of government. Not a great deal is said about his performance: to the extent his performance is judged by the conditions of things in the state, he can make a good case.[10]

Of course, no governor is judged by the electorate or by other political leaders entirely by the "condition of things in the state" that result from his policies. As Cuomo has repeatedly shown he understands, style is as important as substance, the signals in executive speech and behavior as consequential as the effects of concrete action. Insofar as Hugh Carey ignored the implications of what he said and how he behaved for his ability to govern, insofar as he regarded style and substance as separable, the first a private matter and only the second a public concern, he damaged his governorship. But the obverse is also true. A judgment about the Carey administration that considers only the governor's style and ignores his substantive achievements is necessarily flawed.

Political Successes

One New York politician in assessing Hugh Carey's first four years commented that "we thought we were getting Pat O'Brien, but we ended up with Charles DeGaulle."[11] In fact, Carey at the outset looked like "a tough, intelligent and humorous Irish cop," a politician able to reconcile an essentially conservative, white, working-class Brooklyn constituency with a relatively liberal Congressional voting record. First elected to Congress in 1960 at the age of 39 in a closely contested race with Francis Dorn, an eight-year Republican incumbent in the Park Slope section of Brooklyn, Carey defeated Dorn again in 1962 by 383 votes in a district reapportioned by the state GOP, and went on to serve six terms in the House. His record there was that of a mainstream liberal Democrat, with special interests in education, health, and mental health. Carey also, however, did what was necessary to please his constituents. He opposed busing, supported parochial school aid, and spoke out against a civilian complaint review board for the police in New York City.[12]

After supporting Hale Boggs' successful bid for majority leader of the House, Carey gained a position on the powerful Ways and Means

Committee where, as he describes in this volume, he worked to deliver federal revenue sharing, and thus helped rescue Nelson Rockefeller, New York's Republican governor, from a deepening budget crisis in the state. (Later, during his primary race for governor, Carey's opponent Howard Samuels attacked him for calling Rockefeller a "good governor." Carey explained that he simply meant that "all human beings are good."[13]) But Carey's heart always seemed to be in New York City, where politics, he said, was the "biggest game in the world." He failed in attempt for the nomination for president of the city council in 1969, was discussed for borough president of Brooklyn in 1970, and was said too to have his eye on the mayoralty.

Because the city's elections are held in off years, Carey's efforts in this arena did not require him to sacrifice his Congressional incumbency. By 1974, however, the pull of New York induced him to do this, and he entered the race for governor. Though not the nominee of the Democratic convention, which backed Howard Samuels, Carey gained enough votes there (probably as a result of the machinations of Meade Esposito, the Brooklyn Democratic leader) to win a place on the primary ballot without having to petition for it. Esposito's backing did not deter Carey from denouncing Samuels, the convention's choice, for being "in bed with the bosses." There were, the Congressman said, two categories of county leaders: "enlightened leaders, who have seen fit to endorse Hugh Carey, and bosses who have not."[14]

Spending almost $2 million, much of it from his oil magnate brother Edward, Carey defeated Samuels in a primary held on September 10, a date fixed by a Republican governor and legislators who hoped to encourage Democratic divisions for as long as possible in the electoral season. But the Republicans themselves were divided. In December of 1973, a leading GOP gubernatorial aspirant, Assembly Majority Leader Perry Duryea, was removed from contention for the gubernatorial nomination as a result of being indicted for campaign practices in 1972. Duryea detected in this act of "political assassination" the hand of the Rockefeller wing of the party, which favored Malcolm Wilson, Nelson Rockefeller's successor and long-time lieutenant governor, for the nomination. Whatever the origins of the indictment, it immobilized Duryea for 1974, and Wilson was easily nominated.

Once the candidate, however, Malcolm Wilson proved to be an ineffective campaigner against Carey. A brilliant man, the Republican seemed ill at ease in large groups, dressed in a manner some characterized as "mortician-like," and became known for sprinkling his campaign addresses with Latin phrases. Carey ran the conventional Democratic statewide campaign. He charged the incumbent with hiding budget surpluses, promised increased benefits and subsidies for downstate constituencies, and was effective in labeling Wilson as a man of the past. Witness one exchange:

Question: Did you hear what Malcolm Wilson said about you yesterday?

Carey: Malcolm Wilson *is* yesterday.[15]

In the post-Watergate election year, and without the advantage of Nelson Rockefeller's wealth, incumbency, and personal appeal, the underlying institutional weaknesses that had developed in the state GOP over the 1960's became manifest. Though New York State had been Republican-run almost continuously since World War II, Hugh Carey swept to victory by a margin of 800,000 votes, carrying or closely contesting many upstate counties for the first time in decades.

Immediately after his election, and following the pattern of all newly chosen New York governors, Carey was hailed nationally as "potentially the hottest political property" in his party since JFK.[16] For his handling of the fiscal crisis, *Time* magazine considered the governor for its man-of-the-year, and it was speculated that a deadlocked 1976 Democratic national convention might turn to him for President. But the indictment of Carey's Democratic state chairman, Pat Cunningham, for the sale of judgeships at the initiative of Special Prosecutor Maurice Nadjari, and Nadjari's later suggestion, when the governor tried to fire him, that Carey was involved in covering up wrongdoing, effectively blocked the governor's hopes for a place on the national ticket. Carey was later fully vindicated, but the moment could not be recaptured, even in 1980 when he sought to keep New York State's delegation uncommitted so that he might possibly benefit from the bruising presidential battle between Jimmy Carter and Ted Kennedy.

In fact, renomination and reelection for Carey in 1978, even as an incumbent governor, was by no means assured. The fiscal crisis, not even an issue in the 1974 campaign, overwhelmed the state's political and governmental agenda in the governor's first term, and Carey, proclaiming "I'm here to get the hangover. Somebody else drank the champagne," necessarily made New York's financial survival his first priority. Campaign promises went by the board. "I am willing to have egg on my face, to have stones thrown at me, and to walk on nails," Carey said, "in order to prevent default."[17]

After the fiscal situation was stabilized, Carey's priority became restoring the state economy. Tax cuts began in 1977, and continued regularly thereafter, and the state budget was consistently held to increases below the level of inflation. But these actions, though pleasing to the *Wall Street Journal,* angered local governments in need of increased aid, constituencies dependent upon state services, and state workers with partially frozen salaries who delivered those services. An unpopular stand against the death penalty—"I have seen too much of death," the governor said—added to Carey's political difficulties. By June of 1978 he was said by the *New York Times to be* "bleeding from every pore."[18]

Some of the wounds of that June were inflicted by Carey's Lieutenant Governor Mary Ann Krupsak. On the same day that he declared for reelection, she withdrew from his ticket. Krupsak described the governor as "inaccessible" and "unwilling to listen and fulfill the obligations of his office," terms that outgoing Republican Attorney General Louis Lefkowitz later delightedly told his party colleagues to "keep under their pillows" and "in their pockets" for the fall general election. Two weeks later Krupsak decided to seek the gubernatorial nomination in a primary against Carey. Another disaffected supporter of the governor, state Senator Jeremiah Bloom of Brooklyn, who favored the death penalty, also entered the race.

With Mario Cuomo in the lieutenant governor's slot on his ticket, Carey won a Democratic primary conducted in the midst of a New York City newspaper strike. He received 52 percent of the vote, with less than 20 percent of the state's Democrats participating, hardly a ringing affirmation of his leadership.

It was widely believed in the state that Governor Carey would lose the general election to Perry Duryea, finally the Republican nominee, who was ahead of him by 20 percentage points in midsummer polls. With all charges of previous election irregularities dismissed on constitutional grounds, Duryea was now said to have the advantage of "looking like a governor." But his cautious, out-in-front campaign, stressing the death penalty and the less pleasant aspects of Governor Carey's personality, failed to take hold. Carey won by making his tax cuts, traditionally a Republican priority, the key issue. He got help late in the campaign, as well, from allegations of irregularities in Duryea's federal income taxes.

Nelson Rockefeller, Carey's old friend and Duryea's nemesis inside the GOP, also lent a hand. At a well-timed election year ceremony organized by Carey to dedicate the South Mall project in Albany in Rockefeller's name, the former four-term Republican governor, with Duryea looking on, virtually endorsed the Democratic incumbent. "He likes the guy," Rockefeller's wife, Happy, remarked.

The result, after both he and Duryea spent about $4 million, was a Carey come-from-behind victory, but in an election in which the choice offered the voters seemed to be which candidate was less bad, a manifestation of "politics without joy."

A Question of Style

During the 1978 race, in October, the headline on a front page analysis of the New York gubernatorial race in the *Wall Street Journal* proclaimed: "Governor's Personality Shapes Up as Key Issue in New York Elections," and "Democrat has Dual Image of Playboy and Monk."[19] The "playboy" half of this characterization came from a seeming transformation of Hugh Carey's life and associations in the midst of the 1975 fiscal crisis. During the later years of his first term, the governor was frequently seen with celebrity friends in New York City east side night spots. In fact, Carey's social life became so much a part of his public image that for a word association question asked in a poll taken for the 1978 election, respondents most often linked the governor's name to P.J. Clarke's, one of the "licensed premises" that he frequented![20]

His entry into "high society" caused some to think that Hugh Carey had forgotten his roots. His brother Ed, for example, who had financed much of the 1974 campaign, remarked, "I just don't know what he's doing with those people he's with. Phonies, shallow people, New York is full of them."[21] Later, during his second term, an old friend, Jimmy Breslin, took to expressing a similar sentiment through regular reference to the governor, in his syndicated *Daily News* column, as "Society Carey."[22]

But, it was the "monk" in Carey, rather than the playboy, that was of greatest concern to others in state government. David Garth, the political consultant, a close friend of Carey's who ran both of his gubernatorial campaigns, once commented that the governor may "have the best mind I've seen in government—and the most difficult personality."[23] The words used most frequently to describe Carey throughout his years in office were: moody, enigmatic, erratic, aloof, mystifying, mercurial, and dark and brooding.[24] Occasionally, the private Carey: incredibly kind, gregarious, loose, extremely witty, with "a natural gift for blarney and blather" was contrasted with the public man, but generally it was the negative picture that prevailed.[25]

In these characteristics the governor seemed to demonstrate the extremes of temperament so often identified with the Irish heritage of which he was so proud. Carey was self-consciously Irish, aware, as he notes here, of being the first Irish-American governor of New York since Al Smith. With other prominent Irish-American leaders, he took positions, courageous ones, in favor of a non-violent solution in Northern Ireland. Among his staff and commissioners, Carey seemed most comfortable with others of Irish heritage. "Anybody can be a good politician in good times," the governor once said, "but the Irish have a special gift for bad times."[26]

Both Hugh Carey's "black Irish moods" and his interest in night life, not evident before 1975, may have been manifestations of his grief over the death from cancer of his wife Helen, to whom he was deeply devoted, just as he was entering the 1974 campaign. Carey's personal life had been touched by death before—he lost a brother in a plane crash in 1959 and two sons in a car accident on Shelter Island in 1969—and soon after he became governor his first grandchild died as well. Perhaps as a consequence, as Murry Kempton concluded, "all the tenderness left to him resided in the domestic rather than the social side of his composition."[27]

Though Hugh Carey's style itself became a political issue, its real importance was in its consequences for his effectiveness as governor. When, in both the first and second terms, critics spoke of the governor's "difficult personality," it was usually in connection with some other concern: lack of support for staff or commissioners; imperiousness with the legislature; an impulsive, unplanned approach to decision making; an absence of reciprocal loyalty to political supporters; periodic loss of interest in the day-to-day work of his office; and finally, a propensity toward spontaneous comment, already noted here, that resulted in an endless flow of self-inflicted political wounds.

Staff and Commissioners

It first appeared that Hugh Carey, as a manager (like other lawyer-governors before him), would immerse himself in too much detail. The new governor was very deliberate about staffing his government at the top. The process was slowed not only by the need to obtain confirmation for most major appointments by the Republican Senate, but also by the limited pool of Democratic talent knowledgeable about state government after 16 years of GOP dominance in Albany and by Carey's own new, stricter post-Watergate ethics and financial disclosure requirements.

From this process, and other early decision making, it appeared that Governor Carey did not delegate well. Most staff were given a limited brief, and it soon became clear that the agreements they made with others would not necessarily bind the governor; he often revised them or required their renegotiation. This pattern continued even into the second term, and contributed to Carey's reputation for unpredictability. "His mercurial approach has often made for problems with his staff," one observer wrote in 1981, "because it is hard to know what compromise he will accept, a difficulty compounded by his unexplained absences and broken appointments."[28]

In his first years as governor, Hugh Carey did not substantially alter the executive staff structure that he inherited from the Rockefeller-Wilson years. Key positions remained the secretary to the governor, the Budget director, the governor's counsel, and the director of state operations. In addition, there were others of influence in less structured roles, for example, Felix Rohatyn on fiscal issues and Dr. Kevin Cahill, who, until 1980, dominated the entire health policy area.

Whereas the initial criticism of Hugh Carey's management style was that he delegated too little, after the fiscal crisis the dominant concern came to be that he delegated too much to too few people and was himself available too little for the routine work of his office. One to whom he delegated was Kevin Cahill, who in the first term became known as the "man closest to the governor."[29]

Cahill, a distant relative of the governor's through marriage and an internationally known authority on tropical medicine, had cared for Carey's wife during her terminal bout with cancer. The governor was said in 1976 to have an almost "mystical faith" in the doctor, and appointed him to a dollar a year position as "the guardian, the pioneer, the referee, and the counselor in programs of public health."[30] As New York's "health czar," Cahill presided over activities that consumed almost half of the state budget, coming to Albany one day a week, on Wednesdays, to do so. His role, he said, was to induce Carey to make the "right" choices in this top priority area, not the "political" ones. "I work with Hugh, never for Hugh. My role is philosophical. I don't trust people who make political judgments. I'll say, 'Hugh, is this the best we can do? Is this the right thing? Would Helen have approved?' "[31]

Cahill oversaw it all, one analyst commented. He entered into an enormous range of issues, from the complete reorganization of the Department of Mental Hygiene to such matters as creating a workable system of medical malpractice insurance, developing Medicaid cost controls for hospitals and nursing homes, and access for teenagers to abortion services. The doctor sought interagency coordination through a number of panels, and especially through the Health Planning Commission, which he organized and headed. "The human service commissioners, though not always to their liking, answered to him. He had a hand in hiring many of them, and could guarantee an airing of their views."[32]

Admirers praised Kevin Cahill's energy, and his ability to move the health care bureaucracy as a result of his access to and support from the governor. Detractors suggested that his part-time involvement and lack of governmental experience often led to failures of otherwise good policy initiatives because of weaknesses in implementation. By the middle of the second term, the influence of Carey's one-time Savoranola had faded and, saying that his work was finished, Cahill left the administration—and a clear field for Bob Morgado.

One early problem of the Carey administration was that the top aides first appointed to major staff positions—David Burke, Peter Goldmark, Judah Gribetz—were all "strangers in a strange land" in Albany. Their initial unfamiliarity with the people and processes of the capital, and the consuming nature of the fiscal crisis in 1975 and 1976, led these aides and the governor to rely more and more over time for the conduct of daily business upon a young but experienced assistant secretary, Bob Morgado. By the end of the first Carey term, the governor's original secretary, counsel, and Budget director had all moved on. Morgado, who after a battle succeeded Burke as secretary in 1977, emerged as the dominant figure in the administration during the 1978 reelection campaign, and became "the governor's governor" for much of the second term.

"There are two grindstones," Peter Goldmark, Hugh Carey's first Budget director once said, "the legislative forces and the governor. And because of the governor's style, the two grindstones meet in one place—where the secretary is sitting."[33] Kevin Cahill's strength, in the early years, was that he had access to the governor. Bob Morgado's strength, in the later years, was that he controlled access to the governor, for his institutional role as secretary reinforced the close personal relationship he was able to develop with Hugh Carey.

A professionally trained public administrator who had served both parties in both political branches in Albany, Morgado played a dual role for Carey. He sought to "draw fire" away from his boss, and to transform the governor's ideas (often after screening!) into action. His method, as he reports it here, was to target key policy areas and to create ad hoc action groups forcing administrative structures to achieve results within them. Unlike Cahill, Morgado enjoyed an institutional base which allowed effective follow-up, and if he lacked the resources on the second floor, he co-opted those of the Budget Division to his—and the governor's—ends. In Carey's view, his secretary served him well. "He executed," the governor said, "but was not an executioner."

Though Morgado claimed that commissioners could always appeal his decisions to the governor, Lieutenant Governor Mario Cuomo was not the only top level person in the Carey administration to report a feeling of isolation from the decision making process. (One commissioner reported having met Governor Carey only twice in four years.) In 1975 and 1976, preoccupation with the fiscal crisis was given as the reason for the governor's lack of personal attention to the ongoing processes of state government. "The consensus is," one analyst wrote in 1976, "that the Carey administration has yet to take hold of the reins of state government."[34] But, by the end of Carey's first term, "smoothing out the operations of government" still seemed needed. And the problem was there in 1980, as well, causing Assembly Speaker Stanley Fink to comment: "I get constant calls from various commissioners and departments of the state where programs should be emanating from telling me they can't get to the governor."[35]

Clearly, Carey's personality and his preoccupation with personal concerns had an isolating effect during his governorship, one that was compounded by his reaction to the mundane nature of daily business in Albany. As investment banker Felix Rohatyn said in 1977, after the worst of the fiscal crisis had passed: "A lot of the stuff he has to deal with now is a bore, and he doesn't bore well."[36] But, there was also the matter of the governor's conscious choice of administrative style, an approach described by Mario Cuomo as "more like that of a chairman of the board than of a chief executive officer."[37]

Commissioners in any administration are likely to feel neglected by the governor they serve, whose needs differ from theirs. It is the governor's job, and that of his staff, to assure that his department heads serve him, and not he them. The problem in the Carey administration was thus one of degree, rather than of kind. The governor did seem to have an inner circle of commissioners, identified by several of the interviewees in this volume, with whom he was closest. Members of this circle were apparently selected because Hugh Carey was personally comfortable with them and because, too, of the priority he gave to the work of the departments they headed.

Others, such as Muriel Siebert, were kept more distant. And a third group failed to survive. Turnover was high in the Carey administration, and especially, as already noted, in some staff positions and commissionerships: The governor's original secretary, Budget director, and counsel were all gone by the end of his first term. In addition, he had four press secretaries in that term, and three Environmental Conservation commissioners. Over all, fewer than half of Carey's originally appointed commissioners were in the same positions four years later.

Legislative Relations

In his relationships with the state Senate and Assembly, Governor Carey was subjected to the same charges of remoteness and arrogance that were used to characterize his approach within the executive branch. He communicated disdain for the legislature, not only in what he said and did, but in how he said and did it. As one assemblyman commented in 1976: "There's a tone in the governor's comments that makes it seem he doesn't want to be bothered with 'that zoo' on the third floor."[38]

It also rankled legislators that they were often asked by the governor to ignore district concerns and cast politically difficult up-or-down votes for what he said was the good of the state, but were not then acknowledged for doing so. Stanley Fink, for example, commented that in his first two years as speaker there was "never a thank you" from Hugh Carey for his efforts on the governor's behalf.[39] In fact, Carey prided himself as a "no deals" governor, one who would not play "the Albany game." "It's the Albany game that got us in the mess we're in," he said in his first term, "the game of promising jobs for votes, trading off a goodie here, a goodie there."[40] The result was a governor whose behavior was an enigma to such long-time legislators as Senate Majority Leader Warren Anderson, whose relationship with Carey grew more and more acrimonious as time passed.

The governor's protagonists offered two explanations for the often acerbic legislative relations of his years in Albany. The first was that the fiscal crises of their early days in office required that the administration offer solutions to the legislature that, because of their complexity and externally imposed deadlines, could not be altered through negotiation and bargaining. From this experience, a general approach to legislation that was unfortunate developed.

David Burke, for example, commented in 1976: "We had these brand new problems, one after another, and we didn't know what route to follow, so we went it alone because we thought we had to. Then we got used to going it alone. As long as the crisis atmosphere lasted, it worked."[41]

As he says in this volume, Governor Carey knew that during his first two years in office he enjoyed the advantages that accrue to a chief executive during crisis. But the crisis atmosphere could not last, and it did not. And though the administration regularly announced after 1976 that it was working to improve legislative relations, the governor's approach did not change. In 1981, for example, Carey gave legislative leaders an inch-thick bill creating a capital program for the rebuilding of New York City's subways and, citing the transportation emergency in the city, asked for action in 48 hours.

Looking at the bill, Warren Anderson replied, "I don't even know if I could read it in 48 hours," and then said: "Governor, we've been sitting around here since the legislature opened on January 7th without any legislative program being given us, and now you give us

246

one and ask us to deliver it in 48 hours. I don't understand. Where have you been all this time?"[42]

A second explanation offered by Carey loyalists for their chief's difficulties with the legislature was institutional. Both Robert Morgado and Meyer Frucher rightly note here that the New York State Legislature was a much different place when Hugh Carey became governor in 1975 than when Nelson Rockefeller assumed that position a decade and a half earlier. Reapportionment, mandated by the federal courts in the mid-1960's, altered the geographic balance in both houses, and ultimately made possible the Democratic majority in the Assembly that existed for all of Carey's eight years in office. Increased pay and benefits made the position of legislator a full-time job, and attracted a new kind of member, more entrepreneurial and less amenable to taking leadership direction. The decline of political parties in the state contributed to the independence of these legislators, who created their own campaign organizations and were therefore not under obligation to party leaders. And dramatic increases in the size and quality of professional legislative staffs (attributed by some to the simple need to fill up the new Legislative Office Building) gave the Legislature and its leaders the capacity to examine gubernatorial initiatives critically, and to offer alternatives of their own in a range of areas, including such central ones as revenue estimating.

The constrained fiscal environment was also a factor of significance in the gubernatorial-legislative tensions of the 1970's, one that, in fact, was already becoming evident in New York under Nelson Rockefeller as early as 1970. Though Hugh Carey's refusal to make political trade-offs may indeed have been principled, it was also true that with the money not there, there was very little to trade. Carey's twin goals of fiscal stability and tax cuts to restore the New York economy left little money for the increased local assistance payments or enriched state programs for which legislators liked to take credit in their districts when running for reelection.

During his final years in office, a third element also contributed to Hugh Carey's difficulties with the legislature. As reported by Bob Morgado in his comments here, Carey decided in his second term to confront the legislature very visibly on budgeting issues in order to protect his image as a force for fiscal integrity in New York. One consequence of this decision was the governor's much increased use of the item veto in 1980 and thereafter. Thus, in the end, confrontation became the result not only of personal style and institutional development, but of conscious strategic choice. In light of this choice, it is ironic that Hugh Carey is now better remembered for his confrontations with the legislature than for the purposes of these confrontations.

It is clear, furthermore, that the governor's approach to the legislature had significant long-range consequences. In 1976, for the first time since 1870, a gubernatorial veto was overridden. The bill concerned educational aid to New York City, and was later found in the courts to be unconstitutional. But, the spirit of the override—with the governor denounced as a "no good SOB" in the Assembly Democratic conference, and cheers and cries of "Bingo!" on the floor when Marie M. Runyon of Manhattan cast the decisive hundredth vote—not only revealed an overwhelming hostility to Carey by members of his own party, but marked the realization that the veto would now be a somewhat less consequential gubernatorial power.[43] Confirming this, there were other successful overrides in the later Carey years, though the governor was able to sustain his most famous vetoes, those of death penalty legislation.

Other long-term changes were more subtle. Constant confrontations, and missed budget deadlines, raised questions in New York about the competence of state government to deal with resource scarcity. Less trusting of the governor, legislative leaders took to recessing rather than adjourning their bodies, reserving to themselves the option of coming back into session if the need arose. Through litigation initiated by the state Senate, the legislature won the right to appropriate federal funds, theretofore largely under the control of the executive.

Finally, and perhaps most significantly, the institutional roles of the major political branches, especially with regard to budgeting, were altered. Formerly, the governor proposed policy innovations and the legislature accepted them or cut, guarding the purse strings. Under Carey, the governor imposed austerity, and the legislature became the restoring branch, adding money and programs to satisfy group and constituency pressures.

The Record

In their recently published books, Mayor Edward Koch and Governor Mario Cuomo offered different indictments of Hugh Carey as governor. Koch asserted that Carey lacked political courage in various difficult political circumstances during the late 1970's. Cuomo, reflecting particularly upon the MTA financing issue of 1982, was critical of the governor's ad hoc approach, his failure to develop a "strategy."[44]

Both of these criticisms are misplaced. Carey's political courage was clearly evident in his battle against the excesses of Special Prosecutor Maurice Nadjari, in his stance on the death penalty and in his statements on the troubles in Ireland. And his strategic sense was

248

manifest in the consistent priority he gave to the economic recovery of the state through his tenure, and the tenacity with which he held down the growth of state spending in pursuit of this goal.

Perhaps because the worst did not happen—New York City did not go bankrupt, the state's major public authorities were not allowed to fail, the Empire State did not default on its obligations— the achievements of Governor Carey during the fiscal crisis may tend to be minimized as time passes. They should not, for they were enormous.

On his hundredth day in office Carey described the problems he faced to Tom Poster of the *Daily News:* "In New York State, we haven't found only back-door financing. We've got side-door financing and through New York's borrowing over the years— through state government, its authorities and agencies and UDC and MTA—we've got money going out the doors, the windows and the portholes."[45]

Working with aides and advisors both within and outside government, under conditions of the most intense pressure, Carey found solutions. In the city, short-term debt was refinanced through the newly created Municipal Assistance Corporation (MAC), a state agency; interim credit was obtained from both state and federal sources; and an Emergency Financial Control Board was created to monitor and control city spending. Politically, all this was made possible because of an improbable alliance between labor unions and banks, forged by and through the governor.

The state responded to the UDC default by first meeting its moral obligation and then shoring up its public authorities, temporarily and irrationally denied access to the bond market because of the words "New York" in their names. It then helped these building agencies regain the market's confidence by enacting a buildout plan and limiting their overall borrowing authority.

And with regard to putting its own financial house in order, New York marked the end of "the days of wine and roses" in 1976, after a budget balancing tax increase in 1975, with a truly hold-the-line fiscal plan, given teeth through such administrative devices as expenditure ceilings, reductions in force, suspensions of capital projects, hiring and travel freezes, and the impoundment of funds.[46] Tight budgetary control and a series of tax cuts followed in later years but, as the governor notes here, though government spending was restrained from year to year, he did not achieve institutionalization of taxing or spending limits through legislation or constitutional amendment.

Nevertheless, the single greatest achievement of the Carey years was in causing state government to recognize and accept what Mark Lawton here describes as the "new fiscal realities." All agencies had to learn to do more with less; one consequence was the renewed emphasis on management and cost control so evident from the remarks of all the commissioners interviewed for this volume. This, however, was not the only achievement. There was also a significant reordering of priorities in the allocation of the limited resources that were available. On what he called the "caring side" of government, Carey's long-term commitment to Mental Health led him not only to sign the Willowbrook consent decree, but to seize upon it as a vehicle for reform and enriched funding in this area. A tougher stand on punishment for crime, obscured in the public debate because of preoccupation with the death penalty, brought with it a need for more prison cells and the money to operate new and expanded facilities. In contrast, some agencies found themselves less favored by the governor's office under Carey than they had been under his predecessors, for example, the State University and the Department of Environmental Conservation.[47]

There were also unintended consequences of the Carey governorship. One was the redistribution of power in the state political system. Litigation that flowed from the handling of the fiscal crisis ultimately denied the governor the authority to impound local assistance funds in the state budget, and expanded the opportunity for citizens to sue him and others for their official actions on constitutional grounds.[48] In addition, the bond market required certification by key public officials that the state budget was in balance before the massive short-term borrowing needed at the outset of each fiscal year could be undertaken. And Generally Accepted Accounting Principles (GAAP) were adopted for the state late in the second term. Both of these were indicators of a wider sharing of budgetary authority and of the more powerful role played by private financial institutions in New York's political process. These developments, along with the surging assertiveness of the legislature and its leaders, all served to increase the number of significant actors in state politics and to diminish the power of the governor, a fact acknowledged by Hugh Carey in his remarks here.

In dealing with the extraordinary problems that faced the state during his tenure, Governor Carey did much more than "keep smiling," the advice given to him by Nelson Rockefeller in the darkest days of 1975. His achievements, often politically difficult, were substantial. Though he left the governorship weaker than he found it, he left the state stronger, with its government still effective but constrained, and no longer a threatening source of continual fiscal stress.

But though Hugh Carey once said that he "had never done anything out of a desire to hurt," this was not the impression he left when he sought to have a neighbor's home on Shelter Island that blocked his view condemned as a security risk, or told the editors of the *Watertown Times* that they might "go trolling" in Lake Ontario, recently reopened for fishing, with his out-of-favor Environmental Conservation Commissioner Peter Berle, "at the end of the line."[49] Rather than reinforcing his achievements, Hugh Carey's outrageous shoot-from-the-hip style of public comment made the communications effort in his administration a continuous exercise in damage control. The substance was there, but not the sensitivity to the symbolic role of the state chief executive in New York. Thus, though the Carey legacy to the state was a considerable one, it was also, in the end, revealing of the damage that can be done to leadership potential, personal reputation, and political ambition when there is a disregard of public image by a public man.

FOOTNOTES

[1]*The New York Times,* January 1, 1984, p. E7.

[2]Quoted in *The New Yorker,* February 22, 1982, p. 105.

[3]For an elaboration of this point, see Gerald Benjamin. "The Carey-Cuomo Transition," in Thad Beyle (ed.). *Gubernatorial Transitions,* 1982 (Chapel Hill: Duke University Press, Forthcoming).

[4]*Wall Street Journal,* February 22, 1976, p. 1, quoting a December 1975 "Meet the Press" television interview.

[5]John Corey. "Hugh Carey: Portrait of the Politician as a Private Man," *The New York Times Magazine,* June 11, 1978, p. 104.

[6]Michael Kramer. "Carey in Love," *New York,* April 13, 1981, p. 22; and Robert J. Meislin. "Carey's of Albany," *The New York Times Magazine,* October 4, 1981, p. 25.

[7]Mario Cuomo. *Diaries of Mario Cuomo,* (New York: Random House, 1984), p. 387.

[8]Cited in *Empire State Report Weekly,* July 20, 1981, p. 446.

[9]June 18, 1978, p. 46.

[10]Cuomo. (1984), p. 98.

[11]*The New Yorker,* August 7, 1978, p. 64.

[12]Corey (1978) p. 99. For general information about Hugh Carey's pre-gubernatorial career, see Michael Barone, Grant Ujifusa, and Douglas Mathews. *The Almanac of American Politics,* 1974 (Boston: Gambet, 1973), pp. 684-687; and Duncan Spelman. "Hugh L. Carey," *Ralph Nader Congress Project* (New York: Grossman, 1972).

[13]*The New Yorker,* September 30, 1974, p. 111.

[14]*Ibid.,* p. 105.

[15]*Wall Street Journal,* October 31, 1974, p. 1.

[16]The term is Joe Alsop's, from the *Washington Post,* as reported in *The New Yorker,* May 25, 1975, p. 95.

251

[17]Jack Newfield and Paul DeBrul. *The Abuse of Power: The Permanent Government and the Fall of New York,* (New York: Viking, 1979), p. 69.

[18]Cited in *The New Yorker,* August 31, 1981, p. 88.

[19]*Wall Street Journal,* October 20, 1978, p. 1.

[20]Sidney Zion. "How Perry Duryea Lost the Election," *New York,* November 20, 1978, p. 13.

[21]Corey (1978), p. 29.

[22]Cited in Kramer (1981), p. 22.

[23]*The New Yorker,* February 22, 1982, p. 105.

[24]See, for example, Steven R. Weisman. "The Second First Carey Administration," *The New York Times Magazine,* October 3, 1976, p. 19; Corey (1978), p. 27; *The Economist,* March 7, 1981, p. 36.

[25]Weisman (1976) p. 19.

[26]Jim Klurfeld. "The Unfinished Portrait of a Governor," *Empire State Report,* (August 1975), p. 289.

[27]"Hugh Carey's Awkward Win," *New York,* September 5, 1978, p. 15.

[28]*The Economist* (1981), p. 36.

[29]Jim Klurfeld. "Cahill: The Doctor Who Would Be King," *Empire State Report,* July 1976, p. 214.

[30]*The New York Times,* January 18, 1977, p. 33.

[31]Corey (1978), p. 29.

[32]Kathrine Seelye. "Kevin Cahill: Now That He's Gone...," *Empire State Report Weekly,* March 28, 1981, p. 175.

[33]Edward Tivnan. "The Governor's Governor," *New York,* June 9, 1980, p. 44.

[34]Klurfeld (1976).

[35]Tivnan (1980), p. 48.

[36]*The New York Times,* July 17, 1977, p. 8.

[37]Cuomo (1984), p. 25.

[38]Janice Prindle. "Assessing the Legislature's Saratoga Session," *Empire State Report,* September 1976, p. 297.

[39]Kramer (1981), p. 21.

[40]Weisman (1976), p. 83.

[41]*Ibid.,* p. 81.

[42]James Lardner. "A Reporter at Large (MTA)," *The New Yorker,* June 25, 1984, p. 50.

[43]Weisman (1976), p. 78. See also, Joseph Zimmerman. "Rebirth of the Item Veto in the Empire State," *State Government* (1981), pp. 51-52.

[44]Cuomo (1984), *Edward I. Koch. Mayor* (New York: Simon and Schuster, 1984), pp. 73 and 376.

[45]Cited in Timothy B. Clark. "The Rapid Rise and Fast Fall of the UDC," *Empire State Report* (April 1975, p. 110.

[46]For a summary of the action taken to meet the fiscal crisis, see: New York State Division of the Budget. *The Executive Budget in New York State: A Half Century Perspective* (Albany: The Division, 1981), Chapters VI and VII.

[47]For a good summary of the substantive record of the Carey Administration in a number of key policy areas, see: *The Council on*

State Priorities. Report to the Governor (New York: The Council, 1982).

[48]See the decisions of the New York State Court of Appeals in *County of Oneida v. Berle,* 49NY2d515 (1980), and *Boryszewski v. Brydges,* 37NY2d361 (1976).

[49]Corey (1978), p. 29; *Economist* (1981), p. 36; *Empire State Report Weekly,* March 5, 1980, p. 194.

INDEX

A

Abrams, Morris 5
Abrams, Robert 50, 222
Abrams, Sam 231
Adirondack Park Agency 121, 123, 144
AFL-CIO 147, 187
Aid to Dependent Children (ADC) 101
Aid to Families with Dependent Children (AFDC) 89, 90
Anderson, Arthur 61
Anderson, Warren 15, 58, 79, 107, 214, 246
Appleby, Paul 167
Atlantic Alliance 143
Attica 4
Axelrod, David 12, 17, 108, 110, 111, 143, 175-177, 192, 204

B

Banking Board 226, 229
Banking Department, NYS 211-234
Baylor, Vic 192
Beame, Abraham 11
Bellamy, Carol 49, 50
Berger, Stephen 2, 12, 105, 112, 115
Berle, Peter A. A. 128, 130, 251
Berman, Richard 107, 108
Bernstein, Blanche 100
Bigel, Jack 11
Biggane, James 128
Blinken, Donald 66
Bloom, Jeremiah 18, 240
Blum, Barbara 12, 17, 88-119, 192, 204
Blume, Sheila 14
Boren, David L. 109
Breslin, Jimmy 241
Brodie, Gary 232
Budget, NYS Division of the (DOB) 1, 32-34, 38-40, 43, 52-87
                                       94, 95, 103, 110, 141-143, 147,
                                       154, 160, 166, 167, 185, 190, 191
                                       193, 194, 201, 206, 207, 227, 228
Burke, David 3, 5, 9, 11, 13, 14, 19, 39, 244, 246
Business Council 20

C

Cahill, Kevin 5, 8, 12, 15-16, 39, 203-205, 243, 244
Califano, Joseph 106
California State Government 99

Cammerer, John 189
Carter, Jimmy 36
Casey, Al 11
Casey, William 212, 216
Charles, Bernie 232
Child Care Review System (CCRS) 97
Child Welfare Reform Act 90-92, 106, 108
Cincotta, George 214
City University of New York 169
Civil Defense Commission 177
Civil Service, NYS Department of 81, 94, 110, 113,
                         157, 160, 161, 169, 227, 228
Civil Service Employees' Association (CSEA) ... 20, 147, 148, 152,
                                       158, 159, 195
Clarke, Tom 232
Clean Air Act 134, 135
Cohen, Alan 218
Commerce, NYS Department of 1, 14, 66
Community Support System (CSS) 197, 198, 201, 208
Congressional Budget Office 171
Connecticut State Government 143
Consolidated Edison 141
Consolidated Highway Improvement Plan (CHIP) 178, 179
Cornell University 158, 169
Correctional Services, NYS Department of 32, 34, 161
Coughlin, Thomas A. 31, 204
Council of Northeast Governors (CONEG) 21
Council on State Priorities 22, 73, 153, 154
Cummins, Jerry 39
Cunningham, Pat 39, 239
Cuomo, Mario 5, 14, 16, 23, 38, 50, 129, 161, 172, 189,
                         235-237, 240, 244, 245, 248

D

Del Guidice, Michael 11, 19, 225, 226
Dempster, George 14
Dewey, Thomas E. 45, 79, 180
Diamond, Henry 128
Diffley, Michael 11
Disaster Preparedness Commission 175-177
Dorfman, Dan 215
Dormer, Robert 14
Dormitory Authority of the State of New York 43
Dunham, Richard 167

Duryea, Perry 79, 238, 240
Dyson, John 8, 14, 17, 233

E

Eckert, Fred 139
Education, NYS Department of 198
Egan, John 32, 110, 111, 192
Elish, Herb 11
Ellinghaus, William 6, 11
Emergency Financial Control Board 10
Employee Relations, NYS Office of (OER) 147-173
Environmental Conservation, NYS Department of (DEC) 13, 31,
121-145, 176
Environmental Protection Agency, US 122, 124, 143
Esposito, Meade 238
Eustice, Ed 222

F

Federal Deposit Insurance Corporation (FDIC) 212, 217, 219,
220, 222, 223
Federal Emergency Management Agency, US 176
Feinstein, Barry 11
Fink, Stanley 15, 58, 79, 140, 182,
214, 224, 245, 246
Finnerty, Michael 11, 19, 58, 63, 85, 86, 165, 172
Flacke, Robert 31, 32, 110, 120-145, 192, 204
Flynn, Tom 11
Forestry, SUNY College of Environmental Science and 137
Frey, Thomas 15
Frucher, Meyer S. 37, 146-173, 247

G

Garth, David 39, 241
Generally Accepted Accounting Principles (GAAP) 20, 55-64,
73, 76, 80, 250
General Accounting Office 171
General Motors 164
General Services, NYS Office of (OGS) 31, 110, 111, 113
Gentilerio, Hugo 142
Ginsburg, Mitchell 98
Glasse, Lou 108
Glider, Vic 126
Goldin, Harrison 3
Goldin, Jay 50

Goldmark, Peter 8, 9, 11, 14, 39, 71, 172, 244
Gottbaum, Victor 11, 213
Gribetz, Judah 8, 9, 40, 244

H

Haggarty, Jack 213
Hartnett, Thomas 172
Hassett, William 14
Hayes, Fred 93, 94
Health, NYS Department of 1, 12, 13, 33, 96, 143, 176
Health and Human Services, US Department of 100, 109
Hennessy, William 17, 110, 117, 174-195, 204
Highway Act of 1974 178
Hinchey, Maurice 139
Horowitz, Gedale 3
Hover, Bud 127
Human Resources Administration, NYC (HRA) 94, 98, 106
Hurd, T. Norman 1, 167

I

International Free Zone for Banking 30
Interoffice Coordinating Council 199
Introne, James 12, 20, 204
Issac, William 212

J

Job Corps 167
Job Development Authority (JDA) 14, 231, 233
Johnson, Lyndon 167

K

Kahan, Richard 14
Kennedy, Edward 5, 21, 239
Kenny, Michael 232
Kerr, Harris 122
Koch, Ed 21, 36, 49, 135, 155, 248
Kohn, Ernie 227
Kolb, Lawrence 12
Koppell, Oliver 139
Krupsak, Mary Ann 240

L

Labor, NYS Department of 103, 109, 110
Labor, US Department of 109
Lanahan, Peter 126

Lanford, Oscar 63
Lans, Shirley 232
Lawrence, Mary Wells 14
• Lawton, C. Mark 31, 49, 52-87, 95, 142, 165, 169, 249
Lee, Paul 231
Lefkowitz, Louis 222, 240
Legg, Stanley 126
Legislature, NYS 9, 15-17, 44-46, 67, 73-80, 92,
                                                    107, 117, 133, 135, 138-140, 143,
                                                    149, 150, 165, 167-171, 182, 190,
                                                    208, 214, 215, 227, 245-248
Lehman, Herbert H. 73
Lehman, Orin 110, 192
Lehrman, Lewis 235, 236
Levitt, Arthur 3, 55, 60
Levittown 19, 69
Lewis, Al 233
Lindsay, John 21
Logue, Edward 9
Love Canal 127, 180
Low, George 15
Lugavina, Frank 232

M

Maas, Jane 14
Mahoney, Walter 79
Mann, Gene 224
Martinez, Julio 12, 14
Massachusetts State Government 136
Mauro, Frank 58
McCluskey, Orin 6
McGowan, William 20
Mealey, Roger 212
Medicaid 69, 90-92, 96-99, 105, 109, 111, 200
Medicaid Management Information System (MMIS) 92, 95-97, 111
Mental Health, NYS Office of (OMH) 91, 108, 111, 115,
                                                              151, 197-209
Mental Hygiene, NYS Department of 1, 12, 113, 158, 183,
                                                              199, 202, 206
Mental Retardation and Developmental Disabilities,
   NYS Office of (OMR/DD) 66, 108, 151, 202
Mertz, Marty 215
Metropolitan Transportation Authority, NYS (MTA) 184, 185
Michaelson, G.G. 11
Miller, Howard 2, 3, 31, 34, 53, 67, 68, 78, 192
Minnewaska Project 128
Moreland Act 5

Moreland Commission 5, 6, 10
Morgado, Robert 2, 3, 9, 11, 14, 19, 26-51, 111, 112,
117, 121, 165, 192, 203, 214, 218,
224-228, 244, 247
Moynihan, Daniel Patrick 109
Municipal Assistance Corporation (MAC) 11, 69, 249
Municipal Credit Union (MCU) 211

N

Nadjari, Maurice 239, 248
National Governnor's Association (NGA) 21
National Resource Defense Council (NRDC) 123, 128
New Jersey State Government 143
New Jersey Institute of Technology 137
New York City 3, 8, 10, 11, 19, 21, 23, 42, 43, 57, 93,
94, 97-101, 135, 184, 185, 218, 235
Nimetz, Matthew 1
Nixon, Richard M. 18, 122
Nosechuck, Norm 127
Nuclear Regulatory Commission, US 176

O

Oklahoma State Government 109
O'Leary, Vincent 137
O'Neill, Hugh 2
Oberst, Lee 11
Ohrenstein, Fred 214
Opton, Carol 2

P

Peer, Bob 114
Pennsylvania State Government 136
Perales, Cesaer 116
Persico, Dick 126
Political Action Committee (PAC) 21
Prevost, James 31, 196-209
Project Finance Agency, NYS 9
Proxmire, William 224
Public Authorities Control Board 43
Public service 80-84

Q

Quality of Care for the Mentally Disabled,
NYS Commission on (QCMD) 13

R

Rader, Lloyd 109
Ravitch, Richard 8, 9, 14
Regan, Don 213
Reid, Ogden 128
Renssealear Polytechnic Institute 136
Rich, Eldridge 127
Roberts, Lillian 17, 109, 110, 213
Rockefeller, Nelson A. 17, 21, 33, 36, 38, 45, 46, 50,
78-79, 140, 167-169, 175, 188, 190,
191, 205, 235, 238, 240, 247, 250
Rockefeller College of Public Affairs and Policy 162
Rockefeller Institute of Government 137, 138
Rohatyn, Felix 11, 243, 245
Rolison, Jay 214, 215, 224
Rose, Alex 39
Rosen, Mildred 232
Ross, Philip 109, 110
Rubin Task Force 70
Runyon, Marie M. 248

S

Samuels, Howard 238
Schang, Carmen 117
Schell, Orville 5
Schrauf, Jerry 164
Schuler, Raymond 20, 177, 178, 181
Schweiker, Richard 106
Scott, Bill 11
Seebold, Gene 127
Shanker, Al 11
Shapiro, Sydelle 109
Sherill, Don 163
Shinn, Richard 11
Shuman, Stan 11
Siebert, Muriel 210-234, 245
Sierra Club 123, 124, 128
Sloan, Morton 215
Smeel, Frank 3
Smiley, Don 11
Smith, Alfred E. 21, 24, 45, 73, 76, 241
Smith, Bernard 139, 175
Smith, Greg 142
Smith, William T. 117
Social Services, NYS Department of 12, 89-119, 198
Social Welfare, NYS Board of 106

Soss, Neal 231
State of New York Mortgage Agency (SONYMA) 226, 231-233
State Police, NY 176
State University of New York (SUNY) 54, 63-66, 137, 138, 169
State University Construction Fund 63
Steingut, Stanley 15, 140, 214
Stern, Martin 14
Sugerman, Jules 98
Sullivan, Allan 223
Sundram Commission 13
Sundram, Clarence 13

T

Taylor Law 156
Title XIX 95, 96
Title XX 91, 92
Toia, Philip 95, 103, 116, 117
Torgelson, Roy 126
Transporation, NYS Department of (DOT) 13, 66, 175-195
Travia, Anthony J. 79
Truman, Harry S. 21
Tubby, Roger 21

U

Urban Development Corporation (UDC) 3-5, 8, 9-10, 14, 28,
39, 77, 147, 226, 232, 249

V

Van Arsdale, Harry 11

W

Wagner, Robert 21, 39
Wallach, Donald 155
Welfare Management System (WMS) 92, 95, 97, 98
Westway Highway Project 187, 189
Whalen, Robert 12
Wharton, Clifton 64, 66, 137, 138
Whiteman, Michael 33
Williams, Henry 129
Willowbrook 4-6, 17, 29, 46, 102, 113, 164, 207, 250
Wilson, Malcolm 121, 184, 238-239
Work Incentive Program (WIN) 108-111
Wriston, Walter 216

* * * * * * *